W9-DIT-468

after empire

after empire

the art and ethos of enduring peace

sharon d. welch

Fortress Press
Minneapolis

AFTER EMPIRE
The Art and Ethos of Enduring Peace

Copyright ©2004 Augsburg Fortress. All rights reserved. Except for
brief quotations in critical articles or reviews, no part of this book
may be reproduced in any manner without prior written permission
from the publisher. Write: Permissions, Augsburg Fortress, Box
1209, Minneapolis, MN 55440.

Cover design: Brad Norr Design
Author photo: Roger Berg
Book design: James Korsmo

Library of Congress Cataloging-in-Publication Data

Welch, Sharon D.
  After empire : the art and ethos of enduring peace / Sharon D.
Welch.
     p. cm.
  Includes bibliographical references and index.
  ISBN 0-8006-2986-8 (alk. paper)
  1. Religion and international affairs. 2. Religion and politics—
United States. 3. United States—Foreign relations—Moral and
ethical aspects. I. Title.
  BL65.I55W45 2004
  201'.727—dc22

                                                    2004019263

The paper used in this publication meets the minimum require-
ments of American National Standard for Information Sciences —
Permanence of Paper for Printed Library Materials, ANSI Z329.48-
1984.

Manufactured in the U.S.A.

08   07   06   05   04   1   2   3   4   5   6   7   8   9   10

For my daughters,
Zoë and Hannah,
who have helped me see
the wonders of the present

contents

preface

pax americana, pax humana

Imperialism and Its Alternatives

Who are we as Americans?[1] What is our role now on the world stage? Robert Kagan, senior associate at the Carnegie Endowment for International Peace; Jean Bethke Elshtain, professor of social and political ethics; and Niall Ferguson, professor of history, all urge the United States to accept our responsibility as the guarantors of European and American security, international order, and freedom. Jonathan Schell, noted journalist, and Zbigniew Brzezinski, national security advisor under President Carter, propose another path, asking us to be "liberal internationalists," applying "cooperative power" to the "international sphere." Like William Schulz, executive director of Amnesty International USA, they encourage the United States to shape, with other nations, a new "international society," responsive to the "common enemy of terrorism," and resolutely committed to human rights and global justice.[2]

Which path will we follow? We may try to become the beneficent guardians of "peace, prosperity and liberty" envisioned in the National Security Strategy of the Bush administration, preferring alliances but willing to act alone. Or, we may become the "multilateralists" envisioned by Joseph Nye Jr., as skilled in the exercise of persuasive cultural and political power as we are judicious in the use of economic and military might.[3]

We live in a time rife with debates about the best use of our national power, debates that hinge on understandings of the very nature of national and international power, and on interpretations of colonial history. William Schulz, for example, warns against imperialism and asks that we remember that moralistic domination breeds "resentment, resistance, and rebellion." Niall Ferguson takes quite a different lesson from the undeniable brutality yet seemingly irreplaceable achievements of the British Empire and asks the United States to resolutely accept the challenges of establishing and maintaining a Pax Americana.[4]

Many people within the United States acknowledge and embrace the thrill of Empire—the intoxication of mastery, the security of being met with deference if not respect, the challenge of assuming the mantle of destiny, of shaping the world in our image.[5] Those who would be the bearers of Empire most often see themselves as the harbingers of security and peace. From the order of the Pax Romana, through the "civilizing" global reach of the British Empire, to the freedom, democracy, and prosperity promised by imperial America, the rhythms of power, of truth, of unassailable military might, of absolute security swirl, surround, and overwhelm.

There is, however, a different rhythm in the protests of the millions of people throughout the world who tried to prevent the United States' invasion of Iraq in 2003. There are voices throughout the world calling for other ways of maintaining order and security, other means of bringing tyrants to justice, other forms of power, vitality, glory, and community.

Jonathan Schell, William Schulz, Zbigniew Brzezinski, and Joseph Nye Jr. are among those who urge the United States to become something that we have not yet fully been—a shaper, with other nations, of a cooperative international order that can set limits to the excesses of any imperial power, ours included. Robert Kagan, in his influential book *Of Paradise and Power*, derides this vision of a cooperative rule of law as the perennial resort of the weak. He advocates another vital role for the United States: the guarantor, through military supremacy, of global order—the power that is necessary for "paradise." While European nations may choose international law over military struggle, Kagan, like Jean Bethke Elshtain, claims that there are other nations and peoples not so restrained, and some power must be ready to meet the challenges they pose with "military might."[6]

A similar logic is expressed by the framers of the 2002 National Security Strategy of the United States. The document acknowledges that "coordination with European allies and international institutions is essential for constructive conflict mediation and successful peace operations." The reach of these cooperative activities, however, is sharply limited: the serious threats of brutal leaders and global terrorism require military action and may necessitate even preemptive, unilateral action by the United States. "The greater the threat, the greater is the risk of inaction—and the more compelling the case for taking anticipatory action to defend ourselves."[7]

The divide here is clear. Many people believe genuine power and decisive action require military force. Others, however, claim that coercive military force can be counterproductive—that we can, as Schulz states, in our defense of our power lose it. Schulz argues that if we violate the human rights of opponents and dissidents in our defense of national and international security, we lose not only moral integrity but political viability.[8] The divide, though, is greater than a mere debate about the relative utility or folly of military force in particular situations. Kagan and the writers of the National Security Strategy fail to recognize that what is being proposed by other political leaders and scholars is not a strategy of the weak, not a form of inaction in the face of grave threats, but another vision of world community and of the ways peoples and governments can exercise power responsibly in the face of grave threats and great opportunities.

Such momentous choices, so starkly delineated in dualistic terms: imperial America or international cooperation, power or paradise, coercive power or cooperative power, hegemony or survival.[9] To set the debate in these terms misses the creative claims that are being made by many critics of imperial and colonial power. The alternative to the domination of the many by a single unassailable military power is neither isolationism nor a refusal of global responsibility. It is, rather, a third way, another definition of strength and power, and a different way of using and limiting military force. And, while the critics of imperial power warn of the dangers of unchecked military and economic power, many of these advocates of international cooperation are equally aware of the risks that accompany this alternative form of international order.

Although Robert Kagan is critical of this emerging cooperative international order, he does acknowledge that it is grounded in European history. He claims, however, that American history teaches us other lessons. Not only do we lack the "experience of promoting ideals successfully without power" but Europe's move to international cooperation is dependent on the security provided by U.S. military supremacy. Kagan argues that U.S. history supports a different view of power, one that may lead to "a long era of American hegemony."[10]

Kagan could be right. Perhaps we are entering "a long era of American hegemony." There are, however, other ways of reading the lessons of American history and the values and aspirations of the American people.

While Niall Ferguson explicitly advocates that the United States assume the mantle of empire, it is noteworthy that this same rhetoric is not commonly found within the United States itself. Although many people certainly advocate an exercise of power that can arguably be called imperial in its ambition, range, and scope, few explicitly advocate an American Empire. The Bush administration, for example, has repeatedly denied that the United States military presence in Iraq is an occupation. Patrick Tyler, writing for the *New York Times*, cites the words of Paul Bremer as he assumed charge of United States operations in Iraq: "We are not here as a colonial power. . . . We are here to turn over [power to the Iraqi people] as quickly as possible."[11]

Why does "imperial America" still sound like a critique of the hubris of the United States rather than the nonideological description of a laudable goal? In this disjunction—comfort with the unilateral use of power, yet distaste for the name of "empire"—lies great potential and great peril. To simply dismiss this disjunction as the greatest hypocrisy is to miss a creative tension, one that, if fully explored, can lead us to a more just expression of who we are, as a people, as a nation, and as members of an international community.

We may continue to wield overweening power, blinded by our own desires for purity and beneficence to the costs of that power, unwilling to acknowledge resistance to dominance and unwilling to see and mourn the catastrophic consequences in human suffering and death. We may, however, choose another path, taking hold of that tension, exploring it honestly, and building from that prescient discomfort a different expression of national and international power, one as creatively attuned to our weaknesses and limitations as to our strengths.

What is it about *who* we are and *where* we are that leads to these tensions?

We need to understand the urge to use military power and to act unilaterally. At the same time, we must not ignore the continued reluctance to claim unabashedly the role of imperial America.

In this book I explore our story as Americans and propose a vision of national power that is rooted in the best of our values and aspirations as well as in the worst of our excesses and brutality. And, far from being utopian, this is a vision that is eminently pragmatic. Remember the etymology of utopia—literally, "no-place." What follows is a vision of national identity and global responsibility that is emerging from *this* place—from the Hawaiian islands to the mainland to Puerto Rico—and from *this* people—indigenous Americans and the continuing flow of immigrants, voluntary and involuntary, from Africa, Europe, Latin America, and Asia who make this place their home, their culture, and our nation.

It is a vision that also emerges from our encounters with other places, with other peoples, with other stories. It emerges as we learn from others—others who are not the beneficiaries of Empire, but those who bear its costs. Seeing this vision requires learning from peoples who have different views of community, power, national identity, and global responsibility.

Seeing the World
through the Eyes of Others

Seeing difference is a learned art—and an essential task. Learning to hear fundamental critiques of our actions and to critically assess alternative views of human community and of ethical and political responsibility is the task of global citizenship and global ethics. This is also the task of postcolonial comparative religious ethics.

After spending time in a Zen temple, the French philosopher Michel Foucault offered an assessment of the "turning point" in European thought occasioned by the end of imperialism. He claimed that the philosophy of the future would "be born outside of Europe or equally born in consequence of meetings and impact between Europe and non-Europe."[12] What Foucault predicted for philosophy has become true in the comparative study of religion.

The very category of "religion" emerged as a result of European contact with other religious systems.[13] While colonialists were engaged in significant military conflict, they claimed that the indigenous peoples they attacked had no religion, and, were, therefore, practically subhuman. Seen by the invaders as barriers to the march of civilization, they could be removed, even exterminated. Chidester recounts the case of southern Africa where colonialists saw the resistant population as having peculiar "customs" but lacking religion. But once the indigenous population was subjugated, those same 'customs' were then taken as evidence of religion—a religion, however, that was customarily misunderstood in two ways. On the one hand, it was falsely described as ahistorical and uniform (significant differences between peoples and changes throughout time are dismissed as inconsequential). On the other hand, it was often characterized as a primitive or degenerate form of monotheism. Well into the twentieth century, the traditions of non-Europeans were seen as "Other," sometimes in an ostensibly positive sense as an exotic reality to be explored and appreciated, more often in a negative sense, misunderstood as fundamentally irrational and childishly superstitious.[14] The use of material objects in religious rituals and ceremonies, for example, while taken for granted as valid in the Christian reverence for the cross and the use of bread and wine in religious ceremonies, was described pejoratively as the use of fetishes in other than Christian religions.[15]

Contact among religious traditions is now taking a radically different form in the postcolonial era. By "postcolonial," activists and scholars refer to a political situation in which the process of colonization (economic, cultural, and political conquest) is both contested and relatively visible. The term does *not* mean that domination has disappeared. While many of the colonial powers in Africa and the Americas have been defeated, the process of political, economic, cultural, and military domination continues in other forms.[16]

A critique of colonial reason is well established in the field of religious studies and has led to a proliferation of works that describe patterns of misunderstanding and misnaming in regard to particular religious traditions.[17] This critique helps us see more clearly both the past and present contours of exploitation and domination. These critiques recover previously neglected historical materials: the critiques of European and Euro-American colonization by indigenous peoples. If we pay attention to those voices, what we find is a sharp critique, expressed in incredulous laughter, and in searing pain. While the beliefs and habits of the European and Euro-American conquerors often seemed ludicrous, their cruelty and domination was heartrending and unfathomable. Indigenous peoples of the Americas knew warfare, but they were stunned by the massacres of whole villages by Europeans, and by the deliberate mutilation of those who resisted forced labor or conversion.[18] These voices, historical and contemporary, also express different visions of power, community, and global responsibility.

What Foucault claimed as true about epistemes is also true about ethics and politics: we need differences to see injustices that are fundamental, and constitutive of a political, ethical, or religious system. As we listen to these critiques of our interactions with other peoples, as we study histories other than our own, we find that there are compelling ethical and aesthetic alternatives to imperial power.

Our Peace Mandate

Niall Ferguson argues that the real question is not *whether* Empire but *whose* Empire, and claims that a Pax Americana would be preferable to that of any other.[19] With Kagan, he is in a long line of historians, political leaders, and even theologians who see Empire as the inevitable expression of genuine power, the natural outflow of military and moral strength. While there are many who see Empire as desirable, and even more who see Empire as inevitable, there are others who can imagine a variety of constellations of national and international power and order. In this book, I side with those voices, with Brzezinski, Schulz, Schell and Nye Jr., claiming that there are other forms of power and other ways of reading, and playing, American history. This alternative to Empire is neither inevitable nor free of risk and cost. It is, however, an adventure that is, ironically, as pragmatic as it is audacious.

It would be the utmost folly to deny the attraction of Empire. Empire attracts, yet Empire repels. This book is a celebration, an invocation, and an exaltation of the logic that both knows the intoxication of Empire and yet confronts the costs of imperial power. It is a celebration of cultures that have chosen "peace mandates" rather than the heedless or resigned pursuit of military power. It is an invocation of these capacities of heart and mind that enable us to see the costs of Empire, and it celebrates other plays of energy, power, and vitality—the exuberance of other ways of being as peoples and as nations.

Finally, it is a wager. Although he resisted the power of the emerging Third Reich, the great twentieth-century theologian Paul Tillich wrote that history lives under the star of empire.[20] This book celebrates other stars and invokes, with gratitude and wonder, their continued presence—stars of reverence, of compassion, of virtuosity, honesty, curiosity, and respect. Viable alternatives to imperial power are no less assured than is the inevitability of some form of political, economic, and military domination. Is history under the star of Empire? Can humans move from the rule of law *inside* nations to the rule of law *between* nations? These questions cannot be answered in advance of the doing. They are wagers to be lived, risks to be taken, not conundrums to be resolved in theory.

One thing, though, is certain. If we as citizens of the United States are to discover a peace mandate, it will not be a simple repetition of the mandates of other peoples. Our peace mandate will come from our history, from our stories, and from our open engagement with other peoples, other nations, and other visions of community and power. Our peace mandate simultaneously emerges from and transforms who we are as individuals, as political activists, as a nation, and as global citizens. Such a mandate reflects and recasts our personal stories of belonging, hope, and fear; it reflects and recasts our deepest ethical and spiritual commitments. Our peace mandate emerges from our collective history as citizens of the United States and our collective vision of who we have been and of who we may become as citizens in a global community.

In the following chapters we move from an exploration of personal history and commitment (chapters 1 and 2) to a transformed sense of political activism (chapters 3 through 6) and to an alternative geopolitical vision (chapter 7). All three exercises—personal, political, and geopolitical—are invitations to see differently the resources of our individual and collective histories and traditions, resources that may enable us to take up the task of global citizenship, with honesty, daring, and creativity.

chapter 1

memory

Generations[1]

Crying to sleep, soothed by the motion of my parent's car driving through the warm West Texas night, easing from the excitement of the day into the rest of the night, embraced, surrounded by love.

Azure sky, crisp white clouds. Air dry and clear; all is luminous. I am nine years old, the soil, warm and sandy under my feet. Lush green leaves, brilliant red cherries, black stems, juice sweet and tart. The delight of eating them under the watchful eye of my grandfather, relishing his pleasure and my own, bathed in the love and joy he experienced in sharing the fruit so painstakingly cultivated with a much-loved grandchild.

Sitting around the food-laden table at noon, laughing with my father, grandfather, mother, grandmother, and cousins about the day's misadventures working cattle or tilling the fields.

Cold star-filled nights in the New Mexico mountains, returning from a church evening worship service to Mother and Dad's camping trailer—the sweet smell of hot chocolate and buttery popcorn, adults laughing, telling stories about the foibles of that day and ones in the past.

Enchanted by my grandfather's stories of working with his father at six, beginning to farm his own land and take care of his own cattle at the age of twelve. This same gregarious man who loved hard work, at eighty-two, unable to walk because of a stroke, sleeping with his two-month-old great-great-granddaughter on his chest. He lived his last two years with my aunt and uncle, cared for by them, by my grandmother, and by his grandsons, unaware of the passage of time, profoundly aware of the rhythms of life and love.

First stars appear in a velvet sky. Summer ocean breeze, salty and soft. Nursing newborn Hannah, hearing her blissful coos as she tastes, for the first time, warm, sweet, rich milk.

I was raised in a small farming community in West Texas. My grandparents and parents were farmers and ranchers who embodied a profound Christian faith, one that focused on living life fully and well. The main point of their daily prayers was an invocation to be mindful of the needs of other people. When I returned home each year, I was eager to see what avenues of service were central in their lives. Over the years, they worked as members of the school board and of the hospital board (building and expanding the local hospital, thereby maintaining affordable care for a largely working-class and poor population), volunteered at a school for mentally challenged children and teenagers, coordinated drug abuse and HIV/AIDS prevention programs for the county, and exercised leadership in their church. My father was ordained in his early twenties and served many years, first as a local pastor and then as a district president. My mother was ordained in her early fifties, and she, too, served as pastor and then district president. Their ministry was pastoral and political; they worked with church-sponsored economic development projects in Haiti and the

Philippines and were active in supporting gay rights and the parents of gay, lesbian, and bisexual young people.

They lived lives of service but with no sense of guilt, duty, or sacrifice. They acknowledged failure and defeat, but with no sense of fallenness or original sin. They focused on the direction of the Spirit, the ways in which they were being led to new horizons of creativity and service. The variant of Christianity that they followed rejected the division of sacred and profane and claimed that all is spiritual. The heart of their life and work was clear: building the kingdom of God on earth.

🖋

Caring for a colicky baby, finding that fresh air and rhythmic movement soothed us both. Walking for hours the streets of Cambridge, seeing her delight in greeting people, enjoying their warmth toward her. As she grew, observing her curiosity and openness to the world around her—all its sights, sounds, textures, and smells. In the face of this wonder, my habitual stance of perpetual criticism, the prophetic outsider skilled in detecting the nuances of complicity with injustice in art, religion, politics, and economic systems, spending hours deconstructing systems of oppression and denouncing the failings of a militaristic, sexist, racist, and materialistic society, seemed, quite simply, a sacrilege in the presence of Zoë's curious, open, and engaged embrace of life.

🖋

Seeking a spiritual path that corresponded with what I saw and was learning from this very young child, I read the essay of the Pueblo poet, artist, and writer Carol Lee Sanchez in which she describes the Navajo Beauty Way.[2] Her words resonated with my mother's creation of beauty in her home, in her photography, in the imaginative clothing that she designed and made for her granddaughters and daughters. Her words reminded me of my grandmothers' bountiful gardening and baking, their love of feeding their families with the food they had grown and preserved. Sanchez's words resonated with the joy that my grandfather and father took in the hard work of building fence, working cattle, and training horses.

Activism

Although I was raised in a tradition that lived political involvement as the expression of faith and ethical commitment, my understanding of spiritually based political activism was radically challenged by encounters with, and learning from, three other religious traditions: African American Christianity and humanism, Native American traditions, and the engaged Buddhism of Thich Nhat Hanh.[3]

What have I learned from these three traditions, and how do these lessons apply to the contemporary challenges of personal authenticity, social engagement, and national identity, international order, and peacemaking? There are many ways of comparing religious traditions and evaluating their ethical and political claims. The method I am following is described by Mark S. Heim, professor of comparative religions at Andover Newton Theological School, as an exercise that occurs when we "see in another tradition elements authentically relating to the same religious fulfillment sought in [our] . . . own."[4]

Although other traditions may include elements that have an "authentic relation" to our own concerns, this does not save us from the dual dangers of casual and careless appropriation of the insights of others, or from the other elements within our culture that lead to the misunderstanding of traditions and the exploitation of peoples. Jim Harrison, a contemporary novelist, describes both of these elements in his elegiac novel, *The Road Home*. He sharply delineates the dangers of a careless embrace of other traditions. While many whites were attracted to Native traditions, Harrison claims that our misunderstanding of those traditions was as deep as our longing to find something within them that could "heal the alienation and isolation of being the emotional heirs of colonizers and interlopers":

> If you have been horribly swindled and desire reparations to survive you scarcely want to become a totem for the derelicts of the sadistic culture, however benign. If you want to help me don't fawn but go home and kick your congressman in the ass is the plaintive, mostly unvoiced request. You can't greedily suck out of another culture what you have failed to find in your own heart. You may recognize it in another culture but only if it already exists in the core of your own soul.[5]

What I know in my soul I learned from the lives of my mother and father: that it is possible to work for justice without self-righteous condemnation of others, acting instead with good-humored resilience in the face of defeat and with a deep joy and zest for life. Where they saw injustice, they responded and invited others to act with them. They did not waste time denouncing others' apathy or indifference. The range of activities they embraced was vast but united by a common theme: doing something now, with the resources at hand, to make a difference in people's lives.

My parents lived the prophetic mandate for justice without a prophetic denunciation of others. Their lives of service were not lives of self-sacrifice but lives of relishing a larger self, a self fulfilled in creatively using their power to establish conditions of justice in their church, their work, and their community.

What a blessing to be the child of such parents! As my sister and brother and I live out this legacy, we have done so with their support and encouragement, not to repeat their activities, but to find ones that are uniquely ours, vocations that reflect our place in the world and the opportunities we have in our circle of relations and influence.

Were my parents sui generis, a rare and unlikely-to-be-seen-again combination of zest and accountability, wisdom, compassion, and non-guilt-ridden self-critique? Hardly. Thankfully not. It has been a great satisfaction to find a like sensibility expressed, sustained, and nurtured in many peoples, places, and traditions: in the moral wisdom of African American women's literature, in the audacity of jazz, in the irreverence of Native American tricksters.

In the 1970s and 1980s, I was involved in work for nuclear disarmament. In organizing within primarily white, middle-class communities, we noticed a common pattern. No matter what the issue, whether challenging apartheid or working for nuclear disarmament, when we first asked people to take a stand, they would declare that they could not push for specific legislation because they did not know enough about the issue. Responding to that legitimate reluctance to endorse a poorly understood position, we focused on education. The response, however, often remained the same. There was still unwillingness to act, but now for a different reason. Rather than not knowing enough, people knew enough to conclude that the problem was too big to do anything about! In fact, any proposed action could be criticized as woefully incommensurate with the magnitude of the social injustice being addressed.

While at Harvard, I attended the weekly worship services of Harambee, the African American student group at the divinity school. I also was influenced by the writing and teaching of Katie Cannon, then professor of social ethics at Episcopal Divinity School, and her analysis of the moral wisdom found in the black women's literary tradition.[6] I encountered in this moral tradition a radically different ethos and ethic, one that began where white middle-class thought and action often stopped. This ethic began with the realization that we cannot imagine how we will win. There are no feasible five-year plans to end racism, militarism, class exploitation, and sexism. I saw in this community in Cambridge what I had also seen in many African American activists in Memphis and Nashville and in the writings of many African American ethicists, theologians, poets, and novelists: an ethic of risk that is both sharply critical of a white middle-class ethic of control and an ethic that offers an alternative form of resilience and ethical courage. I continued to explore this political, aesthetic, ethical, and literary tradition, finding important resources for ethical and political judgment and action in what Ralph Ellison calls the "art of ambiguity," a sensibility embodied in blues and jazz, and in much African American political life.[7]

Colonial Legacies

As I work with these traditions, I find many ways in which there is an Otherness, an insight and critique that jolts me out of accustomed habits of seeing, thinking, and acting. I also find much that is deeply resonant with the sensibility I saw in my parents as they worked to bring as much as possible out of available resources without being caught in isolating cycles of denunciation, despair, and cynicism.[8]

Because of this heritage of unpretentious, joyous service, two absolutes undergird my life and work. *First, under conditions of even a modicum of justice, life is wondrous, rich, and profoundly meaningful, a glorious gift to be celebrated and cherished.*

As strong as this heritage is, another one, equally strong, is at the core of who I am, and at the core of who many of us are as Americans.

As a child and young adult, I was horrified to learn about the bombing of Hiroshima and Nagasaki, and deeply troubled that Americans were responsible for those atrocities. When I was fifteen, a high school teacher had us study the primary texts of significant moments in American history. I studied the debates about the bombing of Hiroshima and Nagasaki. Under intense pressure to end the war, the United States wanted to demonstrate decisively its military superiority and pressure Japan into unconditional surrender. While there was little debate about the use of the atomic bomb, there was a modicum of debate about the target. Some argued that the site should be deserted; no human lives would be lost, and the immediate impact of the bomb's force would be enough to compel the Japanese to surrender. This alternative was rejected because of fear of humiliation if the bomb failed. The United States bombed two cities without warning, and two hundred thousand people were killed.[9]

Among the mixed and questioned ancestry of my parents, an undoubted strain, on both sides of my family, is German. Although those ancestors had moved to the United States in the late nineteenth century, when I first became aware of the concentration camps of World War II, I felt a disturbing kinship with the bystanders and perpetrators of the Holocaust.

In his deeply challenging work *Righteous Gentiles of the Holocaust*, David Gushee, professor of moral philosophy, reports the horrific fact that *less than 1 percent* of European Gentiles—Christians, atheists, socialists, and liberal democrats—resisted the Nazi genocide.[10] Would I have been part of that 1 percent? While I hope with all my heart that I would have had the courage to resist, to be honest, I must admit that odds are I would not. How did we Christians and humanists allow the Holocaust to happen? How did we allow ourselves to participate in such unthinkable evil? The Nazis, confident in the possession of absolute truth and overweening power, were able to justify the utmost atrocities. We lacked the courage and imagination to stop them. An uneasy question is a continuous part of my awareness: how am I, how are we now bystanders? With our comforts and our scruples, what horrors are we now allowing to occur?

The third historical event at the core of my being is the genocide of American Indians.[11] In West Texas, there was a deep-
seated appreciation of American Indian aesthetics (the
prevalence of "Southwestern" art) and an equally thorough erasure of the history of conquest and genocide. There were, however, occasional breaks in the wall of silence. After seeing *Dances
with Wolves*, my mother was profoundly shaken: "I want to fight
the Indian Wars again, this time, on the side of the Indians." In
the summer of 2003, as we drove across the still grasslands of
the high plains, the comfortable silence was broken by my grandmother's sudden remark, "I hate what we did to the Indians."

The official history of the county where I grew up is typical
of a larger pattern in American culture of cultural appreciation, political exploitation and repression, and denial of responsibility. The history of Castro County does mention the Native
American nations that preceded the white settlers. The Llano
Indians lived in this area of the Great Plains as long as ten to
twelve thousand years ago. The area was also occupied by the
Lipan Apache and the Comanche. A disturbing fact, however, is
mentioned only as an aside. During a period of two years, 1877
to 1878, two white men killed 7,500 buffalo. No explanation is
given for this grotesque butchery, but the results are flatly
stated: "They were killing the last of the buffalo. When the buffalo were gone, the way of life had ended for the Indians who
used the buffalo for their living."[12] It was not, of course, a coincidence that buffalo were slaughtered, and the Comanche left
the High Plains. Given the military victories of the Plains
Indians during the nineteenth century, another strategy of
removing Indian peoples was adopted by the U.S. government.
Whites were paid a bounty to kill buffalo and remove the
means of subsistence for Native peoples, forcing them to give
up their lands to white settlers.[13]

The events in Castro County were not anomalous. Philip
Arnold, professor of American Studies, describes the language

of utopia justified genocide. Arnold writes: "The hope of a technological utopian dream was expressed at the 1892 Columbian exposition in Chicago. At this World's Fair and those that followed, Lakota people specifically, and indigenous people from around the world more generally, were presented as the clear and identifiable impediments to a modern view of progress. . . . In the writing of L. Frank Baum (later the author of *The Wizard of Oz*) there was the explicit claim that 'the realization of this utopian dream . . . required the complete annihilation of indigenous people . . . in order to protect our civilization.'"[14]

A fourth instance further disturbed my ethical and historical naïveté. While it was tempting, and comforting, to see such atrocities as the work of an older, less politically progressive generation, those illusions were decisively shattered by two other historical events. First, I have been a socialist, and I was deeply shaken to learn of the violent, systemic suppression of political dissent in the Soviet Union and other socialist countries. Michel Foucault argues that we cannot dismiss this suppression as an aberration. He argues, rather, that we must see what it is about socialism and this type of utopian dream that evokes and legitimates such horrors. As much as I prefer the socialism of Eugene Debs, Rosa Luxembourg, and Emma Goldman, I must take equally seriously the socialism of Lenin, Stalin, and Mao.[15]

Finally, I have been shaken by the divisions and abuses of power within progressive movements for social change, even those that are feminist and pacifist.[16] While the damage that we have caused is far from the scale of the horrors of mass murder and the imprisonment of dissidents, I have seen how we can be cruel to one another and have little tolerance for deep differences and disagreements.

What are the implications of these five historical events? I offer my second absolute: *I and every person, movement, group, and institution that I trust can be deeply, profoundly, tragically*

*wrong. Not only can we be wrong in minor ways, but our best
ideals can be used to justify cruelty and violence.*

There is logic to the listing of these two legacies, one of
wonder and meaning, the other of horrific brutality. The ability
to acknowledge fully the latter is somehow inextricably tied
with immersion in the former.

With these dual convictions, how do we live? How do we
find an authentic personal path? Second, how do we as
groups—whether in churches or synagogues, whether in professional associations, labor unions, or political parties—work
constructively, effectively, and joyfully for justice? Third, how
do we as a nation and a people learn from our own checkered
history to help ourselves and others bring about democracy,
international cooperation, and peace? This book is an attempt
to answer these questions.

laughter

It is the laughter of people who value love and friendship and plenty, who have lived with terror and death and hate.
—Elenore Smith Bowen
Return to Laughter: An Anthropological Novel[1]

Throughout history, many people have been motivated to work for peace and justice by a profound religious faith. The stories are compelling—abolitionists, pacifists, workers for human rights and for civil rights, labor organizers, feminists—and the faiths manifold—Jewish, Christian, Muslim, Buddhist, Hindu, and the indigenous religions of the Americas, Africa, Europe, and Asia.[2]

It is an ongoing gift to learn from these stories of faith, connection, and hope. It is an ongoing challenge to also learn from centuries of religiously sanctioned violence, domination, and hatred.[3]

We who share a Christian heritage know how Christian faith has been used to justify the terror of the Inquisition, the slaughter of the Crusades, the horrors of slavery, and the systemic subordination and suppression of women and of people who are gay, lesbian, bisexual, and transgender. We may not know that the legacy of many other traditions is as paradoxical, used both to legitimize and to challenge domination and violence.

On July 28, 1937, the Myōwa Kai, a pan-Buddhist organization composed of institutional leaders from each sect of Japanese Buddhism, issued the following declaration, supporting Japanese imperial policy in its war against China:

> In order to establish eternal peace in East Asia, arousing the great benevolence and compassion of Buddhism, we are sometimes accepting and sometimes forceful. We now have no choice but to exercise the benevolent forcefulness of "killing one in order that many may live" *(issatsu tasho)*. . . . We believe it is time to effect a major change in the course of human history, which has been centered on Caucasians and inequality among humanity. To realize the true happiness of a peaceful humanity and construct a new civilization, it is necessary to redirect the path of world history's advance from this false path to the true path.[4]

Brian Victoria, Sōtō Zen priest and professor of Asian languages and literatures, examines what he sees as an unrepresentative yet highly significant time in the history of Zen Buddhism, the period between 1868 and 1945, when most of the leaders of all sects of Japanese Buddhism came to believe that war could be necessary, not merely as a matter of self-defense, not merely as "repaying the debt of gratitude" owed the Buddha and the emperor, but as an expression of the "great benevolence and compassion of Buddhism."[5] Shaku Soen, Zen master and chaplain during the Russo-Japanese War, claimed that the heart-rending sacrifices of war, what he described as "a hell let loose on earth," was nonetheless "an inevitable step toward the final realization of enlightenment."

> In this world of particulars, the noblest and greatest thing
> one can achieve is to combat evil and bring it into complete
> subjection. . . . War is an evil and a great one, indeed. But war
> against evils must be unflinchingly prosecuted till we attain
> the final aim. In the recent hostilities, into which Japan has
> entered with great reluctance, she pursues no egotistic pur-
> pose, but seeks the subjugation of evils hostile to civilization,
> peace, and enlightenment.[6]

The logic of religiously sanctioned violence is straightforward. Whether it be the Buddhist defenders of imperial Japan,
the abolitionist John Brown, or the Muslim leader Osama bin
Laden, the justifications for terror and violence are the same:
they and their followers are the bearers of unassailable truth
and the harbingers of ultimate good, commanded by the
absolute to destroy their enemies and bring about a reign of
peace and justice for all of humankind.[7]

An Ironic Spirituality

To take seriously the religiously sanctioned exercise of violence
leads us to question the relationship between religion and
ethics and to reexamine our understanding of the divine, or of
spirit, itself. Within traditional Western theology, the divine is
seen most often as the transcendent guarantor of the victory of
good over evil, and the absolute measure of the righteousness
and justice of human actions. We might view the task of theology and the realm of the spirit differently, however, if we seriously consider Arendt's reminders of the dangers of
"Robespierre's terror of virtue."[8]

There are many theologians asking fundamental questions
about the nature of theology. What types of claims do theologians
make about "beings-beyond being"?[9] What "symbolic of desire" is

manifest in our concepts and our definitions of religious truth?[10] What realities are we invoking, what behaviors, what states of mind do we conjure in our prayers, rituals, and theological and philosophical explorations of the sacred and the profane?

We often like to think that there was a time when it was easy to know what we were doing when we spoke of gods or "convened the ritual cosmos":[11] we responded to the unambiguous demand of divine revelation; we witnessed to the transformative power of religious experience; we participated in communal rituals that sustained the world.

While I doubt that religious experience and activity within fundamentalisms of the present or in premodern religious communities was as simple as it appears to us who live in a postmodern world, we can be certain of one thing: religious experience and religious reflection are not simple now, and they are not simple for us. After deconstruction, each term of our discourse, each gesture of our rituals, and each movement of desire are seen as contested, indeterminate, and socially constructed. Not only are our concepts, gestures, and desires constructed and indeterminate, but they also are implicated in master narratives that help sustain oppression, domination, violence, and exclusion.[12] The work of theologians and philosophers of religion now highlights these dual concerns. The god of metaphysics and the methods and claims of ontotheology are discredited as much for their legitimization of oppression as for their conceptual idolatry. Where does this leave us theologically and ethically? What are our options in the present moment?

In this chapter I could take up the deconstructive task as described by Grace Jantzen—a critique and an alternative that is a therapeutic intervention in a dangerous symbolic of desire.[13] Placing my work in the camp of feminist theology, I could take up Luce Irigaray's "becoming divine" and with Jantzen construe a symbolic of desire based on natality rather than death.[14] In short, I could propose another symbolic that is more fitting to the epistemic challenges of postmodernity and more suited to the imperative of establishing justice. I could argue that other postmodern thinkers are still implicated in logics of oppression that elide the power of finitude and ambiguity, and provide more adequate symbolics of natality and finitude, informed by African, African American, and Native American symbolics of balance and beauty.

I could play the dualistic game of point-counterpoint, but I will not. I will not repeat the division into legitimate/illegitimate, natality/death, faith/religion, for a simple reason. To take refuge in such a divide (or even in the possibility of such a divide) is to miss the power and peril of the religious and of all religious discourse. *In itself* (a loaded phrase to be sure), religious experience is profoundly meaningful, central to a community's and an individual's sense of identity, and at the same time, intrinsically amoral.

I once claimed that the cause of justice was better served if, rather than focus on God as the source of "right relations," we saw divinity as being "right relations," thus construing divinity as a quality of relations, an adverb rather than a noun.[15] At that time I limited divinity to "right" relations, a move similar to that of other liberal and liberation theologians who describe God as the force of creativity and justice. Now I see creativity and intense relatedness as themselves amoral, and the task of giving them moral expression as socially and culturally mediated.

In describing what this means for a positive although intrinsically ambiguous appreciation of spirituality, I emphasize an ironic spirituality that holds the paradox of being founded by that which is amoral, contingent, and malleable. I speak for those who find the Barthian and Derridean escape untenable, whether expressed as the idea that your encounter with the divine is religious and a projection, while we have received a revelation that has shattered even the pretensions of our Protestant religion and natural theology (Barth), or that your vision of justice is an idolatrous concrete messianism, while ours, in its radical openness and its "universal longing and restlessness," is free from the projections that create religious violence, coercion and fanaticism" (Derrida).[16] In many (all?) Western philosophies of religion and theology, we find an odd logic indeed: sensitive to the potential and actual harm of other religious symbolics, yet certain that we have found the key that can help us escape the same dynamic (the Protestant principle, Derrida's messianic affirmation that is not a concrete messianism).

Just as there is no *universal* longing for a total surprise, there is no definitive escape from injustice and error. I will describe a symbolic of the "fully now" (not the *tout autre*), a desire for the plenitude of presence that can also evoke justice, freedom, and respect. Yet this form of religious discourse stands *alongside*, not over against, Jean-Luc Marion's construals of a God beyond Being and the symbolic of the gift, and alongside Jantzen's and Irigaray's "becoming divine," and alongside Jacques Derrida's *tout autre* and Emmanuel Lévinas's God whose name is the call for justice.[17] Although this construal differs in its placement of error and injustice (acknowledging the amorality at the core of the religious), *it is not, for that reason, more likely nor less likely than any other construal to lead to justice or injustice.* Here I draw on philosopher Richard Rorty, and his evocation of Nietzsche's notion of the longest lie: the belief that "outside the haphazard and perilous experiments we perform there lies something (God, Science, Knowledge, Rationality, or Truth) which will, if only we perform the correct rituals, step in to save us."[18]

It is important to realize that not one of these variants of religious experience *(ours included),* not one of these construals of the divine or divinities or spiritualities inevitably and reliably leads to ethical action. The construal of divinity as

wholly other, as the excess of possibility, the not-yet that desta-
bilizes all concrete messianism, can be found in prophetic
denunciations of social injustice as well as in the cultured
despair of the middle and upper classes and our withdrawal
from political engagement. There is nothing that inevitably
and irrevocably grounds our desire for justice. Justice, in all its
forms, is our work, our creation, our unfinished task.

The Courage of Living

How exquisitely human was the wish for permanent happiness,
and how thin human imagination became trying to achieve it.
                                    —Toni Morrison, *Paradise*[19]

How is it possible that all manifestations of the religious are
amoral, if morality is intrinsic to our names for the religious?
For Lévinas, the name of God is a call for justice; for Derrida,
the *tout autre* challenges the violence and fanaticism of any
concrete messianism; for Irigaray and Jantzen, the imperative
of the religious is to "become divine," which in itself is an act of
justice, the open-ended participation in human flourishing.

   I am not saying the religious is *immoral* and thus such
names are, by definition, unwarranted. Rather, the language of
freedom and openness to others, the language of love and justice, coheres with the ecstasy and claim of the religious as easily as but *no more easily than* the language of exclusion and
self-righteousness.

   Another form of construing the sacred, found in feminist
theology, process theology, and some African and African
American theologies, is also instructive. Here the sacred is
perceived as creativity itself.[20] Let us think, though, about creativity. Creativity itself is amoral, as easily expressed in the
operations of global capitalism, in the production of music

videos and Web sites, and in the design and use of deadly weapons as it is in works of justice.[21] Furthermore, creativity is fed by powerful connections with actually available human and natural resources. The work of scientists in Los Alamos constructing the first atomic weapons, for example, was a vivid manifestation of the power of human connection and creativity. It is remarkable that almost 150 scientists involved in the creation of atomic weapons petitioned President Truman, after the defeat of Germany, and asked that such weapons *not* be used against Japan. Their pleas were unheeded.[22] Could it have been that they could imagine the destructive power of atomic weapons and the moral and political costs of their use because of their connections and creativity? It may well be that the reason pacifist and prophetic movements are relatively weak in the face of military expansion and global capitalism is that *we are less creative* than they, because we, from our vantage point in the ideal, are less connected than they to the human and natural resources of the world around us. If we ground our prophetic social critique in the *tout autre*, in an ideal outside, we might then lack the creativity that comes from working with the resources that are here now. Injustice flourishes because those who love justice are singularly lacking in creativity, content to denounce the structures we see causing harm, inept in producing other forms of art, other economic structures, other political systems.

The experience of creativity and of intense forms of connection is simply this: the crucial synthesis of the energies of people from the past, within the present, and even in the future. We may be energized, but that does not mean our theological and political analyses are true or our ethics and political strategies are just. It is disconcerting to acknowledge that our ecstasy in connection, whether political or conceptual, is simply the energy of connection, an energy that may be used in amoral, immoral, or moral ways. We want the power we experience in connection and the affirmation we encounter in being seen or being loved to affirm the rightness of our choices, actions, beliefs, and desires. While these may be affirmations of our being, they do not affirm how we frame and express that being.

What shape can imagination take, where is its thickness, its vitality, if we are no longer constituted by the desire for perfection? What happens if we are no longer propelled by the goal of perfection and the sanction of a moral divine? What, then, is the symbolics of desire, the symbolics of justice and creativity?

I'll describe a journey, one that begins with a recognition of the ambiguity of our actions and then moves to an imagination that encompasses the amorality of the religious.

Theophus Smith describes the power of conjure in African American religion. Conjure is the eliciting of spiritual power that transforms internalized oppression and evokes and sustains acts of political transformation through a complex interaction of religious symbol systems, ritual performances, and political action.[23] By definition, conjure escapes the dualistic oppositions of good and evil, sacred and profane. Working with Derrida's notion of the *pharmokos*, Smith claims that that which can heal can also harm.[24]

In some African religions and in the African American religions of Vodou, Anthony Pinn writes, we find not only a recognition of the ambiguity of our own sacral activities but also a recognition of the ambiguity of the divine. In his description of orisha service in the United States, the orishas are seen as "neutral energy forces affecting our lives," energy that "can be used for good or ill." It is startling, to the Western eye, to see a clear perception of the amorality of the divine: "Indeed, there is no force in heaven which dictates a morality."[25]

In orisha service, although the forces that create and sustain us and the universe are amoral, there is a strong moral sense. This morality seeks to create and sustain a "proper relationship with the orishas, ancestors, other humans, and the earth."[26] If we learn how to be moral not from God, not from a "being beyond being," what is the source of any particular moral vision? In orisha service, that source is the experiences, teachings, and guidance conveyed to us by other human beings.[27]

Our perception of constitutive energies is socially constructed—the creation and legacy of our ancestors. Our mobilization of these energies is the creation of the interpretive communities in which we are formed. This energy can be used, and is used, for moral and political purposes: justifying our superiority and control of others or, conversely, eliciting greater respect for and openness to others.

Toni Morrison expresses this sensibility in her novels. In *Sula*, for example, she describes a nondualistic view of good and evil, and a clearly humanly based rejection of violence and domination. The time frame of the novel is 1919–1965, a time of violent and systemic racism: lynching, mob violence and harassment, legalized job discrimination and segregation:

> What was taken by outsiders to be slackness, slovenliness or even generosity was in fact a full recognition of the legitimacy of forces other than good ones. . . . They did not believe Nature was ever askew—only inconvenient. Plague and drought were as "natural" as springtime. If milk could curdle, God knows robins could fall. The purpose of evil was to survive it and they determined (without ever knowing they had made up their minds to do it) to survive floods, white people, tuberculosis, famine and ignorance. They knew anger well but not despair, and they didn't stone sinners for the same reason they didn't commit suicide—it was beneath them.[28]

Despair and violence were "beneath them"; this is the gift of a communal legacy of resilience and respect, expressed as well by Patrick Chamoiseau in *Texaco*, a novel that traces 150 years of postslavery Caribbean history, told from the perspective of

Marie-Sophie Laborieux, the daughter of a slave, who leads in the establishment of a shantytown. Chamoiseau writes of those who knew "through which vices to rifle in order to stumble on virtue." In so doing, they received and expressed a humanity of solicitude, tenderness, and dreams. [29] In return for this gift of solicitude, the protagonist of *Texaco*, Marie-Sophie, is able to give life to others:

> The women handed me their swaddled misfortunes which I was unable to undo and which terrified me. All I had to do was look all-knowing, not wide-eyed before their fateful nonsense. And the little I would say to them would be enough to bring them back (for yet another moment) to the courage of living.[30]

What brings us back to "the courage of living" is a matter of alchemy and desire. I see the religious not in terms of right beliefs and sure foundations, but as responses to amoral powers that can be given self-critically moral purposes. There are alchemical processes that have turned the bare bones of ontotheology into fierce, compassionate, and sustained movements for justice. We can do the same.

An Alchemy of Desire

Lives don't make sense in reality, they come and go and often, like tsunamis, with the same crash, and they sweep away the dregs stagnating in your head like they were relics, which are treasures to you but don't stand still.

Chamoiseau, Texaco[31]

I write as one of the masses, immersed fully in the wonder, pain, joy, fears, and hopes of the everyday. What is the religious symbolic, the poetics of desire that evokes meaning, that compels our work for justice without desire for the transcendent, without desire for the *tout autre*, without desire for "becoming divine"? I am an atheist, not just in the sense of the binary opposition of belief/unbelief, but in the sense of the symbolics of desire.[32] I write as one of those who does not desire God. We do not desire to become divine, but rather, we work to be human, "spirit and dust," and our prayers are venues opening us to our embeddedness in nature, in history, its peril and promise.[33]

At times we respond to the needs of vulnerable others; at times others respond to our vulnerability and our needs in an exchange that nourishes and sustains us but cannot be calculated, predicted, or controlled. (Does anyone give more than infants and children? What love, delight, and awe they unleash in the world of those who respect them.)[35]

I am dependent on the theological and political work of other feminists and womanists for a compelling critique of interlocking forms of oppression and an equally powerful celebration of integrity and courage in the most dire circumstances.[36]

The work and lives of the oppressed offer more than an indictment of structures of bias, exclusion, and oppression and of the legitimacy of religious traditions and social and political institutions challenged by lives shattered and voices broken. We also find constructions of subjectivity, community, and agency that are partial *and* powerful.[37]

There are two realities in the writings of many African American and Native American peoples: first, an indictment of the dominating alchemy given to Western culture's most precious and constitutive ideals, and, second, visions of subjectivity, agency, freedom, and community that resonate with the constructions of self, desire, and world that many of us know and cherish.

Patricia J. Williams, a critical legal theorist, uses the analogy of alchemy to describe the centuries-long process of giving political form to the ideals of equal rights, freedom, and justice.

> To say that blacks never fully believed in rights is true. Yet it
> is also true that blacks believed in them so much and so hard
> that we gave them life where there was none before. . . . The
> making of something out of nothing took immense alchemi-
> cal fire—the fusion of a whole nation and the kindling of sev-
> eral generations.[38]

The language of rights and the logic of divine justice can be
mobilized for social justice and can also be part of an alchemy
of distance, isolation, and domination.

Such a plethora of foundational experiences or encounters: a
"god" who evokes love and justice, Schleiermacher's absolute
dependence, Kierkegaardian and Pauline "fear and trembling,"
Carol Christ's "great matrix of love," Tillich's "acceptance,"
Buber's "I and Thou," Derrida's *tout autre*, Jantzen and Irigaray's
"becoming divine." How odd, how human, the impulse to reduce
them to one or to rank them—"ours" as the revelation, "theirs" as
natural theology or mere human projection. What if the matter
of the religious is far more complex and diverse than can be
reduced to any monism or any dualism of authentic/inauthentic,
liberating/oppressive, freeing/reifying?[39] What all of these construals of the religious have in common is not any specific content but their power—a power that is intrinsically ambiguous,
the power of conjure, the power to heal and to harm.

Wonder and Suffering

*Say what you will, do what you will, life is not to be measured
by the ell of its sorrows. For that reason, I, Marie-Sophie
Laborieux, despite the river my eyes have shed, have always
looked at the world in a good light. But how many wretched
ones around me have choked the life out of their bodies? . . .*

*But I never had these bad thoughts. With so many rags to
launder in misery's rivers, I've never had time for melancholy.*

What's more, in the few moments life has left me, I learned to let
my heart gallop on the saddle of intense feelings, to live life, as
they say, to let her be. And note if you please that neither laugh-
ter nor smiles have ever tired the skin of my lips.

—Chamoiseau, *Texaco*[40]

Many long for the wholly other, yet we revel in the fully now.
Our desire is the present in its abundance and wonder, our
desire for justice a way of honoring the integrity of that which
is, our political work an exuberant "virtuosity in the face of
adversity."[41] This is not the religion of the "healthy-minded"
criticized by William James, an unabashed embrace of life's
pleasures and a resolute denial of life's horrors.[42] No, this is a
passion, not for perfection, but for the "vibrantly imperfect"
possible. It is not a passion for transgression, but a passion for
the excess, the depth, the wonder, and the possibilities of the
everyday. We work for justice with the tools of the present and
because of our love and respect for the present texture of lives.
Not all is just, not all is honored, but that which *is valued*
serves as the fulcrum from which to challenge all that devalues
life. To us, it is the passion for the impossible that seems bereft,
isolated from the beauty and vibrant connections that evoke
respect and can be mobilized to work for justice.

As the quote from Chamoiseau makes clear, here we have
a full awareness that life does destroy many people; injustice
destroys lives and drives people mad. And yet, to again quote
Chamoiseau, "To be part of it [City], I chose to act. And like the
local youths say about politics around here: I chose battle over
tears."[43]

Our passion is one of connection, open-eyed and aware of
the fragility of the matrix in which we live. Rita Nakashima
Brock and Susan Thistlethwaite describe a meditation on
breath that can lead us to know the significance of these connections:

> When we are trapped in the musings of our minds, wandering the temporal spheres of memory and future . . . we are not fully in the present. When our whole being is fully attuned to the present . . . enormous energy and life are unleashed. The discipline of learning to breathe in such restorative ways comes in community with others who breathe. . . . In this breathing together we can inspire each other with grace and compassion to conspire for change.[44]

Being in the present can bring stasis and closure. Being in the present may also open us, connect us, and empower us with a dynamic fullness. As Chamoiseau states, "draw in excess from those you love."[45] What we draw from those we love can be described but not trapped in definitive formulations, in truths that can be reflected in the logic of belief/unbelief. Leslie Marmon Silko, for example, describes truths that are communal, intrinsically open and multifaceted. She explains, "The ancient Pueblo people sought a communal truth, not an absolute. For them this truth lived somewhere within the web of differing versions, disputes over minor points, outright contradictions tangling with old feuds and village rivalries." This "living truth" is a truth of engagement and desire, a way of being in a world we can never fully understand, not a metaphysics of how things really are.[46]

This is not a story with an end, although it is a story with many meanings. It is an engagement with life and a passion for its wealth. It is not hope for an end, for a lasting resolution: it is not a longing for the totally new, nor is it the expectation of the repetition of the same, the endless return of the known and the expected. Morrison writes of a desire for and a solace in the rhythms of the present, their openness, and their resonance:

> In ocean hush a woman black as firewood is singing. Next to her is a younger woman whose head rests on the singing woman's lap . . .

There is nothing to beat this solace which is what Piedade's song is about, although the words evoke memories neither one has ever had: of reaching age in the company of the other; of speech shared and divided bread smoking from the fire; the unambivalent bliss of going home to be at home—the ease of coming back to love begun.

When the oceans heave sending rhythms of water ashore, Piedade looks to see what has come. Another ship, perhaps, but different, heading to port, crew and passengers, lost and saved, atremble, for they have been disconsolate for some time. Now they will rest before shouldering the endless work they were created to do down here in Paradise.[47]

Memory and Reciprocity

Write The Word*? No. But tie the knot with life again, yes.*
—Chamoiseau, *Texaco*[48]

Ours is not the desire of becoming divine. It is the passion of "shouldering the endless work" in Paradise, of tying the knot with life again. We "tie the knot" not because of master narratives of destiny and promise, of resolution won, but we live out of the threads of connection, the threads of recognition within which we come to life. Chamoiseau recounts a tale of persistent work, even in the face of defeat: "I wanted to show strength, and so never . . . would I stand round taking pity on my fate like I so often felt like doing. . . . Under the dull eyes of the others, I lifted my poles back up, straightened my partitions, spread my oilcloths. . . . And my tears drowned in my sweat."[49]

How do we gain the will to continue, to let "our tears drown in our sweat"? This persistent affirmation of life does not emerge from an exercise of will; it is not the result of our reason. It is, rather, the gift, the legacy of generations.

Brock and Thistlethwaite point to the fragility of truth and the need of a social movement to hold the truths of compassion and commitment.[50] This holding is communal and generational, a form of power expressed through its fragility and not in spite of it. This power of generations is described well by Garth Kasimu and Karen Baker-Fletcher. In their systematic theology, they add another category to the well-known list of eschatology, ecclesiology, anthropology, Christology, and doctrine of God. They write of generations: the collective matrix of our being; the past that engendered us, the present and future we engender. They cite the cosmological community principle *muntu* of the Bantu peoples of Southeastern Africa: "I am because we are; and we are because I am."[51]

Karen and Garth Kasimu Baker-Fletcher also remind us that "generations must not be romanticized." They write that idealizing our elders causes us to "learn far less of what life has taught them or can teach us" than we can learn by considering their weaknesses as well as their strengths.[52] This legacy of virtuosity, of living fully in the "vibrantly imperfect" possible, is described as well by Leslie Marmon Silko. She sees this as the gift of Laguna storytelling, an oral tradition that recounts even "disturbing or provocative" events. In Laguna stories, "Neither the worst blunders or disasters nor the greatest financial prosperity and joy will ever be permitted to isolate anyone from the rest of the group. . . . You are never the first to suffer a grave loss or profound humiliation. You are never the first, and you understand that you will probably not be the last to commit or be victimized by a repugnant act."[53] We are not the first to suffer and fail, and we will not be the last. We are not the first to also embody a measure of justice, and we will not be the last.

To see the world through the lenses of compassion and empathy, to create our world with this passion for life-affirming justice, is not a duty, demand, obligation, or sacrifice. It is, rather, a blessing and a gift. This life of seeking justice does have costs, but the ability to respect others enough to have a passion for justice, and the ability to mourn and rage our own suffering and that of others, is not an onerous task but a rich legacy. Its source is not our own achievement, but the gift of the generations who shaped us, the ancestors who gave ethical and aesthetic form to the energy of life.[54]

This symbolic of religion has at its core horror and rage at injustice and a fierce longing for justice, for personal and individual institutions that embody respect. Patricia Williams claims that if we live justly, we "give to all of society's objects and untouchables the rights of privacy, integrity, and self-assertion; [we] give them distance and respect."[55] Carol Lee Sanchez describes the respect at the core of the traditions of people of the Laguna Pueblo, recognizing the integrity of "all my relations," human, natural, animal, and the balance that exists between all of us.[56] This is not the vulnerable face of Lévinas, but the compelling *you* of Buber's I-You relationship.[57] Lévinas describes a way some people see otherness—as threat, as vulnerable, as demand—and tries to limit the violence against that other.[58]

Within the work of feminist, womanist, and liberation theologians, we see, though, a basically different perception of otherness.[59] At its core, there is reciprocity. This reciprocity is expressed vividly and concretely in Chamoiseau's description of building the Quarters:

> If someone gives you a hand, you have to stand ready with at least one canari of vegetables, with a piece of cod, a gallon of rum, glasses and madou. Once I was ready, I rang out the call . . . . Then things went very fast. My hutch attracted other hutches. . . . The very people on the slope lent a helping hand, gave advice, helped, shouldered each other.[60]

This is not caring for the vulnerable other. Nor is this reciprocity calculated or constrained. It is, rather, the exuberant expression of mutuality.

Many of us cannot see the other, the face, the way Lévinas does. Our alternative seeing—one of curiosity and respect—is not a choice, but the gift of the ancestors. We see as we were seen; we love as we were loved.

What would it mean for political organizing if we began with the premise that our passion for justice is not our achievement, but a gift? What if we realized that caring about injustice is not the result of our astute sociopolitical analyses, our compassion, our courage, and our will but is, rather, the result of being loved, recognized, and seen by others? Longing for justice and mourning and raging in the face of injustice are the gift of the ancestors, the gift of "all our relations."[61]

This recognition of our dependence calls us away from prophetic denunciations of other people's hard-heartedness and closed-mindedness. It calls us from any satisfaction in merely denouncing structures and peoples who exploit or ignore others. When we acknowledge the strength and dignity of others, when we empathize with the suffering of others, and when we cast our lot in acts of creating justice, our selves are enlarged by the blessings of openness, the blessings of an open heart, and the blessings of an enlivened imagination.

"Return to Laughter"

What then, is the religious? This is the name we give to those encounters and energies that are constitutive but amoral, those encounters and energies that are vivid, compelling, and meaningful, but fragile. This symbolic of desire is not better than other conceptions of the religious, for it has its own peril and promise.[62] It may lead to justice, and it may also sustain structures of isolation and domination.

I am not as aware of the fundamental, constitutive dangers of this logic as I would like to be, but I can identify four. One of the greatest dangers is complacency. If we are relatively safe and comfortable, removed from the immediate costs of oppression, it is easy to relish the beauty of life and leave the work of building justice to those who are suffering the costs of direct injustice in their daily lives.

Another constitutive danger is settling for too little. If we forgo the illusion of utopia and choose instead "connections that are real and hopes that are realizable," we may settle for reforms that are less far-reaching than is actually possible.[63] An element of madness, folly, and excess exists in any work for justice—an exuberant overreaching of the limits of the present. Embedded as we are in complex networks of other actors, with other hopes and desires, we cannot tell the difference between what we can change and what we cannot. We cannot tell in advance of the struggle if we will succeed or fail; we cannot predict the ramifications of our actions in the present or the future.

Another constitutive risk, one true of any construction of the religious that valorizes religious ecstasy and the intensity of religious experience, is that this mysticism, or this intense connection to other people, separates us from life and leads us to have disdain for "ordinary" life and "ordinary" people, who supposedly, do not know this ecstatic connection. The dangers are twofold: First, it is often difficult to translate the ecstasy of mystical experiences into the possibilities and demands of daily life. Rather than mysticism being a way of "illumining the everyday," it can be an escape from the everyday, or seen as more than the material, that is, more valuable than the daily tasks of life.[64] These intense experiences and connections can also lead to disdain for other people. If this sense of connection and energy seems new and our prior life seems meaningless or shallow in contrast to what we now know, we may project our prior meaninglessness onto others, assuming, to quote the camp song, that we share a love, a peace, a joy "that the world does not know."

In her novel *Paradise*, Toni Morrison recounts the tragedy of a town that, in escaping slavery and exclusion, defined itself as exclusive, and violently so. This town, in trying to give its youth safety, denied their vitality and creativity. *Even the energy of generations is amoral;* it can be used to stifle and bind, rather than to frame and nourish. Morrison writes:

> How exquisitely human was the wish for permanent happiness, and how thin human imagination became trying to achieve it. Soon Ruby will be like any other country town: the young thinking of elsewhere; the old full of regret. The sermons will be eloquent but fewer and fewer will pay attention or connect them to everyday life.[65]

There is no fundamental divide between us, the righteous, the vanguard, the enlightened, and the "unsaved, the unworthy and the strange." We can "return to laughter," learning from the stranger within and the stranger outside, blessed with the legacy of seeing all as worthy of dignity, privacy, and respect.[66] We can return to laughter, the generous laughter that relishes the irony of knowing that what funds our morality is itself amoral, and morality—far from being the demand or gift of the divine—is the perilous and at times beautiful human response to the energy and wonder of life.

chapter 3

virtuosity

You are America and my father.
your honesty
your uncompromising faith in
participatory democracy
your belief in "the rights of the people"
I take from you
as my own—
to pass on to future generations.

—Carol Lee Sanchez[1]

Consider how we might establish a democracy that is deep, inclusive, and creative. What would it mean to fully include the histories and insights of all Americans as we continually revise the social contract that makes up our society? Despite deep-seated divisions of race, class, and gender, many people persist in calling us to a more just social order. Vine Deloria Jr. (Standing Rock Sioux), professor of history, claims that "forces of reconciliation and reparations do indeed exist," and these forces "continually present us with the opportunity to get involved in the creation of a society more in tune with human needs and highly compatible with the best of Indian

and non-Indian beliefs and practices." He challenges people in
the United States to move forward together to create a "con-
tinental culture" focused on "providing everyone with a sense
of integrity and identity."[2]

In this chapter we explore the work of contemporary
Native American scholars and activists. David Moore, a scholar
who examines the relationship of critical legal theory to tribal
sovereignty, clearly indicates what we can expect to find from
listening to contemporary Native Americans: a vision of "*e
pluribus unum* as community built on difference."[3]

In responding to Native American scholars and activists,
we both continue and revise a tradition that predates the
American Revolution. The continuity lies in recognizing that
there is much to learn from Native peoples about democratic
governance. Historian James Wilson writes that in the eighteenth century, European philosophers and New World settlers alike, seeking "principles for less despotic political
systems" and principles for "self-government and independence," were "genuinely curious about the possible model to be
found in the egalitarian and non-coercive League of the
Iroquois."[4] Thomas Jefferson and Benjamin Franklin studied
the constitution of the Iroquois and found much to emulate. A
century later the women's suffrage movement was inspired by
the political and cultural power and freedom of Iroquois
women.[3] As Carol Lee Sanchez writes, "The basic principles of
democracy, the freedom of the individual and equality among
the people of both genders, come directly from the Native
American nations the first European immigrants lived among
in the Americas."[5]

The League of the Five, later Six Nations (the
Hotinonshonni) was a stable form of governance that had
ended years of destructive warfare between the Cayuga,
Mohawk, Onondaga, Oneida, and Seneca. Many scholars have
noted how intrigued European and Euro-American political

thinkers were with the Great Law (the Kaianerekowa) of the Hotinonshonni. The League was founded by Deganawida, the Peacemaker. The Kaianerekowa is a system of government marked by a balance of powers between men and women, and between individual nations and the League. Within the League, decisions were made after lengthy discussion. If agreement could not be reached, the parties—whether a nation or a faction within a nation—could do as they pleased, as long as they did not harm any other League member.[6]

Euro-Americans, including Henry Morgan, a nineteenth-century lawyer, recognized and appreciated the balance of powers within the League. But few, if any, understood the nondualistic assumptions about human nature and human society that led to this form of governance. Morgan wrote, "Their whole civil policy was averse to the concentration of power in the hands of any single individual, but inclined to the opposite principle of division among a number of equals." Why was it so important to avoid the concentration of power? The founder of the League, Deganawida, was described as a man who saw his task as that of healing wrongdoers, not defeating them. Healing is a process that requires the restoration of limits and balance to individuals and to society. Hence, the enduring opposition to any concentration of power.[7]

The Hotinonshonni brought this concern with balance to their negotiations with Europeans. They were able to imagine European and Native societies coexisting, neither trying to control or conquer the other. The "Two Row Wampum" belt symbolized this vision:

> "You say that you are our Father and I am your son." We say "We will not be like Father and Son, but like Brothers." This . . . belt confirms our words. These two rows will symbolize two paths or two vessels, traveling down the same river together. One, a birch bark canoe, will be for the Indian

People, their laws, their customs and their ways. The other, a ship, will be for the white people and their laws, their customs and their ways. We shall each travel the river together, side by side, but in our own boat. Neither of us will make compulsory laws or interfere in the internal affairs of the other. Neither of us will try to steer the other's vessel.[8]

In spite of the genuine interest Anglo-American settlers and European political theorists felt about the Iroquois social order, they lacked an appreciation for much that was central to that order, a lack that had fatal consequences for hundreds of thousands of Native peoples. We see this fatal lacunae in Benjamin Franklin's grudging acknowledgment of the wisdom of a 1744 speech by the Iroquois leader Canasatego. In that speech to the commissioners of Pennsylvania, Virginia, and Maryland, the Onondaga sachem Canasatego spoke of the possibility of harmonious relationships between the League of Five Nations and Anglo-Americans, and urged the latter to follow the example of the League:

We heartily recommend Union and a good agreement between you, our brethren. . . . Our wise forefathers established union and amity between the Five Nations; this has made us formidable; this has given us great weight and authority with our neighbouring nations.

We are a powerful Confederacy; and by your observing the same methods our wise forefathers have taken, you will acquire fresh strength and power.[9]

In 1754 Benjamin Franklin referred to Canasatego's speech while arguing for the political union of American colonies: "It would be a very strange thing if Six Nations of ignorant savages should be capable of forming such a scheme for such a union, and be able to execute in such a manner as that it has subsisted ages, and appears indissoluble; and yet that a like union should be impracticable for ten or a dozen English colonies."[10]

Franklin was not alone in dismissing the integrity and wisdom of the Hotinonshonni (League of Six Nations). While some colonists extolled the political acumen of the Hotinonshonni or the agricultural expertise of the Powhatan, they still withheld recognition of their full humanity. Such bigotry fueled the military campaigns of the English and later the nascent United States against the Nations, whose governmental system they had so admired. George Washington, for example, ordered brutal attacks against the Hotinonshonni in 1779. Troops under General John Sullivan, following Washington's orders that the territory not "merely be overrun but destroyed," razed crops, burned villages, and massacred women and children.[11]

For Americans to create a truly inclusive social contract, we must recognize the devastating costs of colonial domination, as well as the resilience of Native peoples. Just as the Onondaga sachem Canasatego offered a vision of living and working together in 1744, contemporary Native American leaders and writers enjoin us to listen and learn from the survival strategies of Native peoples, and to work together to establish a democratic society for *our* time. For example, Regis Pecos (Cochiti Pueblo), director of the Office of Indian Affairs for the State of New Mexico, challenges us to learn from the "bold intellectual and spiritual understandings that have enabled us [the Pueblo peoples] to survive in the midst of incredible hardships and [devastating federal] policies." He states, "Our ceremonies and community life are filled with important lessons that we should all consider in our efforts to make the next five hundred years an era in which all people enjoy the freedom and protection of rights guaranteed to us by the Constitution of the United States."[12]

How do we work together now, creating a more democratic and just present and future, while fully acknowledging the history of colonialism and the attempts to destroy the culture and language of hundreds of Native nations? Kathryn Shanley (Assiniboine/Nakota), professor of Native American asks non-Indian peoples to stop the onslaught of "neo-colonial cultural appropriations," in which we selectively take elements from Native cultures but ignore the specificities of history and language. Shanley suggests that the task for Western academics is to acknowledge the importance of Native histories and insights for public discourse, and "to offer to be an audience and then to amplify those voices barely heard, or not heard at all without a committed audience."[13]

A New Social Contract

Creative possibilities for framing a new democratic spirit exist in social contract theory, especially in light of contemporary and historical Native American critiques of Euro-American politics and culture, and in light of contemporary Native American practices of social order. Why social contract theory? It is a fitting vehicle for acknowledging the past and then forging a creative, forward-looking reciprocity between peoples within the United States. By working with social contract theory, we begin with an understanding of political legitimacy and political obligation that is widely understood and accepted, albeit still debated, within the United States and Western Europe. The writers of the American Declaration of Independence declared that "governments derive their just powers from the consent of the governed." Today people widely accept the idea that "political legitimacy, political authority, and political obligations are derived from the consent of those who create a government (sometimes a society) and who operate it," whether by voting, electing representatives, or following its rules.[14] Within a social contract, women and men create together the institutions and laws that regulate our collective life. These laws and institutional structures, the obligations that we have to one another, are not derived from natural law or divine decree, but are chosen by us.[15]

The philosophers who developed social contract theory in the seventeenth and eighteenth centuries described this process of choosing obligations in terms that are primarily counterfactual and ahistorical. Hobbes (1588–1679), for example, writes of an imaginary situation of a "war of all against all" and individuals choosing social constraints rather than violent anarchy.[16] It is possible, however, to read the development of a social contract as an ongoing historical process, the efforts of human beings to shape our social life, building on the collective wisdom of humankind. We do not need to refer to an imaginary "state of nature." We can critically examine our past.

Social contract theory is being creatively reformulated by theorists in the present. Martin Jay, professor of modern European intellectual history, describes the renewed interest in social contract theory and human rights found in the work of "new French thinkers." Unlike their poststructuralist predecessors, these philosophers are interested in liberal Western political theory and express "a desire to revitalize the tradition of human rights as a fundamental dimension of a liberal polity."[17] In exploring their work, Jay argues that three basic problems remain:

1. For purposes of discussing "human rights," we need to clarify who counts as fully human. How do we acknowledge and address the "abjection of the 'other'"—that is, the exclusion of certain peoples, due to race, gender, and ethnicity, from the fully and normatively human? How do we define the human self and its "integrity"? What do we do with different understandings of human integrity and the relationships among self-sufficiency, autonomy, and social interdependence?

2. Significant debates also remain over the foundation of the social contract and any commitment to human rights. A commitment to liberal democracy and human rights is hardly "self-evident," given the widespread political and philosophical debates over the content and value of human rights.

3. Finally, we face the conundrum of how to adjudicate among competing and possibly incommensurable rights. As an example, Jay points to the well-known tension found between "social rights"—for example, the "right to work" and the "right to a standard of living adequate for the health and well-being of his [sic] family" found in the 1948 United Nations Universal Declaration of Human Rights—and the "allegedly absolute right to private property."[18]

Jay provides a concise summary of these challenges yet to be addressed: "the uncertain boundaries of the category of the 'human,' the difficulty of finding a foundational *point d'appui* for transcendent rights, and the possible incommensurability of those alleged rights." He suggests that as we seek ways to meet those challenges, we "begin to rely more on our own conceptual resources and traditions."[19]

To take up that task, I draw primarily on the resources of Native American philosophers. There is a crucial reason for beginning fundamental change by building on the ingredients that exist in the present to redress the horrors of the past (*wrongs* is too weak a word for the monumental atrocities of the massacre and betrayals of Native peoples). In working with a political strategy already in place, albeit partially and erratically implemented, we follow the example of African Americans who made sense and meaning out of American ideals of human rights and social equality that far exceeded the conceivable implementation of those ideals by Jefferson, Locke, and Paine. In *The Alchemy of Race and Rights*, critical legal theorist Patricia Williams writes of the complex process entailed in giving life to aspirations for justice and equal rights, of the centuries-long process of giving practical form to cherished ideals.[20]

This chapter takes up only one dimension of the task of giving life to a just and honorable social contract: a critical reexamination of what it means to be American in light of Native American history and the insights of contemporary Native American peoples. The same, of course, needs to be done (and is being done) in light of the history and insights of all exploited and marginalized peoples in the United States who have shaped this country and are part of its present and future without, however, receiving due recognition and respect.[21]

Framing a new vision of a just and honorable social contract entails a long process. The beginning is not, however, arbitrary. From the insights of Native peoples and their understandings of learning from atrocities and mistakes, their understandings of reciprocity and respect, we can learn what is required to base a social compact on the wisdom and history of *all* Americans, learning from the complex interaction of our mistakes, our atrocities, and our noble ideals. We find a pattern for *e pluribus unum* that does not eradicate differences but holds together acts of good and evil, justice and freedom, massacre and legalized theft—seeing them all, acknowledging them all, including them all as part of who we are.

The Diversity of Native American Societies

When *e pluribus unum* includes Native American peoples, it encompasses a wide range of social structures and religious traditions. Represented within the United States are more than six hundred tribal traditions and eight major language groups.[22] Native American societies, in the past and in the present, exhibit vast differences, not only of language, but of kinship systems, gender roles, class divisions, ceremonial practices, means of economic subsistence, and ways of dealing with enemies. There are warrior societies such as the Cheyenne, the Apache, and the Lakota, as well as peoples committed to peace (the Arawak and the Pueblos). There are significant differences in social organization, even within linguistic groups. In the nineteenth century, among the Salish-speaking peoples of what is now Washington State and British Columbia, for example, we find both the egalitarian systems of the Sanpoils and the Southern Okanogans of the Interior Salish, as well as the social class differentiation and slavery of the Coast Salish and the Bella Coola.[23]

We find considerable differences as well in the status of women. The Cherokee were noted for the independence, power, and freedom of women, while the nearby Muskogee had strict divisions of gender roles and subjected women to paternal authority.[24] Religious ceremonies are equally diverse, not only in terms of specific rituals and symbols, but in the intensity and focus of religious life. While some societies, like the Lakota, focus more on ecstatic visions, others, like the Pueblos, are attuned more to the ceremonial significance of daily life. Even those peoples who practice similar healing rituals often do so in fundamentally different ways. The Lakota, Arapaho, Assiniboines, Crows, Pawnees, Shoshones, Utes, and Mandans, for example, have long included piercing in the Sun Dance, the ceremony in which individuals undergo intense physical pain for the good of their families and for the life of the community. The Kiowa, and now the Cheyenne, do not.[25]

Native American peoples have changed in response to conquest and modernity. Change was also integral to precolonial Native American life. Alfonzo Ortiz (San Juan Pueblo), professor of anthropology, describes the "shifting clusters of experiences and meanings" that unify the forty thousand Pueblos of New Mexico and Arizona. Pueblos speak "six mutually unintelligible languages" yet share a homeland, trading practices, and a history of "adaptability and cultural tenacity." Ortiz claims that there is no "invariant cultural property" that marks Pueblo identity. There is, however, a common thread, as important in the present as in the past: "revitalization as a way of life."[26]

Gerald Vizenor (Anishinaabe), writer and professor of literature and American Studies, sees such transformative resilience in the so-called return to traditional practices. Rather than simply repeating a static or uniform past, Vizenor claims that Native peoples are participating in the continuing evolution of dynamic traditions of knowing and being. He coins a word, *survivance*, to capture this dynamic play of survival and transformation.[27]

While tremendous diversity among native societies and languages exists, there is a politically compelling reason for speaking of Native American political claims, ethical and political critiques, and moral and religious worldviews. This is, of course, a complicated task. Jace Weaver (Cherokee), professor of religion and law, clearly insists there is no unitary Native American worldview, but following the postcolonial theorist Gayatri Spivak, he advocates a "strategic essentialism," describing a view of religion, community, land, and knowledge that differs sharply from dominant views in Europe and the United States for "visible political interests."[28] As Weaver states, "To speak of Native views of religion, land and culture is not so much erroneous, as it is imprecise."[29] He refers whenever possible to specific traditions and urges all of us to become cognizant of the reasons for the differences among those traditions.

There are, however, common political, ethical, and epistemological reasons for the focus on particularity within Native traditions. It is these principles of knowing and of being—principles held by most, if not all, Native communities—that are elucidated by scholars and activists such as Jace Weaver, Vine Deloria Jr., and Carol Lee Sanchez.[30] There is, furthermore, a compelling political reason for a strategic essentialism. Europeans and later Euro-Americans initially treated the diverse indigenous peoples in the same way. We find in the accounts of Native people throughout the Americas a devastating critique of their treatment by Euro-American settlers and governments: humanity denied, land stolen, treaties abrogated, and cultures first derided and exterminated, later seemingly valued but still fundamentally misunderstood. In addition, Native peoples, in their diversity, make similar claims to political rights, out of a common history of pre-Columbian sovereignty and postcontact domination, conquest, and survival.

Jace Weaver and the contemporary writer Sherman Alexie (Coeur D'Alene) remind us of a further challenge in listening to the insights and critiques of Native American activists and writers. Euro-Americans have a long history of romanticizing, and thereby dehumanizing, indigenous peoples.[31] Alexie, Weaver, and Gerald Vizenor, among others, delineate the vitality and the devastation that are part of contemporary American Indian culture. Weaver acknowledges the diversity of Native American communal life, and he also highlights the ambiguity of Native American history: "It is not my intent to . . . romanticize pre-Contact society. There were conflicts and problems as in any other cultures. America was not some Edenic paradise. It was simply ours."[32] These writers do not deny the brutality, greed, and disappointments within Native communities in the past and in the present. The complete story of a community, its despair and achievements, its good and its evil, is, rather, the matrix within which identity is forged and meaning is found. We can learn from and with traditions other than our own without assuming that these communities are any less free of conflict, failure, and challenges than are we.

Elements of a Communal Ethic

Tribal Sovereignty

The first claim raised by Native American peoples that must be taken seriously by all Americans is as simple and straightforward in principle and theory as it is contentious and complex in practice. Native peoples want much of their land returned, and Native peoples call for recognition of tribal sovereignty. How much land should be returned? What can tribal sovereignty mean in our contemporary society? David Moore describes a few of the emerging models, including the lease of reservation land to white residents and, in South Dakota, a plan to convert public lands into a Great Sioux National Park.[33] The specifics of land rights are up to negotiation, but the negotiations must be undertaken from a position of reciprocity, respect, and acknowledgment of the abuses of the past.[34]

According to the 2000 census, Native Americans make up 1.5 percent of the population of the United States.[35] Despite the small numbers, some Native peoples continue to hope for and work for a return of all of America to indigenous peoples. Leslie Marmon Silko, in *Almanac of the Dead*, decries the corruption of Euro-American society and recounts the hope for the return of all tribal land: "It might require a hundred years of spirit voices and simple population growth, but the result would be the same: tribal people would retake the Americas; tribal people would retake ancestral land all over the world."[36]

Most Native peoples, however, see the challenge as one of living with the immigrant groups who now make this land base their home. For that coexistence to be truly reciprocal, we who are Euro-American are challenged to acknowledge the centuries-long theft of Native lands and to seek means of restoring significant amounts of land, and of protecting and honoring what has been already restored. Moore also challenges us to move past the strictures of "a binary colonial mind" and imagine, and create, a "multicultural state" that encompasses "coexistent tribal sovereignties."[37] To negotiate land claims fairly, to develop a social contract that recognizes Native rights and our mutual obligations, Native activists and scholars challenge Euro-Americans to understand the significance and meaning of land, religion, and community for Native peoples.

Sacred Places

According to Jace Weaver, a key factor in the inability of American jurisprudence and culture to respect Native American rights has been an inability to understand the full scope of Native people's claims for land and religious freedom.[38]

Many of the first European explorers and settlers failed to see Native ceremonies and ways of life as religious. The conclusions drawn by Christopher Columbus about the Taino (Island Arawak) are well-known. On Thursday, October 11, 1492, Columbus wrote: "It appears to me, that the people are ingenious, and would be good servants and I am of opinion that they would very readily become Christians, as they appear to have no religion." A few days later, October 14, he also noted that "the people here are simple in war-like matters. . . . I could conquer the whole of them with fifty men, and govern them as I pleased."[39]

By the nineteenth century, Euro-Americans recognized Native religious practices as a vital yet dangerous form of religion, outlawed, therefore, as barriers to assimilation and as threats to social stability. Vine Deloria Jr. states, "By the time of the Allotment Act of 1887 (Dawes Act), almost every form of Indian religion was banned on the reservations. . . . Even Indian funeral ceremonies were declared to be illegal, and drumming and any form of dancing had to be held for the most artificial of reasons."[40] The comprehensive ban of Indian religion was revoked in 1934 under the Indian Reorganization Act. With their renewed religious freedom, Indian people began to practice ceremonies openly. The religious freedom of Native peoples continues, however, to be limited by narrow definitions of what counts as constitutionally protected religious practices.

The dominant understanding of religious freedom in the United States was based not on all religions in North America (Native, Muslim, Christian, and Jewish) but on Enlightenment views of Christianity in which religion is seen as primarily a matter of individual belief. According to Weaver, the constitution and subsequent legal interpretations have difficulty incorporating a view of religion in which there is "no distinction between everyday life and . . . spirituality" and in which "Native religious traditions are intimately and inexorably tied to the land and often cannot be practiced merely anywhere."[41] As Joe S. Sando (Jemez Pueblo) states, "Religion . . . was life itself."[42] Weaver cites a 1988 Supreme Court case, *Lyng v. Northwest Indian Cemetery Protective Association*, in which the court declined to forbid construction of a timbering road that would have devastated northwest California land considered sacred by the Yurok, Karok, and Tolowa tribes. The reason given was a stark rejection of claims that hunting and fishing are religious activities for these tribes and other Native American tribes: "While that may be true, in an anthropological sense, the federal Constitution does not recognize such a broad concept of 'religion.'"[43]

Land

Euro-Americans were able to justify to themselves the necessity and legitimacy of the eradication of Native American societies because of two major convictions: (1) certainty in the universal validity of our concept of individual and property rights; and (2) an inability to understand a different view of land and its significance within human community. Two examples, though separated by 350 years, together illustrate the conviction of knowing, without a doubt, the correct way to organize society and utilize natural resources.

In 1641, John Winthrop, governor of Massachusetts, described the Native peoples of New England as follows:

> This savage people ruleth over many lands without title or property; for they inclose no ground, neither have they cattel to maintayne it, but remove their dwellings as they have occasion, or as they can prevail against their neighbors. And why may not Christians have liberty to go and dwell amongst them in their waste lands and woods (leaving such places as they have manured for their corne) as lawfully as Abraham did among the Sodomites?[44]

Compare Winthrop's words with those of then-president Ronald Reagan, speaking in Moscow in 1988, and answering a question about Native Americans:

> Let me tell you just a little something about the American Indian in our land. We have provided millions of acres of land for what are called preservations, or the reservations I should say. They, from the beginning, announced that they wanted to maintain their way of life as they had always lived, there in the desert and the plains and so forth, and we set up these reservations so they could and had a Bureau of Indian Affairs to help take care of them, at the same time we provide education for them, schools on the reservations, and they are free, also, to leave the reservations and be American citizens among the rest of us, and many do. Some still prefer, however, that early way of life and we've done everything we can to

meet their demands on how they want to live. Maybe we made a mistake. Maybe we should not have humored them in that wanting to stay in that kind of primitive lifestyle. Maybe we should have said: "No, come join us, be citizens."[45]

Most Euro-Americans did not see themselves as stealing Native lands. They claimed, rather, that Native peoples were not fully or properly using a vast and fertile continent.[34]

The resilience of the myth of a largely unpopulated wilderness is surprising, and the power of the rationalization remarkable, given the magnitude of evidence against it. When the Spanish arrived in what is now New Mexico, they found agricultural communities, Pueblo villages that had existed since 700 CE. In Chaco Canyon are the vast remains of an elaborate ceremonial complex built between 850 and 1100 CE. The English in New England found people who hunted and farmed, lived in stockaded villages, and according to current scholarship, had under cultivation nearly all of the arable land in New England. Similarly, Native American hunting patterns in the western Great Plains required vast expanses of land. The Cheyenne, Lakota, and Apache followed the migration of the buffalo over millions of acres.[46]

Recall John Winthrop and the land "manured for their corne." Not only was much of the land actually "used," in even a European sense of use, the lands of the Americas were valued, respected, and perceived in ways inconceivable to most European settlers. For many Native American peoples, the land is not simply theirs, or ours, to use. The connections between people and land are far more complex. Jace Weaver writes that the community that shapes the self is not limited to other humans. Weaver illustrates this sensibility by defining the Cherokee world *eloh'*. Although the word is sometimes translated "religion," its meaning simultaneously includes "'history,' 'culture,' 'law'—and 'land.'"[47] Land is as much a part of community as is the relationship with other people. Weaver explains, "Natives tend to be spatially oriented rather than temporally oriented. Their cultures, spirituality, and identity are connected to the land—and not simply land in a generalized sense but *their* land. The act of creation is not so much what happened *then* as it is what happened *here*, it is the story of the formation of a specific land and a particular people."[48] Whereas European settlers saw themselves as properly using land that was uncultivated and underappreciated, Weaver claims that few, if any, Europeans understood what was at stake when Indian tribes were forced to leave their ancestral lands: "When Indian tribes were forcibly removed from their homes, they were robbed of more than territory. Taken from them was a numinous world where every mountain and lake holds meaning for their faith and identity."[49]

Native peoples cultivated land without the correlative assumption that humans are superior to the land. As Weaver states, "It [the land] was held in common by all. It was not property but community." Weaver cites the words of Tecumseh (Shawnee), spoken in 1801 as he urged all Native peoples to work together to stop Euro-American land theft: "The only way to stop this evil is for all the redmen to unite in claiming a common and equal right in the land, as it was at first, and should be now—for it never was divided, but belongs to all. No tribe has a right to sell, even to each other, much less to strangers, who demand all and will take no less."[50]

Weaver describes the centuries of conflict over land use and anticipates that the claims of Native peoples will continue to be disregarded. He does not see this, however, as simply a matter of sheer power, the stronger disregarding the claims of the weak. Rather, the struggle is epistemological as much as political. Many Euro-American settlers, lawmakers, and jurists cannot even comprehend what was at stake for Native Americans in their claims to land: a view of religion as ritual practice, part of daily life, and tied to a particular place.[51]

Like Weaver, Deloria argues that the very experience of religion, the very "presence of the sacred," is tied to what he calls the specific places that "are the foundation of all other beliefs and practices." He says each generation must learn that sacred spaces "properly inform us that we are not larger than nature and that we have responsibilities to the rest of the natural world that transcend our own personal desires and wishes."[52]

The meaning of sacred lands, honored for centuries by many Native peoples, is a lesson that Deloria argues non-Natives can and must learn: "Today our society is still at a primitive aesthetic stage of appreciating the personality of our lands, but we have the potential to move beyond mere aesthetics and come to some deep religious realizations of the role of sacred places in human life."[53] For Deloria, this lesson is necessary if we are to avoid destroying the land we occupy.

Community: "That the People Might Live"

Jace Weaver writes of a "communitist" sensibility in which individual meaning is found in belonging to and contributing to a particular social group.[54] In this worldview, individuals are recognized as selves in society, and the meaning of individual life is found in being recognized by a community. As Carol Lee Sanchez states so clearly, how else do we discover who we are than by examining who we are in relation to others?[55] Vine Deloria claims that within Native communities, individual names reflect individual strengths, religious experiences, and actions that are most fully expressed on behalf of the people. Individual achievement is seen as coming from within a specific community and as having its full creative expression in giving back to that community.[56] This is the measure, the meaning and power of stories that heal, of visions that give shape and direction to individual and collective life: participation in a communal process in which even "sin" is seen as a matter of a failure of responsibility to the whole, and not merely individual failing. As Weaver writes, "The Sun Dance, practiced by numerous Plains Indians (and increasingly in a pan-Indian context), is illustrative. It is generally said to be performed 'that the People might live.'"[57]

In spite of this fundamental valuing of community, Native peoples live within and move between many different kinds of communities, named by Weaver as "reservation, rural village, urban, tribal, pan-Indian, traditional, Christian." Varying locations lead to diverse understandings of what is required for Native cultures to thrive. While there are different forms of community, Weaver claims that the importance of the larger group is paramount. From this strong sense of community, Weaver derives a "we-hermeneutic": an understanding of life and its possibilities in light of webs of connection. While the history of this form of hermeneutics is culturally specific, Weaver claims that it moves beyond the narrow confines of us against them: "Though it [we-hermeneutics] seeks to be inclusive, as much as possible, of the entire Native American community, it does not stop there. Nor does it stop at the entire human community; rather, it seeks to embrace the entire created order, including plants, animals, Mother Earth herself."[58]

All My Relations

Jace Weaver explains the significance of the Lakota term *mitakuye oyasin*, translated "all my relations." The meaning is broader than "family" or even "humanity"; it includes "the web of kinship extending to the animals, to the birds, to the fish, to the plants, to all animate and inanimate forms that can be seen or imaged." Furthermore, "all my relations" alludes to the expectation that a person accept the responsibilities that accompany participation in this web of kinship. Weaver comments, "A common admonishment is to say of someone that they act as if they have no relations."[59] What is the significance of this view of "self in society" for ethics and politics?

According to Deloria, the earth is bountiful, but living abundantly from that bounty requires discernment and effort. Deloria ascribes to tribal religion the dual task of determining "the proper relationship that the people of the tribe must have with other living things" and developing "the self-discipline within the tribal community so that man acts harmoniously with other creatures." The context for these efforts is a world "dominated by the presence of power, the manifestation of life energies, and the whole life-flow of a creation." In this creation, people recognize that human beings hold an important place but at the same time depend on everything in creation for their existence.[60]

Deloria states that within the "tapestry of life," "humans are 'younger brothers' who learn survival and respect from other life-forms." Respect requires self-discipline. It also requires covenants that ensure the well-being of humans and of other life-forms. It is, of course, not easy to discern what is "mutually agreeable" for other people, much less other life-forms. Deloria advocates attention to balance and reciprocity, taking what humans need to survive without destroying the ability of other species to reproduce and sustain themselves. He contrasts this attention to reciprocity and limits with "Anglo-Saxon" views "in which the most powerful swallows up the weak and the unprotected."[61]

As difficult as it is to discern patterns of relationship and develop covenants in accord with them, the covenants may need to be modified as life unfolds and basic patterns change. In that regard, Sanchez writes of the challenge of learning to use new technologies "in a sacred manner." As new technologies are introduced, we must carefully measure and observe their significance and impact.[62] To live this way is to experience both belonging and discipline, a sense of the world that sustains and limits us.

Ceremonies

The Motion of Songs Rising

The October night is warm and clear.
We are standing on a small hill and in all directions,
around us, the flat land listens to the songs rising.
The holy ones are here dancing.
The Yeis are here.

• • •

The Yeis are dancing again, each step, our own strong bodies.
They are dancing the same dance, thousands of years old. They are here
for us now, grateful for another harvest and our own good health.

> *The roasted corn I had this morning was fresh,*
> *cooked all night and taken out of the ground this*
> *morning. It was steamed and browned just right.*

They are dancing and in the motion of songs rising,
our breathing becomes the morning moonlit air.
The fires are burning below as always.

> *We are restored.*
> *We are restored.*
> —Luci Tapahonso (Navajo)[63]

Through ceremonies, humans give the simple gift of awareness and respect, and receive, in turn, the healing restoration of balance and connection. Ceremonies bring a people into honest and grateful connection. They are a way of acknowledging our proclivity to overstep our bounds, and of centering us again in webs of reciprocity. They remind us that all exists in connection, and they restore connections that have been broken.

Weaver calls ceremonies an integral part of daily life, reminders that "no element stands in isolation." He describes, as illustrative, the hunting rituals of the Clackamas of Oregon: "Hunting involves more than the act of stalking and killing the animal itself. It also involves preparation, the making of arrows and rituals for success prior to the hunt. It involves rituals performed after the kill to show respect for the sacrifice of the prey and to ensure future game."[64]

Linda Hogan (Chickasaw) writes of the deep connections with the elements that are integral to traditional Indian people, connections that are acknowledged and restored in daily ceremonies. She tells of the brilliant Sioux leader Crazy Horse, who wore under his arm a stone he had received from an elderly medicine man. Hogan says, "The stone was his ally. For Indian people, even now, the earth and its inhabitants all have spirit, matter is alive, and the world is an ally." Hogan calls on us to remember and learn this lesson, "that we are energized by the stars, by the very fire of life burning within all the containers and kinds of skin, even the skin of water, of stone."[65]

Our connection to "the fire of life" can be, and often is, broken. We find ourselves lost, all awry. Ceremony not only reminds us of connection but also invites us to take into ourselves again the elements that constitute our lives. Hogan celebrates this restorative process: "We speak. We sing. We swallow water and breathe smoke. By the end of the ceremony, it is as if skin contains land and birds . . . The land merges with us . . . We who easily grow apart from the world are returned to the great store of life all around us and there is the deepest sense of being at home here in this intimate kinship."[66]

Ceremonies are "part of a healing and restoration," but the healing does not end with the ceremony. In Hogan's terms, the "real ceremony" is manifest in "compassionate relationships" with one another and with the world.[67] Ceremonies are opportunities to connect with cosmic processes; ceremonies are also occasions of healing, of grieving, of acknowledging loss and restoring broken connections. They ground our subsequent actions in a richer sense, a reminder of our belonging to the land and of our responsibilities to the land. Weaver adds another dimension to what is healed through ceremony: the "erosion of self and community" caused by centuries of European colonialism in America.[68]

Deloria states that here we find a fulcrum for ethical judgment that is as pivotal as notions of progress or a return to a golden age are for Western culture: what is most important is the restoration of community relationships in the present.[69]

Wisdom and the Sacred

Conflicting Truths

Western peoples have many motives for trying to understand indigenous traditions. Some motives are dangerous and inevitably misleading, such as attempts to rank indigenous religions in a scheme that is already set, with Western philosophy or religion at the pinnacle of human achievement. David Chidester, in his study of comparative religion in South Africa, describes the political uses of the categorization of indigenous religions as either degenerations from a prior truth or as primitive attempts to understand and manipulate the world. In both cases, conveniently for the operations of conquest, colonizers claimed that indigenous peoples either needed Western tutelage or deserved extermination.

Another motive for understanding mixes respect and conquest, the attempt to chronicle a way of life that is valued but seen as inexorably vanishing. In this case, the disappearance of Native culture may be genuinely mourned, but the assumption of the inevitable march of history occludes two crucial factors: our responsibility as Euro-Americans for that disappearance and the resilience, changes, and survivals of Native traditions.

Yet other motives are less dangerous. Some people approach indigenous traditions with a genuine desire to understand and respect another culture and religion. Aware of the colonial processes of exploitation and denigration, they seek in Native American traditions something they see lacking in their own. Many Westerners reject the assumptions and values that fuel conquest: the goal of individual and national mastery; materialism and consumerism as satisfying expressions of creativity; an isolating individualism and autonomy; a sense of humans as superior to and apart from nature; a pursuit of individual and national wealth with little concern for the poverty of others or the long-term ecological and economic impact of how that wealth was obtained.

When Westerners genuinely try to understand Native traditions, however, understanding is often blocked by assumptions that are as foundational as they are unconscious. The Western understanding of truth, of the methods that lead to accurate and sympathetic knowledge, keeps many of us from seeing Native traditions as they are seen by Native peoples.

Let me give two examples. The first is the work of Edward Curtis, well known now, although not during his lifetime, for his elegiac portraits of Native peoples within the United States from 1896 to 1930. His project was massive, and his work complex. In twenty volumes he compiled photographs of every major tribe west of the Mississippi. Curtis was profoundly moved by Native American life, and his photographic records of eighty tribes are valued by Natives and non-Natives alike. His work was, however, marked by the obvious misconception that this honored way of life was inexorably vanishing. While certain traditional practices were suppressed and many others were changing, Curtis did not distinguish between losses caused by conquest and colonial repression and changes that reflected survival and adaptation. In his film of the Northwest Kwakiutl, for example, he orchestrated a reenactment of what rituals might have been like, leaving out the elements of the contemporary fishing rituals that included new aspects of Native life. While many of the surviving Kwakiutl recount enjoying the elaborate play, they claim that the depiction of actual life was misleading. Not only were contemporary objects removed, but for dramatic effect, people were portrayed doing daily tasks in ceremonial dress.[70]

The more serious barriers to understanding, however, can be seen in Curtis's photographs of sacred ceremonies. While Curtis's desire to commemorate such ceremonies is understandable (he thought the religious rituals were the most beautiful aspect of Native life), his insistence on doing so reflects two erroneous assumptions. Curtis thought that the Native way of life was inevitably disappearing. He did not imagine that Native traditions could change and adapt. In fact, he thought that the only hope for survival for Native peoples was assimilation into modernity, leaving sacred traditions behind. His whole life was an attempt to capture a vanishing way of life before it was too late. Furthermore, while he saw the beauty of the rituals, he did not understand the meaning of the sacred and the reasons for limiting ceremonies to those who were members of the tribe. He insisted, for example, that he be allowed to participate in the sacred Snake Dance of the Hopi. His twelve-year pursuit to be included in order to understand was a clear example of his fundamental lack of understanding.

In an introduction to a volume of his photographs, written in 1906, Curtis described the difficulty of fulfilling his goal of photographing "all features of the Indian life and environment." Not only was "long and serious study" of particular ceremonies necessary, but he and his assistants had to "[overcome] the deep-rooted superstition, conservatism, and secretiveness of the Indian people."[71]

Curtis never understood why some ceremonies were secret, although he did appreciate the years of training required to be part of them.[72] Similarly, in our time, Deloria, with others, is highly critical of New Age practitioners of Native American spirituality who copy songs, ceremonies, and dances and is equally critical of the people who sell their healing spiritual expertise to non-Natives, rather than using them within Native American communities.[73]

What is the problem here? The disjunction has a simple root: a clash of epistemes. To the Western mind, truth is universal, generalizable, knowable by all rational people, and conceptual. If a proposition is true anywhere, it is true everywhere. In morals as in science, truth is one. Kant's categorical imperative is a clear example: an action is morally justified if we could will that it be universally followed. This epistemological clash has multiple components:

- What is the scope of truth—universal or particular?
- Who is the bearer of knowledge—the individual, a people, and/or the cosmos?
- Where is human knowledge carried—primarily, solely a faculty of reason, or also carried in the body and in the emotions?
- What *is* an individual? How is the body related to the mind? Are there multiple souls? What is the connection of the individual self and society and the natural order?

According to Jace Weaver, Native American epistemology is polycentric, built on the recognition of the value of multiple sites of meaning. For example, a ritual carried out in one place is the center of the universe, as are the rituals carried out in other places, by other peoples. *All* are centers of the universe. *All* embody truths particular to that place, that people, and that history. As Weaver states, "Though no culture's worldview can be privileged in any universal sense, it can and must be privileged for that particular culture."[74] Alternative stories, perspectives, and worldviews are valued, worth studying for what they contribute to a picture that "is not yet and may never be wholly complete."[75]

Illustrating this polycentric epistemology, Vine Deloria cites a story told by Charles Eastman (Sioux). In Eastman's story, a Christian missionary told a group of Native American people the Genesis account of the creation of the earth and the creation, and then fall, of humanity. The Native peoples responded by recounting their creation story. The missionary was appalled:

> "What I delivered to you were sacred truths, but this that you tell me is mere fable and falsehood!"
>
> "My Brother," gravely replied the offended Indian, "it seems that you have not been well grounded in the rules of civility. You saw that we, who practice these rules, believed your stories; why, then, do you refuse to credit ours?"[76]

Here we have an understanding of truth as multiple; it is meaningful for and grounded in a place, a region, a community of peoples and ecosystems.

Furthermore, as Christopher Ronwanien:te Jocks (Mohawk) writes, "Knowledge requires a network of knowers, or more accurately, of actors."[77] Knowledge emerges from the careful observation of life over generations. Take, for example, the solar and lunar patterns traced in the architecture of Chaco Canyon. Chaco Canyon is a complex of twelve large pueblos, with buildings three to four stories high, and 200 to 350 smaller villages spread over twelve miles. They are part of a larger complex that includes 70 towns and 5,300 villages in a 35,000-square-mile area located in what is now New Mexico, Colorado, Utah, and Arizona. The buildings are placed in a way to enhance their size and convey an "aura of magnificence." Some of the buildings are aligned with the solar equinox and solstice. Others trace the 18 1/2-year cycle of the passage of the moon. Recognizing this lunar pattern would require close observation for generations. Pueblo people constructed the buildings at Chaco over a period of two hundred years (900–1130 CE), carrying collective knowledge for generations and embodying this knowledge in buildings of timber, stone, and mortar.[78]

Knowledge is held not just in the mind—it is not only a matter of reason, concepts, and facts—but also in the body. Ceremonies and rituals of healing often take many days. The insight gained in ceremony is achieved as much through sound and physical transformation and openness as through understanding of ideas. The embodied reality of knowledge leads Deloria to emphasize that Native American religions are primarily religions of practice, not beliefs.[79] What matters is not shared belief, but the knowledge held and expressed in the interactions people have with one another and with the place in which they live.

Truth is multiple; truth is also conflictual and paradoxical. Leslie Marmon Silko (Laguna Pueblo) writes of the impact of varied stories about a single event: "I know Aunt Susie and Aunt Alice would tell me stories they had told me before but with changes in details or descriptions. The story was the important thing and little changes here and there were really part of the story. There were even stories about the different versions of stories and how they imagined these differing versions came to be."[80] The multifaceted truths that emerge within and structure Native society are best conveyed in narrative, in stories in which contradictions are acknowledged as part of the complex truths to be remembered and acknowledged.[81]

This narrative, polycentric, and embedded understanding of truth has many implications. First, there is no reason for proselytizing, and conversion is difficult. To "convert" is not to take up a set of beliefs but requires being adopted into a people—living within that community, taking a role and responsibilities within it. Deloria is quite clear on this point: "It is virtually impossible to 'join' a tribal religion by agreeing to its doctrines. People couldn't care less whether an outsider believes anything."[82]

Furthermore, specific stories and ceremonies are not to be casually copied or repeated. Deloria claims that a story or a ceremony has meaning at particular times and in particular places, and cannot be practiced or told anywhere at any time. Meaning is violated when taken out of context and cannot be properly understood without a complex process of belonging to a particular community and a particular place. Deloria questions the possibility of taking religious experience out of its original context and "distilling" it into an abstract principle that applies universally in different places and at different times without severely harming the message itself and the society that receives it. He claims that for Native Americans, "revelation was seen as a continuous process of adjustment to the natural surroundings and not as a specific message valid for all times and places."[83] Truth is found in responsible grounding in a particular place. Taking elements of a ceremony or a story and repeating them out of context is a dangerous fragmentation of knowing and belonging that reflects the isolation of the one doing the copying, a fragmentation that is likely to lead to further disruption and imbalance.

What would it mean to recognize the importance of particularity and context? Paula Gunn Allen (Laguna Pueblo/Sioux) extols "an epistemological protocol of caution and respect in

Native communities" and advocates an "ethos [that] fosters a different kind of academic rigor attentive to the values in uncertainty, in ignorance, in lack of domination, even in fallibility, not as anathema but as a welcome element in a mode of communication that would tolerate the unknown in a continuing, pragmatic process."[84] Natives who belong to other nations, and non-Natives, can learn to acknowledge and accept that there are vast realms of knowledge that cannot and will not be shared. We can, however, learn to listen carefully, respectfully, and critically to that which is openly exchanged with us and with other peoples.

Although knowledge is specific and grounded in a place and a people, some principles can be publicly discussed. As Deloria, Weaver, and Sanchez emphasize, we in the Americas now share a land base, Native and non-Native. We can learn patterns of attention and habits of respect as we create our own ceremonies of gratitude, accountability, and responsibility, and as we tell the stories that are part of our collective history.

These principles and habits include a strong sense of the sacred dimension of all that is. To recognize that all is related, that all is sacred, is a precious gift, celebrated in ceremonies and sustained in careful, grateful awareness of each aspect of daily life. Sanchez states that the ways we greet the day, notice the animals and plants around us, and perform the tasks of individual and collective survival can be acts of recognizing the sacred dimensions of all that we do: "If we believe that everything is sacred, then the most mundane tasks take on a deeper meaning." With this awareness, she states, we can "ritualize ordinary actions," from awakening each morning, to preparing meals, to accomplishing our other daily tasks. As an example, Sanchez tells how the Apache day is begun: "An individual male arises at dawn, leaves the house, faces east, and begins singing a song to assist the sun in its journey over the horizon. This is considered a sacred duty, and the song is one of joyful greeting."[85]

Trickster Stories

The sacred surrounds us, is in us, and is a power that can disrupt and destroy as easily as harmonize and heal. Weaver elucidates the nondualistic understandings of the sacred, and of power, carried in the trickster stories of numerous Native peoples. He analyzes in some detail the function of the trickster in the stories of the contemporary theorist and novelist Gerald Vizenor: "This comic but compassionate clown undermines people's expectations and punctures the pompous—contradicting and unsettling lives, but, in the very process of disruption, imaginatively keeping the world in balance. By the trickster's actions, the world is defined and recreated."[86]

Weaver writes that the trickster—the "mischief maker" and "breaker of barriers and eraser of boundaries"—is also found in non-Native cultures. Tricksters "move between heaven and earth, deity and mortals, living and dead." These figures are powerful, yet ambiguous. "He makes trouble for everyone, including himself. He comes to a bad end as often as he succeeds as a result of his actions. Trickster stories are thus teaching stories, imparting to listeners societal values and mores, through humor." As one example, Weaver refers to the story of Raven, trickster figure of the Northwest coast: "Before Raven, the world is in darkness. Through trickery, he steals light from the other world and returns to earth with it. True to form, however, he does this not out of any feeling for humanity but so that he will have light by which to feed."[87]

Learning from these stories and this sensibility has powerful effects. Trickster stories challenge us to forgo linear thinking and embrace the paradoxes, contradictions, and mixed motives that often accompany our actions. Although our motives are often mixed and our insights less than pure, our actions may yet be profoundly healing and life-giving. Weaver cites the work of Lewis Hyde, who notes that the trickster is "amoral but not immoral." Hyde writes, "When someone's hon-

orable behavior has left him unable to act, trickster will appear
to suggest an amoral action, something right/wrong that will
get life going again. Trickster is the mythic embodiment of
ambiguity and ambivalence, doubleness and duplicity, contra-
diction and paradox."[88] If we cannot find the "right" thing to do,
we may find the vital thing to do and in that partial response
unleash greater energy for living justly and well.

According to Weaver, the stories of the trickster "teach the
naturalness of humanity, including human sexuality."
Reinforcing these lessons, the trickster usually is cast as an
animal that lives close to humans. Such animals—coyotes, for
example—have adapted well to humans and "have often
learned how to thwart the attempts of Euro-Americans to trap
and exterminate them."[89]

Gerald Vizenor declares that if we look at Native survivance (survival and thriving), we find far more than stories
of "real destitution" and oppression. He claims that non-
Natives rarely understand the "native survivance stories" that
"are renunciations of dominance, tragedy and victimry." He
extols the use of such stories, claiming, "Many natives were the
past masters of trickster stories and, in that aesthetic sense,
always prepared to outwit missionaries, social scientists, and
manifest manners."[90]

Vizenor describes the characters in trickster stories as profoundly liberating. We find in trickster stories accounts of the
transformation of men to women, animals to birds, and
humans to animals. The stories elicit an awareness of survival
and continuing transformation, but not a sense of closure:

> The sources of natural reason and tribal consciousness are
> doubt and wonder, not nostalgia or liberal melancholy for the
> lost wilderness; comic not tragic, because melancholy is cul-
> tural boredom, and the tragic is causal, the closure of natu-
> ral reason. The shimmers of imagination are reason and the
> simulations are survivance, not dominance; an aesthetic

restoration of trickster hermeneutics, the stories of liberation and survivance without the dominance of closure. Tribal
consciousness is wonder, change, coincidence.[91]

These wildly ironic, comic stories of transformation and
subversion, these "compassionate tricksters who heal through
story and humor," remind us to not take ourselves too seriously.[92] At the same time, these stories and this sensibility
enable something that is very serious indeed: the healing of
individual and collective imbalance and disharmony.
Unbalanced power is deadly to all concerned—the ones who
bear it, as well as those who are affected by it. The trickster
shows us the costs of unbalanced power and jolts us back into
a properly chastened respect for the fierce and unpredictable
power that we and others can exercise. Lewis Hyde writes of
the danger when Euro-Americans have misunderstood the creative ambiguity of trickster stories: "The erasure of trickster
figures, or unthinking confusion of them with the Devil, only
serves to push the ambiguities of life into the background. We
may well hope that our actions carry no moral ambiguity, but
pretending that is the case when it isn't does not lead to
greater clarity about right and wrong; it more likely leads to
unconscious cruelty masked by inflated righteousness."[93]

Jace Weaver's response to this analysis is succinct: "Anyone
familiar with the history of Christian/Native encounter over
more than five centuries will find little to dispute in Hyde's
assessment."[94]

Contact, Conquest, Identity

What can the trickster teach us about our attempts to shape an
equitable, resilient, and creative social contract? In *Playing
Indian*, the historian Philip Deloria (Dakota) provides an

insightful analysis of the misadventures, insights, and tragic misunderstandings that have occurred in earlier attempts by Euro-Americans and Europeans to understand and learn from the political insights of Native Americans. While some Europeans and Euro-Americans found in Native American culture a vantage point from which to see the greed, injustice, and brutal militarism of European cultures, there were, at the same time, cultural and political tendencies that led to extermination. In particular, there was an inability to see Native culture as not only equal to Western culture but, quite possibly, superior in fundamental respects. Deloria sees the tension between valorization and extermination in the ideology of "noble savagery":

> If one emphasizes the noble aspect . . . pure and natural Indians serve to critique Western society. Putting more weight on savagery justifies (and perhaps requires) a campaign to eliminate barbarism. Two interlocked traditions: one of self-criticism, the other of conquest. They balance perfectly, forming one of the foundations underpinning the equally intertwined history of European colonialism and the European Enlightenment.[95]

We might try to unlock these intertwined traditions, building on the history of Enlightenment self-criticism and using it as a critical tool to disenchant Americans from the pursuit of colonialism, conquest, and empire. To break the historical cycle of imperial conquest, it is first helpful to have a fuller understanding of its many manifestations in American history.

Philip Deloria gives a thorough account of the complex ways in which Euro-Americans have simultaneously taken spiritual power from Native Americans while exercising political power over them: "The self-defining pairing of American truth with American freedom rests on the ability to wield power against Indians—social, military, economic, and political—while simultaneously drawing power from them."[96] Euro-Americans have taken as their own a Native sense of freedom, of belonging to the American continent, and of spiritual quest, without seeing the responsibilities and connections to the land and to other peoples that are part of Native American traditions. We have failed to be responsible to Native peoples, repeatedly valuing art and spiritual practices while treaties are abrogated and land stolen. Deloria claims that for two centuries, American social and political policy with regard to Native peoples has alternated between "assimilation and destruction." He argues that this oscillation is grounded in two opposing motivations: "Americans wanted to feel a natural affinity with the continent, and it was Indians who could teach them such aboriginal closeness. Yet, in order to control the landscape they had to destroy the original inhabitants."[97]

Vine Deloria Jr., Jace Weaver, Philip Deloria, and Carol Lee Sanchez all hold out the possibility of a respectful engagement with Native traditions and peoples in the present and the future. Sanchez, especially, highlights a crucial and surprising ingredient in transformative encounters between Native Americans and Euro-Americans. She asks that we pay as much attention to the failings of Native American communities as we do to the successes and creative insights.

In her essay "Animal, Vegetable and Mineral," Sanchez points out that the basis of a Native American environmental ethic is not a genetic or romantic proclivity toward closeness with nature but is rather a deliberately chosen and developed culture of ceremonies that foster balance and reciprocity with the natural world. The need for those ceremonies is grounded in an *awareness of the many errors in the past,* times in which balance was lost because of greed or misuse of the environment (overhunting, overfishing, and failing to share resources in an equitable manner):

Detailed explanations of the ecological disasters that were
brought about by the Meso-American pyramid and apart-
ment builders have been preserved in the oral histories of
various Tribal groups that descended from them. Many of
these stories tell us that the people began to deviate from
their Sacred Ways and became greedy and quarrelsome.
Some of the recorded Pueblo stories tell how the men gam-
bled all night and slept all day; how they violated the women
and ceased performing their sacred duties. The stories speak
of the women neglecting the children and gossiping with each
other for hours instead of performing their sacred duties.
They tell of a time the people took more than they really
needed from their creature relatives and Earth Mother . . .
They became more and more disconnected and continued to
commit acts of violence against each other and the things in
their environment. As a direct result, the plants, the creatures, and the elements *abandoned* the people.[98]

The Pueblo peoples, and others, honor nature as a way of
remembering those errors and avoiding them in the present.
According to Sanchez, imbalance often occurred with the first
introduction of a new technology, and time was required to discover how to use that technology in a sacred manner.[99]

In addition to her account of the roots of some American
Indian ceremonial practices, Sanchez also describes an alternative basis for social action. She describes the Navajo Beauty
Way, a principle common to many tribal peoples. Sanchez
teaches many things to those of us who are not Pueblo, but
there are many things she does not share. She teaches principles of attention and patterns of reciprocity, but not the specific
ceremonies, stories, and prayers that belong to the Pueblo people. In her workshops on tribal principles for nontribal peoples,
she argues, for example, that we will not learn to resolve our
ecological problems unless we learn to honor and respect the

land with which we live.[100] Here the focus is not on critique but on gratitude. The basis for our work for justice and peace can be love for the world, awe and respect for the wonder that surrounds us. This stance is sharply different from that of the prophetic outsider, who bases his or her political work on denunciation and critique. Sanchez tells us that such continual denunciation poisons our relation to the world around us. "Focusing on destructive forces all the time causes feelings of despair and, too often, a sense of powerlessness to do anything to change these dreadful circumstances."[101] Focusing on injustice to the exclusion of other forms of attention prevents us from seeing and receiving all that is healing and isolates us from "all our relations," human, animal, and nature. Sanchez encourages us to base our activism on gratitude for all that is beautiful and precious. The practices of attention include awareness of the past, in all its complexity, and openness to the "beauty and wonder" of creation. She suggests specific ways of seeing the healing forces around us:

> Where you live now was once home to your Native American ancestors hundreds or, possibly, thousands of years ago. Who were they? What is their history of the place where you live? . . . Identify the prominent landmarks surrounding your home place. . . . How did the Tribe(s) relate to these landmarks? What significance was assigned to them (for example, special sacred places for receiving visions, for locating healing plants of the region)? . . . Consider what has changed about your environment since European contact. How have the creatures and plants adapted to the change? Then center yourself in the region where you make your home and introduce yourself to the spirits of your place. Greet the plant, creature, mineral, wind, water, earth, and sky spirits. Make a song to them . . . Approach each day in a sacred manner and with a healthy sense of humor. Our relatives will help us if we ask them to help. Our relatives will forgive us if we ask

for their forgiveness and make a serious commitment not to repeat our previous mistakes.[102]

What does it take to acknowledge the sacred around us? How can we tell our own stories of error and concomitant devastation? How can we create our own prayers and ceremonies to check our arrogance and thoughtlessness? Sanchez teaches us that practices of gratitude are central to the lives of Pueblo communities, and she invites us to create our own ceremonies, practices of respect and attention that may help us see the sources of healing and the possibilities for growth all around us.

Sanchez's pedagogy is a joy to watch, transformative for me and for many of the students who participate in dialogue with her. Sanchez brings students into a different relationship with their familial history of migration and abuse of resources, with the particularities of their locale, and with Native American peoples. Her interactions embody survivance; she is a member of a vital, evolving culture engaging us in deep reflection from a position of equality. Sanchez's stance is clear: we are all here together now, and this is what my people have to bring—a process in which we can discover, together, more clearly who we are and who we can be.

The foundation for a social contract that both respects all forms of life and limits our abuse of power is twofold: ceremonies and practices that open our hearts and minds in gratitude to the world around us, and ceremonies and practices that enable us to discern, acknowledge, and understand our mistakes and our abuses of power in the past and present. These foundations are both thoroughly pragmatic and historical— first seeing and then learning from power dynamics in the past and present. Equally central to the stories of learning from the natural world is openness to the stories of our errors and cruelty; equally central are ceremonies that help us avoid repeating that cruelty in the present.

chapter 4

respect

Although learning from error and abuse is of utmost importance for a just social contract, Carol Lee Sanchez does not recount the history of atrocities committed by the Spanish or the Anglo-Americans against her people. Jace Weaver, while analyzing specific atrocities in a later chapter in his book, does not begin with that history and, in fact, argues against doing so.

Sanchez points out the dangerous ways that beginning with atrocities correlates with our tendency to think of Native peoples as the "Vanishing Indian." Beginning with the past reiterates the assumption that there are no longer any "real" Indians: they were all slaughtered, or their culture suppressed and adulterated beyond repair. Sanchez challenges this nostalgic erasure in her poem titled "the two worlds of the red nations":

> 'For those who live/ in the two worlds:/
> There are so few of us, let us/ be good/
> to one another.'
> (from Caroll Arnett [Gogisgi], *South Line:*
> *Poems* [New Rochelle: Elizabeth Press, 1979])

-there's no such things as Indians
in north america-
that professor sd to me.
-not like they were, they're
all gone, you know.

(sun dance pole / sweat house pit
four corners marked and colored true
above, below and middle place
corn mother dances green today)

i paused to think what he might mean
and he continued on:
-panama has **real** ones, still **wild**
and **primitive**, not contaminated yet.

(white deer dance / bear dance / eagle dance songs
whale blow / raven step and seal feast
wind spirit whistles / koshare clowns)

-i've spent three summers there (he sd
-to study them. they're pure.
up here, well, they're Americans
like the rest of us. no pure
culture to be found.

(morning star and mountain ways / stomp dance
circle dance / northern and southern styles-clock
and counter clock / up river salmon ceremony / root
digging songs / yei be che huuhuuhuu / shalako blessing)

-they dress and drive and eat fast food, the same
as us. oh-there's remnant bits of this and that,
a few folks speak their native tongue

(blue jeans / cowboy shirts / ten gallon hats
fry bread / navajo tacos / corn-venison-mutton stew
lambing-sheep camp-sheering time / cowboy boots)

-but all in all that's not enough to say
there's any indian culture left
in north america (he sd

(basket / rainbow / corn and butterfly maidens
acorn mash and corn meal grinding songs
strawberry festival and ribbon shirts / pinon harvest)

five centuries fall away unnoticed
spring plant to harvest to hunt to
silent winter sleep.

long-time stories still live around here
sweet sage, tobacco, cedar and corn pollen
still offered around here.
old time spirit talk and medicine songs
still sung around here.

five centuries, now, we walked in two worlds
weaving new stories into baskets and blankets
adding ribbons, beads and bright colored threads
to things we use and wear. work copper, gold
silver, nickel and brass in indian fashion.

five centuries living and dying unnoticed.
five centuries walking silent and hidden.
five centuries in-between "the two worlds."[1]

In her poetry, as in her teaching, Sanchez conveys the powerful presence of a culture that has continued to evolve during five centuries of contact and conquest, a culture, imperfect like any other, yet vital enough to hold the promise of further changes, and further transformations of American life.

Atrocity and Evasion

For there to be further transformation, we must first recognize that fundamental change is needed. As a country, we have not yet fully confronted, much less understood, our colonial past. If we focus primarily on our experience of resistance to British colonialism, and our defense of democratic values at home and abroad, we fail to see the complexity and contradictions of our colonial history—resisting British exploitation while exterminating the indigenous peoples of the Americas, enslaving Africans, and subjugating women.

When learning of this brutal history, some Euro-Americans react with paralyzing guilt and shame; others, with defensive rejection or disingenuous nostalgia.

Defensive Rejection

The first reaction, defensive rejection, takes the form of denying the magnitude of the atrocities committed by Euro-Americans in one of three ways. One uses the myth of the open frontier to deny both the extent and the complexity of Native societies in precontact America. A second denial is to emphasize the devastation caused by infectious disease, denying the actions of Euro-Americans in spreading or capitalizing on such disease. The third is to focus on pre-Conquest warfare among Native peoples without also examining the measures they took to limit the devastating scope of that warfare. While there was war between Native America nations, these wars did not result in near extermination.

Although precontact North America was settled by between two million and eighteen million people, the rhetoric of an untamed wilderness was, and still is, ubiquitous. We find a dangerous disparity in the writings of the early colonizers. While justifying their control through the myth of the untamed wilderness, they also wrote of their awareness of the extent to which land was cultivated and their own dependence on that cultivation by Native peoples for survival.[2] James Wilson describes this disparity between rhetoric and reality: "Although the idea that American Indians 'roamed' remained a basic tenet for advocates of—and apologists for—European colonization, the recorded experience of early travelers and settlers give a very different picture of native life." As examples, Wilson mentions Thomas Hariot, who in 1585 described the "ingenious" agriculture of the Algonquians, including the use of "a graine of marveilous great increase; of a thousand, fifteene hundred and some two thousand fold"; a Jamestown colonist who estimated that the Kecoughtans had three thousand acres of cornfields; and the fact that the survival of the earliest English colonies depended on the support from the Wampanoags—support that would have required surplus production from Indian farming.[3]

To justify the conquest of Native peoples, Euro-Americans offered two contradictory rationales. The land was seen as largely empty, yet the peoples who lived on the land and claimed an ancestral right to occupy it were dismissed as savages. Repeatedly we find a dual stereotype—the contrast between the "noble savage," the bearer of a way of life that is inexorably vanishing, and the "bloodthirsty savage," who irrationally defies the spread of civilization. In both cases, Euro-American conquest is presumed to be inevitable, and the agency of Euro-Americans in both cases denied—denied as provoking defensive attacks to protect Native land claims, denied as deliberate policies that led to the destruction of Native ways of life.[4]

Imperialist Nostalgia

By the nineteenth century, many white Americans denied their culpability for the destruction of Native cultures, even mourning their disappearance, as though their demise were caused by something other than economic and political conquest. Philip Deloria offers the following claim by Supreme Court justice Joseph Story in 1828: "By a law of nature, they seem destined to a slow, but sure extinction. Everywhere, at the approach of the white man, they fade away. We hear the rustling of their footsteps, like that of the withered leaves of autumn, and they are gone forever. They pass mournfully by us, and they return no more."[5] These evasive, nostalgic sentiments were also found in many novels and plays written by Euro-Americans. Deloria recounts one such "Indian death speech" that exemplifies the "imperialist nostalgia" found in many plays written between 1828 and 1838:

> The dying chief Menawa, [extends] his blessings to the new nation (in the form of George Washington) before departing for the happy hunting grounds: "The Great Spirit protects that man [Washington], and guides his destiny. He will become the Chief of nations, and a people yet unborn, hail him as the Founder of a mighty Empire! Fathers! Menawa comes." *(Menawa sinks slowly into the arms of his attendants, strain of music, curtain falls.)*[6]

The disappearance of Native peoples was not, of course, an act of nature but was accomplished through wars and treaties deliberately designed to force Native peoples to relinquish their land to white control. Deloria describes the process by which most Native people were forced to leave the eastern half of the United States by the mid-nineteenth century: "From 1813, when the final defeat of Tecumseh . . . marked the end of

Indian attempts to offer a unified, interregional resistance, until the 1830s, when President Andrew Jackson defied his own Supreme Court and forced the Cherokee to take what became known as the Trail of Tears, Americans waged war, signed treaties, and used guile and force to relocate hundreds of thousands of native people."[7]

We cannot understand who we are as citizens of the United States, and who we can be, if we fail to grasp the ramifications of this tragic dissonance. We Euro-Americans saw ourselves as the bearers of freedom, progress, and prosperity, even blessed by those whose lives and lands we had taken through violence and deceit. Deloria's words challenge us to look at a reality that was so resolutely denied. He decries the fiction whereby "Indian figures offered up their lands, their blessings, their traditions, and their republican history to those who were, in real life, violent, conquering interlopers."[8] What we saw as Manifest Destiny, Native peoples experienced as unrelenting violence and treachery.

Rejection, Resistance, and Resilience

It is not easy to take up the challenge posed by Philip Deloria. It is far easier to mourn a lost way of life than to encounter the violence of our civilization. Vine Deloria reminds us that there is far more at stake here than facts about Native American ceremonies, stories, and culture, far more than even facts about Euro-American atrocities and treaty violations.[9] What does it mean to genuinely understand the impact and meaning of this history of brutal territorial expansion? What effects would such knowledge have on actions in the present? What practices can enable us to know this history without defensiveness and denial, without guilty paralysis or cynical resignation? We are dealing here with the fundamental human challenge of remaining fully alive—open in mind, body, and heart—in the face of suffering.

At the conclusion of his book in defense of human rights, William Schulz makes an eloquent case for fully confronting human suffering: "What I will not accept is those who tell us that it [human suffering] doesn't matter, that other things are more important, that we ought to offer a hand to anguish only in the narrowest of circumstance." Schulz claims that we cannot deny suffering and remain fully alive: "To look on human agony and consistently remain unmoved is to be dead in all the ways that truly matter, dead to the mystery of pulse and breath, dead to the gifts of grace and kindness, dead to the fragility of Creation."[10]

In his analysis of why so many people in the United States currently deny the importance of human rights, Schulz offers suggestions that can illuminate what is happening in regard to our denial of the Euro-American genocide of Native Americans. According to Schulz, seeing openly the suffering of others caused by us or by our people requires that we face two limitations: "moral limitations ('How have I contributed to this carnage?') and political limitations ('Maybe I don't have the power to stop this')."[11]

Facing these limits requires strength and determination. Where might we find these qualities? For an answer, we might return to Schulz's wording and reverse its call: we need to be *alive* to "the mystery of pulse and breath," alive to "the gifts of grace and kindness," alive to "the fragility of Creation."

Sanchez begins her work with Euro-Americans by turning our attention to the gifts of life, helping us express gratitude to our families and to the creatures who live around us and appear to us, for a very profound reason. We cannot acknowledge suffering, we cannot have the strength to stop, redress, and rectify that suffering, unless we are sustained by and grounded in something much larger than ourselves. The

Beauty Way celebrates this process of being alive to pulse and breath, grace and kindness, the fragile and terrible beauty of Creation.

Close observation of the natural world that gives delight and provides information needed for survival also provides checks to mistakes, greed, and brutality. The principles of close attention to all our relations, as lived and not merely believed, shape our desire to honor and maintain harmonious connections.

The process of close observation also gives us the resilience to see errors, absurdity, and tragedy. Our intelligence and energy can as easily lead us astray, into self-indulgence and imbalance, as into responsibility, harmony, and balance.

Once grounded in a deep connection to nature and to other people, there are pointed critiques by Native American writers of Euro-American actions that we can, and must, hear. Native American critics, from the time of first contact up to the present, have criticized Euro-American ineptitude, greed, brutality, and denial of culpability.

Ineptitude

The historian Cornelius J. Jaenen describes the views that some Micmac, Montagnais, Algonquian, Huron, and Iroquois peoples had in the seventeenth century of French culture. They were not impressed by European dress, finding it inadequate for cold weather, and did not see the necessity or value of European-style housing. Jaenen cites the words of an unnamed Micmac chieftain, as recorded by a French missionary:

> But why now, do men of five or six feet in height need houses which are sixty to eighty? For, in fact, as thou knowest very well thyself, Patriarch—do we not find in our own all the conveniences and advantages that you have with yours, such as

reposing, drinking, sleeping, eating, and amusing ourselves with our friends when we wish? This is not all. My brother, hast thou as much ingenuity and cleverness as the Indians, who carry their houses and their wigwams with them so they may lodge wheresoever they please, independently of any seignior whatsoever?[12]

Many French missionaries were surprised by the resolute rejection of European customs and practices by the Micmac, Montagnais, Algonquian, and Huron peoples. Jaenen cites a 1616 missionary report that reflected a deep-seated confidence: "For all your arguments, and you can bring a thousand of them if you wish, are annihilated by this single shaft which they always have at hand, *Aoti Chabaya* ... 'That is the Savage way of doing it. You can have your way and we will have ours; every one values his own wares.'"[13]

Not only did the Micmac "value their own wares," they often criticized the French for being "parsimonious and inhospitable," and were wary of French motives for coming to the Americas:

Thou sayest of us ... that we are most miserable and most unhappy of all men, living without religion, without manners, without honour, without social order, in a word, without any rules, like the beasts in our wood and our forests, lacking bread, wine, and a thousand other comforts which thou hast in superfluity in Europe ... I beg thee now to believe that all miserable as we seem in thine eyes, we consider ourselves nevertheless much happier than thou in this, that we are content with the little that we have; and believe also, once for all I pray, that thou deceivest thyself greatly if thou thinkest to persuade us that thy country is better than ours. For if France, as thou sayest, is a little terrestrial paradise, art thou sensible to leave it?[14]

The Iroquois, Montagnais, Algonquians, and Hurons also criticized the rigid French administrative system and the elitism of French leaders. The Iroquois found their own system of justice superior to that of the French system. Unlike the French, who merely punished the criminal, the Iroquois system also attempted to "give satisfaction" to the one wronged.[15]

Native peoples were also critical of the harsh methods of French education and childrearing, preferring their own culture in which the education of children was an inseparable "part of the everyday life of work and play." Given the many shortcomings that the Iroquois also saw in European culture, it is not surprising that they were uninterested in the offers by the English to give their children a British education. Vine Deloria cites the rejection by the representatives of the Iroquois confederacy of the offer made by English colonists at the Treaty of Lancaster in 1744 to educate six Iroquois boys:

> We know that you highly esteem the kind of learning taught in those Colleges, and that the Maintenance of our young men, while with you, would be very expensive to you. We are convinced, that you mean to do us Good by your Proposal and we thank you heartily. But you, who are wise must know that different nations have different Conceptions of things and you will therefore not take it amiss, if our Ideas of this kind of Education happen not to be the same as yours. We have had some Experience of it. Several of our young People were formerly brought up at the Colleges of the Northern Provinces: they were instructed in all your Sciences; but when they came back to us, they were bad Runners, ignorant of every means of living in the woods . . . neither fit for Hunters, Warriors, nor Counselors, they were totally good for nothing.[16]

The Iroquois rejection of English education was quite shocking to the colonists. As the historian James Axtell reports in his analysis of educational efforts in colonial America, one of the primary motives expressed in colonial charters was the desire to convert Native peoples to Christianity and share the benefits of Western civilization. The English colonists had an unquestioning belief in the superiority of English life and Christian religion, and "were confident that the Indians would want to be converted." They were baffled by the reaction of Native peoples to what they saw as a magnanimous offer. Axtell cites Cotton Mather's reaction in 1721 to the refusal by many Native peoples of the northeast of the benefits of Christian civilization:

> Tho' they say a People Arrive among them, who were Clothed in *Habits* of much more Comfort and Splendour, than what there was to be seen in the *Rough Skins* with which they hardly covered themselves; and who had *Houses full of Good Things,* vastly out-shining their squalid and dark *Wigwams;* And they saw this People Replenishing their *Fields,* with *Trees* and with *Grains,* and useful *Animals,* which until now they had been wholly Strangers to; yet they did not seem touch'd in the least, with any *Ambition* to come at such Desirable Circumstances, or with any Curiosity to enquire after the *Religion* that was attended with them.[17]

The English colonists supposed that the Wampanoag, Huron, Powhatan, and Narragansett would eagerly seek conversion to Christianity, and they believed as firmly that "no civilized person in possession of his faculties or free from undue restraint would choose to become an Indian." Axtell reports that both of these assumptions proved erroneous. During the colonial period, he says, very few Indians adopted the ways of "civilized Englishmen," and most (if not all) who received an education from the English returned to Indian society as soon as they could.[18]

Not only did the English colonists fail to convince Indians of the superiority of Western culture and religion, but many English colonists chose to join Native nations. In 1753 Benjamin Franklin described the startling imbalance of Natives choosing to return to tribal life after having experienced the benefits of Western civilization and colonists who had been taken captive preferring Native life:

> When an Indian Child has been brought up among us, taught our language and habituated to our Customs, yet if he goes to see his relations and makes one Indian Ramble with them, there is no persuading him ever to return. [But] when white persons of either sex have been taken prisoners young by the Indians, and lived a awhile among them, tho' ransomed by their friends, and treated with all imaginable tenderness to prevail with them to stay among the English, yet in a Short time they become disgusted with our manner of life, and the care and pains that are necessary to support it, and take the first good Opportunity of escaping again into the Woods, from whence there is no reclaiming them.[19]

Similarly, Axtell cites the dismay of Hector de Crevecoeur, who wrote in 1782, "Thousands of Europeans are Indians, and we have no examples of even one of those Aborigines having from choice become European!"[20]

Most Native peoples rejected European education and social mores. Many also saw Christianity as a powerful force, but not a desirable one. Rebecca Kugel gives an account of the type of missionary work that led the people of an Ojibwa community to reject Christianity as socially disruptive. She writes of a village near present-day Duluth, Minnesota, and recounts the 1839 Ojibwa critique of Reverend Edmund Franklin Ely of the American Board of Commissioners for Foreign Missions:

Ely continually violated Ojibwa values, norms, and deeply
held beliefs. The Ojibwa stressed harmony in interpersonal
relations; Ely delighted in confronting people and rebuking
them loudly and publicly for transgressions against an alien
and, from the Ojibwa view, incomprehensible moral code. His
strictures against work or travel on Sundays, for instance,
struck the Ojibwa as ludicrous, and, in such cases as refusing
to help procure food during a long, difficult, winter journey in
"intensely cold" January weather, as downright dangerous.[21]

Not only did Ely publicly denounce the Ojibwa for violat-
ing a Western code of behavior, he did not understand the
codes of reciprocity and social harmony that structured
Ojibwa society. For the Ojibwa, "reciprocity defined human
society." Ely was oblivious to the value of reciprocity, and when
he did occasionally agree to share his food or clothing, "he hag-
gled over the amounts." The Ojibwa saw Ely's actions not as
merely personal failings, but as indicative of larger spiritual
dangers. Characteristics such as his lack of generosity marked
Ely as a person possessing "fundamental hostility to organized
human social life." Ely also created social division by attempting to isolate the few who showed an interest in his religious
message: "He was obviously a person who gloried in chaos and
disharmony, and thus, was one who might easily abuse spiritual power."[22]

Greed

Many Native American writers were also highly critical of the
deeply pervasive and seemingly insatiable greed of European
colonists. The continuous encroachment of settlers on Native
lands seemed to be motivated by a boundless desire for wealth,
as were the poverty and class divisions that marred the social

harmony of European nations. The French essayist Montaigne reported on the reaction of Micmac visitors to France when they encountered poverty. He wrote that they "thought it strange that these needy halves should endure such an injustice, and did not take the others by the throat, or set fire to their houses."[23] LaVonne Brown Ruoff finds a similar reaction in the writings of Samson Occom (Mohegan, 1723–1792), who went to England in 1765 to raise money for Eleazar Wheelock's Indian Charity School in Connecticut. A decade later, addressing "Christian Indians," Occom had these observations about the British class system: "[The] Nobles and the great, and they are very Proud and they keep the rest of their Brethren under their Feet, they make Slaves of them. The great ones have got all the Land and the rest are poor Tenants."[24]

Another critic, Joseph Brant (Mohawk, 1742–1807), had supported the British in the Revolutionary War but was highly critical of British life after he visited England in 1786. He wrote of the superiority of Mohawk governance: "The estates of widows and orphans are never devoured by enterprising sharpers. In a word, we have no robbery under the color of the law."[25]

Many Native peoples valued social harmony more than material acquisition. According to Jaenen, the willingness to share freely among themselves and with European settlers was astounding to many European explorers and colonists. The French missionaries to the Huron and Montagnais nations were surprised to find that there were no beggars among these nations, and they reported the Huron and Montagnais shock at learning of such poverty in Europe. One missionary, Sagard, reports, "They found it very bad hearing that there were in France a great number of needy and beggars, and thought that it was due to a lack of charity, and blamed us greatly, saying that if we had some intelligence we would set some order in the matter, the remedies being simple."[26]

Repeatedly we find Native leaders encouraging European colonists to accept "simple remedies" for European greed. In 1609 Wahunsonacock, a Powhatan leader, addressed the British colonists and pointed out the folly of their violent usurpation of Powhatan land and food: "Why should you take by force that from us which you can have by love? Why should you destroy us, who have provided you with food? What can you get by war? We can hide our provisions, and fly into the woods; and then you must consequently famish by wronging your friends."[27]

In August 1793, the leaders of the Seven Nations of Canada and twelve other tribes refused the offer by settlers to buy land north of the Ohio River. Instead, they encouraged the settlers to use the money they would spend to buy their lands to address the poverty within their own societies:

> Brothers, money to us is of no value, and to most of us unknown; and as no consideration whatever can induce us to sell the lands, on which we get sustenance for our women and children, we hope we may be allowed to point out a mode by which your settlers may be easily removed, and peace obtained.
>
> Brothers, we know that these settlers are poor, or they would never have ventured to live in a country which has been in continual trouble ever since they crossed the Ohio. Divide therefore this large sume of money, which you have offered to us, among these people . . . and we are persuaded they would most readily accept of it in lieu of the lands you sold to them.[28]

These reasonable offers were rejected, and throughout the history of Euro-American settlement of the Americas, we find a devastating pattern: treaties made in which boundaries are set and some Native lands protected, followed by the breaking of these treaties under the unrelenting pressure of white settlers for more land. Of the 370 treaties made by the United States with Native Americans, *all* were violated by U.S. citizens. Charles Eastman describes how his uncle explained the greed of white settlers: "The greatest object of their lives seems to be to acquire possessions—to be rich. They desire to possess the whole world."[29]

When Missouri, Iowa, Wisconsin, Arkansas, Michigan, and Florida became states, the Osage and the Oto were forced to move and were given supposedly permanent homes on land that is now part of Kansas and Nebraska. Within a decade, these agreements were violated. Once again, Wilson writes, we find "the usual abuses—fraudulent land deals, exploitation by traders, outright theft and sexual assaults on women."[30]

Brutality

Spanish Conquest. The first contact with Europeans was also marked by the first cruelty. In his diaries, Christopher Columbus described the gentleness and hospitality of the Taino peoples. He wrote that fortifications were unnecessary, "as the people heare are simple in war-like matters . . . I could conquer the whole of them with fifty men, and govern them as I please."[31] Conquer them he did. By 1513, the peaceful Taino had been decimated by war and slavery, their population reduced from 125,000 to 14,000.[32] In 1520 Bartolomé de las Casas denounced the actions of his fellow Spaniards in the land they named Hispaniola:

> Here those Christians perpetrated their first ravages and oppressions against the native peoples. This was the first land in the New World to be destroyed and depopulated by the Christians, and here they began their subjection of the women and children, taking them away from the Indians to

use them and ill use them, eating the food they provided with their sweat and toil.[33]

Wilson describes the ways in which Don Juan de Oñate and the soldiers who were part of his expedition into the American Southwest continued the pattern of greed, sexual assault, and brutality. Early in the expedition, which began in January 1598, soldiers sexually assaulted an Acoma woman and stole food from the Acoma Pueblo. Members of the Acoma Pueblo then killed thirteen soldiers. Don Juan de Oñate responded by waging all-out war:

> After three days of fierce fighting, some 800 Indian men, women and children were dead, and almost 600 more had been taken prisoner. All the survivors over the age of twelve were condemned to slavery, and the children were given to the friars to be distributed as servants . . . Every man over the age of twenty-five had one of his feet amputated, and two Hopis . . . lost a hand each and were sent back to their own people as a stern warning.[34]

Other Spaniards condemned the greed and brutality of Don Oñate and his men, and the Franciscans forced his resignation in 1607, having heard the Natives' logical question, "If . . . Christians cause so much harm and violence, why should [we] become Christians?" Although critical of the brutal massacres and mutilations of thousands of Pueblo people by Don Oñate, the Franciscans were themselves extremely cruel, using violence to enforce conversion to Christianity. During the seventeenth century, Pueblo people found to be "invoking the devil" (that is, practicing their Native rites) received public beatings, sometimes resulting in death.[35]

The Spanish were not alone, however, in their brutal assaults on the peoples of the Southwest. The "Missouri volunteers"—settlers who moved into land held by the Pueblo, Hopi, and Navajo peoples in 1840—repeated the pattern of arrogant, violent conquest: "Like the Spaniards before them, the newcomers proclaimed themselves the vanguard of civilization and then promptly set about robbing, raping and brutalizing the indigenous population." The Pueblo nation fought back and killed the first United States governor in New Mexico and twenty Anglo-Americans. In response, soldiers from the United States killed two hundred Indians and destroyed much of Taos in heavy artillery bombing.[36]

The Northeast. Throughout the colonial period, Native peoples fought back, and Native writers denounced the brutality of colonizers. William Apess (Pequot) challenged the "demonization of the Pequots," attributing the wars and bloodshed to the settlers' behavior. He told how settlers depended on Indians and then stole from or brutally attacked the same people who had fed them. He also described a situation in which "Captain Miles Standish and his men prepared a feast for the Indians and massacred their Native guests when they sat down to eat."[37] Not only were the colonists supported by the Wampanoag, Powhatans, and Paspaneghs, but these prosperous people offered to teach the English how to feed themselves through farming and fishing. The English rejected the offer, preferring to grow tobacco for export and coerce these Native peoples into giving them food.[38]

In 1622 Opechancanough led the Powhatan uprising against the English immigrants, who were "becom[ing] more aggressive, unpredictable, and hostile." In the attack, 347 colonists were killed, one-fourth of the colonists. In response, the English declared that they now had "license to take [Powhatan] land." Wilson cites the words of Edward Waterhouse: "We, who hitherto have had possession of no more ground than their waste, and our purchase . . . may now by right of Warre, and law of Nations, invade the Country, and destroy them who sought to destroy us: whereby wee shall enjoy their cultivated places." The goal of the English colonists was clear: to eradicate the Native Americans from the earth. "In one incident alone," writes Wilson, "200 Indians died when the English concluded a treaty with the rebellious Chiskiacks and then gave them poisoned sack to toast the two peoples' 'eternal friendship.'"[39]

Wilson recounts the many ways in which the English colonists continued to respond with disproportionate violence when the Pequot peoples tried to prevent them from taking over their land and farms. In 1636, for example, the Massachusetts Bay Colony responded to the killing of two English traders by ordering Captain John Endecott to attack Block Island and slaughter every Indian male. Writes Wilson, "Ninety Indians were murdered, most of them Narragansetts who were unconnected with the Pequots."[40]

The Indian nations of New England were horrified by the "virtual extermination" of the Pequot people by the English in 1637. The scope of the planned attack seemed excessive even to some of the British. Those who opposed the planned massacre were appeased, however, after the chaplain assured them the plan met with divine approval. Wilson writes, "The ruthlessness of the attack appalled most of the colonists' Indian allies: this, clearly, was warfare of a kind they had never seen or imagined before. In the initial attack, the colonists reported killing and burning to death 600–700 men, women and children. In the next few months, they killed almost all of the Pequot people."[41]

Not only did the English continue to kill thousands of Narragansatt and Pequot people, but their attacks were marked by indiscriminate brutality, targeting not only warriors but also women and children. In another attack in 1671, for example, English settlers killed two thousand Narragansatt men, women, and children, "most of them burnt to death." The colonists waged war by any means available, including the deliberate spread of smallpox. After the Ottawa had significant military victories, taking nine British forts and killing two thousand settlers, Lord Jeffrey Amherst determined that he would destroy them entirely. Amherst launched what Wilson calls "a primitive kind of germ warfare." Writes Wilson, "The commander of Fort Pitt invited some of the besieging Delawares to a parley, and gave them smallpox-infected blankets from the fort hospital as a token of esteem." An epidemic began, crippling the Natives' ability to fight. The Ottawa and Delaware surrendered in 1766.[42]

Wilson describes the extent of devastation caused by disease by contrasting it with the loss of life in modern European wars:

> The death rate far exceeded anything that modern Western nations have experienced: the First World War, for instance, which is often seen as the apotheosis of mass destruction, killed around 2 per cent of the British population over a four year period. Many Native American communities lost 75 percent or more of their members within just a few weeks, the kind of losses predicted for a nuclear holocaust, and certainly greater than those suffered at Hiroshima.[43]

The Southeast. Disease, violence, legalized land fraud—all continued as Andrew Jackson defied the order of the Supreme Court and ordered the removal of the Cherokee from their homelands, a territory of over forty thousand square miles. Cherokee land was distributed to whites in a lottery, and the Cherokee people were brutally forced from their land. Major Ridge (Cherokee) described the atrocities and wrote to President Jackson for protection: "The lowest classes of the white people are flogging the Cherokees with cowhides, hickories, and clubs. We are not safe in our houses . . . This barbarous treatment is not confined to men, but the women are stripped also and whipped without law or mercy." Most of the Cherokee people were "rounded up at bayonet-point and held in stockades, where hundreds died from hunger and disease, before being moved to Indian territory" in the winter of 1838 to 1839. The thousand-mile forced march further devastated the Cherokee population. Between four thousand and eight thousand people died on the "trail of tears."[44]

The Far West. As white settlers moved into the far West, the hatred of indigenous peoples and the scale of cruelty against them did not abate but, rather, intensified. Wilson writes that at the time of Columbus, the West Coast had a significant Native population. In California there were, by his count, six major language families, 150 societies, and about seven hundred thousand people. By the 1830s, the indigenous population had been subjected to the brutal forced labor of the Catholic missions and had dropped below two hundred thousand.[45] When gold was discovered, there were even more devastating attacks on the Native population. Miners and settlers killed and raped Pomos, Yuki, Yana, Winta, Yurok, and Hupa peoples with impunity. Wilson writes, "Many of the miners seems to have been driven by a deep-rooted racial hatred . . . Between 1850 and 1863 an estimated 10,000 California women, many of them children, were sold or indentured . . . Armed bands of Anglo murderers . . . would exterminate whole communities. More Indians probably died as a result of deliberate, cold-blooded genocide in California than anywhere else in North America."[46] The attacks by miners and settlers were unrelenting. The Yana, a nation of two thousand to three thousand, were "virtually exterminated." Groups of Anglo men killed ten thousand Yuki, fifty or sixty at a time in hunting trips conducted two or three times a week.[47]

These attacks were not only widely encouraged but also financially supported by other settlers. A newspaper in Marysville, California, reported a subscription campaign to finance such attacks in 1859: "A new plan has been adopted . . .

to chastise the Indians for their many depredations during the past winter. Some men are hired to hunt them, who are recompensed by receiving so much for each scalp, or some other satisfactory evidence that they have been killed. The money has been made up by subscription."[48]

While many white settlers bemoaned the so-called depredations of Native people, we can also find contemporary reports by army officers and civilians who denounced the unspeakable violence of miners and settlers against people who could not legitimately be accused of any theft or crime. Wilson cites the 1860 report of Major G. J. Raines:

> I have just been to the Indian Island, the home of a band of friendly Indians between Eureka and Uniontown, where I beheld a scene of atrocity and horror unparalleled not only in our own Country, but even in history, for it was done by men self acting and without necessity, colour of law, or authority— the murder of little innocent babes and women . . . barbarously and I can't say brutally—for it is worse . . . Volunteers, calling themselves such, from Eel River, have employed the earlier part of the day in murdering all the women and children of the above Island . . . midst the bitter grief of parents and fathers . . . I beheld a spectacle of horror, of unexampled description—babes, with brains oozing out of their skulls, cut and hacked with axes, and squaws exhibiting the most frightful wounds in death which imagination can paint—and this done . . . without cause . . . as far as I can learn, as I have not heard of any of them losing life or cattle by the Indians. Certainly not these Indians, for they lived on an Island and nobody accuses them.[49]

While some settlers denounced the atrocities of their people, the Native population in California was not given legal standing to challenge the attacks, and those Anglo-Americans who were horrified by the atrocity did not, or could not, stop them. Wilson writes that Native Americans in California lacked citizenship status and standing to testify in court, "so they had no legal recourse when settlers occupied their territory, kidnapped women and children or carried out vigilante attacks on their villages." The violent attacks by the encroaching settlers were unrelenting, and by 1900, in all of California, only fifteen thousand Native Americans were still alive.[50]

The Great Plains. While the images of the U.S. Cavalry and its war against the Sioux, Arapaho, Cheyenne, and Apache are still resonant in American popular culture, the successful resistance of Plains Indians to that military campaign is far less known. As Euro-Americans moved into the Great Plains, taking land that had been occupied by thirty different Native nations, the United States government was initially defeated, then developed new strategies to force Native peoples to relinquish their land. The first assaults were, however, the same as in the past: brutal and duplicitous military campaigns, justified by the settlers and the military as being sanctioned by God. Wilson describes the 1854 massacre at Sand Creek, led by a Methodist minister, Colonel John Chivington:

> Members of the Colorado militia launched a series of indiscriminant raids against Cheyenne camps. They were commanded by Colonel John Chivington, a Methodist preacher . . . who . . . publicly advocat[ed] the murder of Indian children . . . In terms that echoed the ferocious rhetoric of Captain John Mason during the Pequot War more than two centuries before, he declared: "Damn any man who sympathizes with Indians! I have come to kill Indians, and believe it is right and honorable to use any means under God's heaven to kill Indians."[51]

The Cheyenne were ordered to stay near the army post, ostensibly for protection. Colonel Chivington led an attack of two hundred soldiers. Although Chief Black Kettle of the Cheyenne attempted to surrender, the brutal attack was unabated. Wilson cites the description by Lieutenant James Connor of the "massacre site": "I did not see a body of man, woman or child but was scalped, and in many instances their bodies were mutilated in the most horrible manner."[52] Over one hundred Cheyenne were killed.

Those who escaped told other nations of the attack. A force of one thousand Sioux, Arapaho, and Cheyenne retaliated, together defeating over three thousand U.S. soldiers. This was not the only victory. In a series of military campaigns between 1861 and 1868, the Sioux, Cheyenne, and Arapaho successfully defeated United States military forces. In an 1868 concession of defeat, the secretary of the interior of the Grant administration reported that the war against the Sioux and their allies cost the United States "almost $1 million per Indian killed."[53]

The concession was, however, only temporary. The United States government was determined to force white settlement of the Great Plains, so it developed a new strategy to defeat the Sioux, Arapaho, Cheyenne, and Apache. First, the government would cause starvation by paying hunters to slaughter the bison herds. Second, it would offer food and money to the Native peoples who agreed to move to reservations.[54]

Unlike the military campaigns of the previous thirty years, this campaign accomplished its goals. As of 1895, the remaining bison numbered under a thousand, not only causing widespread starvation among the Plains nations but also destroying "the core of their spiritual and ceremonial world." By first starving the Sioux, the United States military was then able to defeat them militarily. One of the last military actions was the massacre at Wounded Knee, in which the Seventh Cavalry first disarmed and then shot three hundred Sioux.[55]

Boarding Schools. After taking what land they wanted, Euro-American settlers began a federal educational campaign designed to force what they had not been able to accomplish voluntarily: the assimilation of Native peoples to Western culture. From 1873 until World War II, the federal government built schools, including boarding schools located off the reservations. Federal agents "used whatever means they had to force the parents to enroll their children."[56] Many Native parents and children fiercely resisted boarding school education, denouncing the harsh educational methods and the deliberate destruction of Native language, culture, and history. The proponents of such education were unmoved by the protests, continuing to justify their educational work as a faithful response to a divine mandate. Wilson cites Merrill Gates, who in 1891 stated that "the time for fighting the Indian tribes" had passed: "We are going to conquer barbarism . . . We are going to do it by the conquest of the individual man, woman, and child . . . We are going to conquer the Indians by a standing army of schoolteachers, armed with ideas, winning victories by industrial training, and by the gospel of love and the gospel of work."[57]

This "gospel" of love and work was no more attractive than the English education first offered to the Iroquois in the seventeenth century. In fact, it was extremely brutal, and the results of this seventy-year-long assault on Native culture still reverberate in the lives of many Native peoples. Luther Standing Bear (Lakota), who was captured in 1879 and forced to attend the Carlisle Indian School in Pennsylvania, described the harshness of the education: "The change in clothing, housing, food, and confinement combined with lonesomeness was too much, and in three years nearly one half of the children from the Plains were dead . . . In the graveyard at Carlisle most of the graves are those of little one."[58]

Ruoff cites the description in Zitkala-Sa's (Yankton Sioux) 1901 autobiography, *The School Days,* of the trauma she endured at the White Manual Labor Institute. Zitkala-Sa wrote that she "lost her spirit" when she was caught hiding from her teachers and, as punishment, was tied to a chair, and her hair was "cut in a style only cowards wore: 'In my anguish, I moaned for my mother, but no one came to comfort me.'" Ruoff recounts another such story, that of E. Pauline Johnson (Mohawk), who described the trauma of being "forbidden to speak her language and denied permission to return home for a visit, lest she regress to her Indian ways . . . 'I wanted my own people, my own old life, my blood called out for it, but they always said I must not return to my father's tepee. I heard them talk amongst themselves of keeping me away from pagan influences.'"[59] Weaver reports the story of Isabell Knockwood (Mi'kmaq), who told of the coercion used by teachers in a Canadian residential school, in which students were beaten for speaking their own language. Knockwood reported, "When little children first arrived at the school we would see bruises on their throats and cheeks that told us that they'd been caught speaking [their native language]. Once we saw the bruises begin to fade, we knew they'd stopped talking."[60]

Culpability and Accountability

The world of 2004 is, in some ways, very different from previous centuries. Native Americans have full citizenship and can now legally challenge attempts to take their land. The Indian Reorganization Act of 1934 made it legal for Native peoples to practice their religions, and the Indian Education Act of 1972 ended the boarding school system and returned control of Native education to Native peoples. Under the Nixon and Ford administrations, some sacred sites were returned, most notably the sacred Blue Lake of the Taos Pueblo, taken in 1906. In 1970 President Richard Nixon supported the repeal of the termination policy previously passed by Congress on moral and legal grounds and affirmed "the integrity and right to continued existence of all Indian tribes and Alaska native governments, recognizing that cultural pluralism is a source of national strength."[61]

With the return of sovereignty, many tribes have developed gaming operations. The long-term viability of such operations is still a matter of serious debate within tribes. Wilson cites a common justification for casinos: "By exploiting the Euro-American addiction to gambling and smoking, they [their supporters] argue, they are merely continuing the old struggle to protect and sustain their communities by other means."[62] Euro-Americans fill Native American casinos, and many tribes find these to be highly lucrative. The Pequot, for example, have been able to send the majority of their young people to college. The Choctaw in Mississippi have developed a complex set of operations, not only casinos, but auto dealerships, a greeting card plant, and an automotive dashboard instrument company. As a result, the Choctaw have become one of Mississippi's five largest employers and have reduced the unemployment rate among the Choctaw from more than 50 percent in 1970 to only 4 percent in 2002.[63]

Not only is there a modicum of space for economic and political independence, but Euro-Americans, by and large, no longer revile Native art and traditions, instead embracing such practices as an alternative to the emptiness of consumer culture. Philip Deloria describes the ambiguous use of "Indian play" by Euro-Americans to address the cultural and spiritual anxieties of modernity:

> At the turn of the twentieth century, the thoroughly modern children of angst-ridden upper- and middle-class parents wore feathers and slept in tipis and wigwams at camps with multisyllabic Indian names. Their equally nervous post–World War II descendants made Indian dress and pow-wow-going into a hobby, with formal newsletters and regular

monthly meetings. Over the past thirty years, the countercul-
ture, the New Age, the men's movement, and a host of other
Indian performance options have given meaning to Americans
lost in a (post)modern freefall. In each of these historical
moments, Americans have returned to the Indian, reinter-
preting the intuitive dilemmas surrounding Indianness to
meet the circumstances of their times.[64]

Vine Deloria Jr. also describes the ambiguity of New Age
attempts to learn from Native cultures. On the one hand, he
sees a positive effort: "In seeking the religious reality behind
the American Indian tribal existence, Americans are in fact
attempting to come to grips with the land that produced the
Indian tribal cultures and their vision of community. Even if
they avoid American Indians completely, those Americans
seeking a more comprehensive and meaningful life are retrac-
ing the steps taken centuries before by Indian tribes as they
attempted to come to grips with this land."[65] On the other hand,
Vine Deloria is critical of the superficiality of many attempts to
understand Native traditions. Similarly, Weaver points to the
danger of such a superficial exchange of religious ideas: "It
takes in well-meaning White seekers who are searching for
meaning and healing in their lives and believe that they are
getting 'authentic' Native teachings and practices. It excludes
natives and their contemporary issues entirely in favor of feel-
good self-actualization and empowerment." This process,
Weaver concludes, excludes any possibility of "serious discus-
sions of Native cultures and values."[66]

Although many Euro-Americans value Native art and spirituality, other forms of economic exploitation and political domination still occur. Tribal sovereignty is hotly contested, and
land claims remain a matter of intense dispute. Vine Deloria
argues that the pattern that was recognized in 1876 continues
today: "Whenever an Indian reservation has on it good land, or

timber, or minerals," the Commissioner of Indian Affairs stated
in his Annual Report for 1876, "the cupidity of the white man
is excited, and a constant struggle is inaugurated to dispossess
the Indian, in which the avarice and determination of the
white men usually prevails."[67]

Current challenges to the economic activities of the
Choctaw nation exemplify this tendency, as does the decision by
the Bush administration in November 2002 to rescind the protection of sacred lands in the Modoc National Forest granted
under the Clinton administration. Although Kathleen Clarke,
the head of the Bureau of Land Management, and Dale
Bosworth, chief of the Forest Service, claimed to have listened
carefully to the claims raised by the Pit River Tribe, they
approved the construction of a geothermal power plant. The reason given for the rejection of the Pit River claims was stark: "a
clash of cultures, your culture and the culture of capitalism."[68]

Philip Deloria, Vine Deloria, and Jace Weaver criticize the
tendency to copy Native spiritual practices without looking at
current political and economic issues such as these and working toward a fair resolution of these conflicts. Treaties continue
to be broken, and agreements rescinded. Behind these treaty
violations, behind the continued encroachments on tribal sovereignty and the use of sacred lands, is an inability to grant the
legitimate and distinct differences of Western and Native views
of religion, of property, of the interrelationship between the
individual and the community.

As Euro-Americans, we are challenged by Native
Americans to acknowledge our abuse of economic and political
power in the past and in the present. To accomplish this monumental task, Weaver insists, we must realize that all of the
acts of rape, theft, massacre, and betrayal are not isolated acts,
not "mere mistakes," but part of a larger pattern of national
identity and expansion.[69] We can learn from Native critics to
see, without excuses, our capacity for brutality, greed, and

dehumanization of other people. Because of this capacity for the callous disregard of the rights of others, and for brutal coercion of those who resist the imposition of what we deem as a just social order, we need ongoing checks on our proclivity toward colonialism and domination.

In developing such checks, we can learn from the nondualistic paradoxes and insights of trickster stories. The trickster is not simply good or evil. Rather, the trickster is creative and vital yet can also be overreaching and destructive of self and others. There are tendencies within us to create, to act vigorously and thoroughly, *and* to overreach, to act with haste, impatience, and disdain for the needs of other peoples. To ignore these tendencies is to ignore our own likely complicity in patterns of exploitation and oppression. Our intelligence can become mere cleverness; our vitality can become violent and reckless.

This does not mean, of course, that we stop acting. Carol Lee Sanchez describes the challenge well: We must continue to act, invent, and develop new technologies and forms of social organization. But in all of these actions, we must remember the failures of the past and our need to learn how to use these technologies and how to govern in a sacred manner.

It is not easy to accept this challenge. The Western definition of *sacred* leads us to the supposition that there are divine mandates and absolute standards of just and righteous behavior. The understanding of the sacred found in the writing of Sanchez, Weaver, and Deloria is less dualistic and more fluid. To govern or to use technology in a sacred manner is to be aware of the effects of our actions on "all our relations"; it is to be open to challenges to our wisdom and power; it requires that we acknowledge our weaknesses as frankly as we celebrate our strengths.

Jace Weaver criticizes our Euro-American absolutism and false innocence, our claims to Manifest Destiny, progress, democracy, and Christian civilization. *All too often in American history, the nobility of our ideas has blinded us to the brutality of our practices:* the violent extermination of Native peoples, the enslavement and forced conversion of others, the violation of treaties and the theft of land, forced removal to inadequate reservations, the cruelties of mission schools, and the outlawing of Native religious practices. Weaver indicts the "inflated sense of self-righteousness" that fuels conquest and genocide. What others rightly see as a deadly mix of hubris and self-righteousness we experience as the intoxicating power of fulfilling a grand and glorious destiny.[70]

Although it is vital to acknowledge these bitter lessons, accountability in the present requires far more than mourning the past actions of our ancestors. Vine Deloria Jr. claims, "Being guilty for remote sins is easy; accepting responsibilities for current and future sins is difficult. It is this contemporary attitude toward aboriginal peoples that must be changed rather than compensation for past wrongs."[71]

Why, then, if our attention should be on the present, is it exceedingly important that we analyze the atrocities of the past? We confront what was done in the past and examine the justifications, rationales, ethical structures, and political policies that allowed those atrocities to occur, not to simply denounce our ancestors but to learn from them. If they could commit genocide, so can we. We cannot repent for the actions of others. We can, however, examine the ways in which the attitudes, mores, and unwitting assumptions of conquest are also part of our actions now. We can take responsibility for our own policies and actions, and we can work with the situation as it is, and with people as we and as they are: capable of self-critique and grand delusions, capable of kindness and generosity, and capable of the most grotesque brutality.

Working with the situation *as it is* sounds, on the surface, rather simple, yet Vine Deloria argues that an inability to work with peoples and ecosystems as they are is precisely part of the Euro-American culture of domination and conquest.[72] Unable to work with the realities of a land already occupied by civilizations that had lasted for thousands of years, we Euro-Americans convinced ourselves that the Americas were destined to be ours, and the Native inhabitants were an impediment to be destroyed or assimilated to our superior way of life. As Shanley states, if any of their culture remained, it was to be solely on Western terms.[73]

In the past, the illusion of Manifest Destiny justified conquest and domination; in the present, the temptations of global capitalism led by American power seem to justify a new form of empire. Vine Deloria argues that we can choose another path and can "reject the concept of history as an inevitable and controlled or controllable process." We can work together, "demand[ing] protection of natives and of their lands, cultures, and religions . . . honestly fac[ing] the problems of . . . Western societies and consider[ing] what real alternatives now exist for those societies to survive in a world that is growing smaller."[74]

Let us begin to work together, creating the ceremonies and telling the stories that will allow us to participate in the framing of a more just and equitable social order.

chapter 5

ceremony

We are in the process of establishing a new kind of American identity, apart from the Pilgrim tradition, and it is a very painful process of sorting out values. We must not take any easy or superficial answers.

—Vine Deloria Jr.[1]

As we try to respond with integrity, clarity, and creativity to the atrocities and betrayals of the past and present, we do well to follow Vine Deloria Jr.'s injunction. Deloria asks Native American peoples and Euro-Americans to move beyond symbolic politics to real solutions.[2] Real solutions and specific policies can be developed, not from a position of speaking for others, but from the practice of inclusive democracy. What kind of revision of the social contract, and of our practices of democratic deliberation, are necessary to enable us to establish a new American identity?

Iris Marion Young is a political philosopher who provides guidelines for the practice of inclusive democracy. We can work with her description of the methods of inclusive democracy and revise them in light of Native American insights in two crucial regards: the specific practices that are necessary for inclusive democracy, and the tone and import of engaging in practices of inclusion and deliberation.

Transforming Democracy

First, let us look carefully at the significance of inclusive democracy. Jace Weaver, with his fruitful concept of "we-hermeneutics," interprets life and its opportunities and challenges in light of the self and community. He offers as a possibility and model for all of us what he extols as part of Native traditions: a challenge to acknowledge our embeddedness in community.[3] From this perspective, we can see the social contract not in primarily individualistic terms, as a matter of individuals deciding how to balance freedom, rights, and limits to that freedom. Rather, in Weaver's expansive terms, the social contract can be an analysis of the collective wisdom of generations.

In this sense, democratic processes are akin to Native American ceremonial practices. They can be the concrete means by which we recognize and remind ourselves of our need for, and responsibility to, one another. These concrete acts of political processes can be experienced as sacred, as an act of gratitude for "all our relations," human and natural, and as concrete means of observing and regulating the impact of our actions on the natural and social world.

Contrast this view of democratic politics as ceremonial practice with Young's description of the tedium of democratic processes:

> Democracy is hard to love. Perhaps some people enjoy making speeches, or confronting those with whom they disagree, or standing up to privileged and powerful people with claims and demands. Activities like these, however, make many

people anxious. Perhaps some people like to go to meetings
after a hard day's work and try to focus discussion on the
issue, to haggle over the language of a resolution, or gather
signatures for a petition, or call long lists of strangers on the
telephone. But most people would rather watch television,
read poetry, or make love.[4]

Young argues, "If democracy is valuable at all, it is for instrumental reasons primarily."

Why does Young focus on the "angers, frustrations, fears,
uncertainties, drudgery, disappointments, and defeats that are
democratic daily fare"? Young is, to a large degree, right. Many
of the practices that she mentions as central to democracy are
intrinsically isolating and alienating, such as telephoning long
lists of strangers; others, such as confronting people with
demands, *can* be alienating. Many practices of democracy, however, can also be the occasion for recognizing community and
recognizing fallibility. For example, consider one aspect of democratic politics that Young deplores: "In a democracy nearly
everything is revisable, and because unpredictable public opinion often counts for something, uncertainty shadows democracy." This frustration, from the perspective of trickster
hermeneutics and the recognition of our own fallibility, can be
experienced as one of the ironic joys and gifts of participatory
democracy.[5]

Although Young focuses on the instrumental values of
democracy, she writes that some people do find "intrinsic values" in the practices of democracy. These include its ability to
broaden the lives of active citizens and its potential for developing our ability to think, exercise judgment, cooperate, and
achieve social recognition and acclaim.[6]

Young offers what she sees as two strong reasons, albeit
instrumental ones, for democracy: "restraining rulers from the
abuses of power that are their inevitable temptations"; and

influencing "public policy to serve or protect [our] interests."[7] Carol Lee Sanchez, Jace Weaver, and Vine Deloria challenge us to participate in democratic practices for vastly different reasons: not only to check the abuses of power by others, but to check *our* abuses of power; to express our own interests, *and* to bring us into critical awareness of and engagement with the interests of "all our relations." As a result, we may have our interests challenged, expanded, and transformed. If we are grounded in the Beauty Way, we have a different set of reasons for democratic practice and, quite possibly, different forms of organizing that do not require tedious practices that reinforce isolation and alienation—actions that have all the appeal of the man preaching to presumably sin-bound riders on a Friday-evening train, haranguing and denouncing all of us, with no attempt at real conversation or connection.

Politics without Polemic

Young's description of the tedium and alienation of much democratic practice is extremely important. We can use her analysis as a catalyst to develop forms of democratic practice that are less alienating and less enervating. We can work with her insights in the way that Michel Foucault develops his criticism of much leftist political rhetoric. Foucault writes of the dangers of polemics and speaks of his desire for a different form of social critique.

In an interview conducted by Paul Rabinow in 1984, Foucault answered a simple question, "Why don't you engage in polemics?" by emphasizing that "a whole morality is at stake, the morality that concerns the search for truth and the relation to the other." Not only are polemics unproductive ("Has anyone ever seen a new idea come out of a polemic?"), but the rhetoric of polemics functions as "an obstacle in the search for truth." Foucault describes three forms of polemics found in Western political and philosophical thought. The first is the religious model, which "sets itself the task of determining the intangible point of dogma, the fundamental and necessary principle that the adversary has neglected, ignored, or transgressed; and it denounces this negligence as a moral failing; at the root of the error, it finds passion, desire, interest, a whole series of weaknesses and inadmissible attachments that establish it as culpable." Similarly, the judiciary model sets up adversarial roles: "Polemics allows for no possibility of an equal discussion: it is processing a suspect; it collects the proofs of his guilt, designates the infraction he has committed, and pronounces the verdict and sentences him." Finally, with the political model, "Polemics defines alliances . . . it establishes the other as an enemy, an upholder of opposed interests against which one must fight until the moment this enemy is defeated and either surrenders or disappears."[8]

Foucault challenges us to forgo the ready satisfactions of polemics while yet being attentive to the continuing presence of error and domination. He asks us to avoid "polemical and repetitive jeremiads" against people and against global structures of imperialism and domination, and recommends another type of critique, one that enlivens, rejuvenates, and emboldens people to act with daring, creativity, and courage:

> I can't help but dream about a kind of criticism that would try not to judge but to bring an oeuvre, a book, a sentence, an idea to life; it would light fires, watch the grass grow, listen to the wind, and catch the sea foam in the breeze and scatter it. It would multiply not judgments but signs of existence; it would summon them, drag them from their sleep. Perhaps it would invent them sometimes—all the better. All the better. Criticism that hands down sentences sends me to sleep; I'd like a criticism of scintillating leaps of the imagination. It

would not be sovereign or dressed in red. It would bear the lightning of possible storms.[9]

What keeps us from realizing Foucault's dream? Much of our critical work has precisely the opposite effect—not "multiplying signs of existence," but amplifying our sense of isolation, cynicism, and despair.

There is a fundamental tension within the American practice of democracy. For many people, commitment to democracy is superficial at best. The democratic system of checks and balances and of equitable inclusion of all parties is seen as an obstacle to be overcome or manipulated when individuals or groups are convinced that they have the truth and feel, therefore, justified in imposing that truth on others.

What if we come to political organizing from a different perspective, recognizing that no one group possesses *the truth*, but that *truths* about how to organize our economic and political lives emerge from the fits and starts, the trials and errors of what Foucault calls the collective "experiments with truth" of human history?

Coalition

The experience of democratic debate and inclusion as more of a burden than a sacred responsibility is shared by people at both ends of the political spectrum, the left wing as well as the right. Protest activities in the United States are often fueled by a sense of being a prophetic outsider, denouncing the ills of a corrupt system from the vantage point of those who are marginalized, exploited, and oppressed. I have been an enthusiastic part of movements that protested, with all our might, sexism and militarism, at the same time that we, perversely, romanticized and even valorized our ineffectiveness at bringing about social change. No matter how fierce the condemnation or impenetrable the indifference to our protests, we would continue to speak out against injustice. Our unwavering commitment to justice, however, could mask contempt for those unpersuaded by our moral clarity and uncompromising vision.

Ronald Dellums is one of many who warn us of the dangers of not examining critically why our protests are ineffective. In *Lying Down with the Lions*, Dellums and Lee Halterman recount the history of Dellums's work in politics and the commitments and strategies that have shaped his work. His career is marked by his continual openness to the voices of those who have been marginalized and exploited, hearing their stories of injustice and hope. Dellums uses words like *chorus, harmony, counterpoint,* and *syncopation* to describe the "music of protest" he heard from various ethnic groups, women, lesbians and gay men, the disabled, and environmental and peace activists. Dellums recalls that this "music" inspired him, as did the writing of June Jordan: "In her essay 'Where is the Rage?' June Jordan, an African American and an extraordinary activist, poet, and professor, captures the legacy of that era: 'unabashed moral certitude and the purity—the incredible outgoing energy—of righteous rage.'"[10]

Although he affirms the "moral certitude" and "righteous rage" of those who are oppressed, Dellums's own political engagement led him away from self-righteous denunciations of other people and social structures. In responding to the voices of suffering and rage, Dellums recounts that he had to choose whether to be a "rhetorical activist" or "an effective legislator committed to securing social change through the process of governance." Dellums chose the latter path, and describes for us two elements of being an effective legislator committed to social justice. These principles are easy to understand yet difficult to practice. He learned from his mother "that you have to start by dealing with people as they are and seek to change their views from where they start, not from where you want them to be." This insight was reinforced by his professional training as a social worker. "Another professional tenet I'd learned forbade either condemning or condoning behavior: by forbidding passing judgment on a person, this principle allowed the social worker to focus on understanding behavior and its roots, and better understanding enhances the prospect of problem solving."[11]

Dellums learned the importance of these principles early in his political career. In a speech in Milwaukee in 1971, he referred to colleagues in the House of Representatives as "mediocre prima donnas . . . with no real understanding of the pain and human misery being visited upon our people." When Dellums returned to the floor of the House, Representative Wayne Hayes verified that the statement was accurate and then asked, "I just wonder if you then want a bunch of mediocre prima donnas to pay more serious attention to your amendment?" Dellums writes that the lessons here were clear:

> I had not come to Congress to attack and alienate my colleagues; I had come to challenge their ideas. I needed to step back from the personal . . . I needed to become better informed, to understand my opponents and be able to best them in open debate. I had to bring them along with me, not demand that they reject themselves . . . I needed to develop arguments that my fellow legislators could take home to *their* constituents and imagine articulating at *their* constituents' day meetings.[12]

The form of Dellums's work was educational and transformative. There was confrontation, of course—but not in the form of polemics. Rather, inspired by the work of Dr. Martin Luther King Jr., this confrontation invited debate, dialogue, and further discussion.[13]

While his political goal was coalition, Dellums also argued against easy compromises. Genuine coalition is built on a mutual process of education—not only educating others, but also being willing to learn from them. The process takes time and offers no promises of control, no "guarantees of success or lasting progress." Rather, Dellums found that what he could ensure was "my own faithfulness to the ideas and principles of our movement, and a willingness to do my work diligently in pursuit of the legislative goals that could achieve them." In the end, Dellums found, simply "showing up and being prepared for the fight" could at times have "powerful unanticipated consequences."[14]

Dellums's acknowledgment and acceptance of "unanticipated consequences" is crucial. His is a political and ethical philosophy of fallibility, accountability, and unanticipated and unpredictable effects. Dellums argues that even our successes are inevitably temporary. What we have accomplished will be challenged in the future, and we will face other unforeseeable political and social challenges. Even as he recalls successes at arms control, environmental protection, and racial discrimination, Dellums writes:

> Everything we have struggled for remains under attack— and in some measure it always will. Some will always reject equality as a first principle and will do no more than pay lip service to the idea that the common good means including everybody . . . Some will always believe that war is the inevitable solution to international affairs . . . Some will always seek to consume rather than preserve the environment . . . And so it will go.[15]

Dellums's work manifests the power of fluid, educational, transformative political engagement. He maintained his connection with those who are oppressed and also created connections with opponents who became allies in the work for justice. He recounts the joy of finding common ground with people who had earlier rejected his political analyses, and the joy of maintaining connection with others equally committed to justice.[16] In the words of Foucault, Dellums's work can be seen as critical engagement with "transformable singularities."[17]

Democracy as Ceremony

We can learn much from Congressman Dellums about the attitudes and commitments that can bring us closer to a just social contract and the practice of inclusive democracy. Like Dellums, we can choose to engage in democratic practices because of our grateful participation in particular communities and particular histories of connection, respect, self-critique, and virtuosity.

The meaning of this form of social engagement can be seen in the approach to social justice taken by Carol Lee Sanchez. Her description of the Navajo Beauty Way can itself be interpreted as an "analytics of power" that "multiplies signs of existence." It is a technology of the self, grounded in practices of respect, self-critique, and gratitude.[18]

To work for a fitting response, but not a final or definitive response, is to respond with beauty and evocative creativity to the ambiguity and domination of life. This work is not cynical, nihilistic, or utopian. It is not triumphalistic but evocative, for it embodies an intelligent, vital engagement with the complexity of life.

Vine Deloria highlights another significant dimension of Native American political life. He points to the greater tolerance for the foibles and failures of leaders within Native communities: "For some obscure reason, nontribal peoples tend to judge their heroes much more harshly than do tribal peoples."

Although Deloria states that he finds the judgmental nature of nontribal peoples to be obscure, in the same passage he describes an openness to change and fallibility that I would claim is precisely what leads to greater acceptance among tribal peoples. While Young decries the uncertainty, disappointments, and frustrations that "shadow" democratic practices, Deloria argues that as we acknowledge forthrightly both the achievements and the failures of our elders, "we are cushioned in our despair of disappointment and bolstered in our exuberance of success."[19]

What undergirds the acceptance of change, ambiguity, and defeat? Deloria asks us to accept a simple fact: "Life is exceedingly hard and . . . no one accomplishes everything they could possibly do or even many of the things they intended to do." What we do accomplish, however, we achieve not through our own insight and courage, but because of what we have learned from our communities.[20]

If we follow the insights of Sanchez, Deloria, and Weaver, we find a logic of social critique that is vastly different than that of Western polemics. First, we do not come to this critique on our own. We depend on others who gave us these tools and who enabled these insights. Second, these critics lead to an insight similar to that of Ronald Dellums. If our protests are ineffective, could it not be due to our own lack of creativity and compassion, rather than solely or primarily due to the obstinate indifference of other people? Maybe Dellums is right; maybe we have not found the language, images, and strategies that can connect to other people's passion for justice and fairness.

If we protest from a communal matrix, we call a community to its best. We seek to connect to what is positive and possible, and we practice what William Jones called "internal criticism," finding the ingredients in a particular culture's own values, history, and hopes that can lead to responsible social action.[21]

Practices of Inclusive Democracy

If we decide that we need the wisdom and insight of all social groups to develop just social policies, what do we need in terms of concrete practices to make that possible? Iris Marion Young points to the many ways that public voice is often sharply limited by forms of external and internal inclusion. For external inclusion, Young cites voter registration rules that are discriminatory, meetings held at a time and place that limit participation, the ability of some factions to spend far more than others on media time and political campaign contributions, and the secretive process in which policies are "determined privately" and then "introduced to the public as accomplished facts." As examples of internal exclusion, Young says people may find that "others ignore or dismiss or patronize their statements and expressions . . . The dominant mood may find their ideas or modes of expression silly or simple, and not worthy of consideration. They may find that their experiences . . . are so different from others' in the public that their views are discounted."[22]

In contrast, Young states, there are practices that enable genuine dialogue and exchange. If we follow those practices, even when compromise is required, even when one side may win and another lose, policies developed through such procedures may be more acceptable because of the openness of the process. Young writes, "Inclusive democratic practice is likely to promote the most just results because people aim to persuade one another of the justice and wisdom of their claims, and are open to having their own opinions and understandings of their interests change in the process."[23]

What happens if we center our reflection on this aspect of democratic process—the awareness that interaction with others is likely to transform our own opinions and our understandings of even our own interests? Young describes three practices that enhance such open-ended, inclusive communication:

specific forms of greeting, the use of rhetoric, and the function of narrative.

Young argues for using forms of greeting that acknowledge "the presence and point of view of diverse social segments in the political public."[24] Through intentionally inclusive greetings, Young claims that we have "gestures of respect and politeness" in which "a speaker announces her presence as ready to listen and take responsibility for her relationship to her interlocutors, at the same time that it announces her distance from the others, their irreducible particularity."[25] Sanchez and Deloria describe the importance of such greetings for ceremonial practices, the deliberate acknowledgment of place and of the broad community of "all our relations"—people, animals, and the land itself. Although Young does not acknowledge the broader natural community, her articulation of the power of greeting can easily be expanded to include this larger sense of where we are and with whom we are in relation.

After specific greetings, how do we proceed? Young challenges an exclusive focus on rational argumentation. While argumentation may be possible in certain situations, it assumes a level of homogeneity and a set of shared premises that is often absent in significant political disputes. Also, the rhetorical norms in argument—that the participants be articulate, dispassionate, and orderly—may exclude certain people, "not because of what is said, but because of how it is said." To correct this form of exclusion, Young states, we need to expand the range of acceptable rhetoric to include multiple forms of discourse that effectively situate people who are trying to understand and learn from one another. She suggests that we allow a wider range of what she calls emotional tone, no longer privileging "calm and distance" but instead welcoming as well "fear, hope, anger, joy, and other expressions of passion." A larger sense of effective rhetoric can open our minds to appreciate communication methods other than speech—for example, "visual media, signs and banners, street demonstration, guerrilla theatre, and the use of symbols in all these contexts."[26]

Given that argumentation depends on shared premises, we need a way to communicate when such premises are absent. For this, Young advocates the importance of narrative and describes three "political functions of storytelling":

1. Storytelling may bring into public discourse an experience of oppression that is not recognized within existing categories of immoral or criminal activity. The example that Young gives is sexual harassment. Through personal stories, such experiences have moved from being regarded as merely private matters to a widespread recognition of the social and political ramifications of such an abuse of power.

2. When people disagree about what counts as a social problem or how social conflicts can best be addressed, narrative may reveal "the source of values, priorities, or cultural meanings."[27] It is easier to engage in productive disagreement and conflict when we more thoroughly understand the multiple reasons that people have for holding ideas we may see as erroneous or dangerous.

3. Narrative can help us understand the effects that policies and actions are likely to have on individuals in different social situations. No matter how open our understanding, we cannot know the world from all locations and from all points of view. We need the insights of others to overcome our stereotypes and limited vision.[28]

Working within the frame of inclusive greeting, rhetoric, and narrative, Young articulates a norm of reasonableness that includes a willing recognition of our own errors, as well as the erroneous assumptions and conclusions of other people: "Reasonable people often have crazy ideas; what makes them reasonable is their willingness to listen to others who want to explain to them why their ideas are incorrect or inappropriate." On this basis, part of being reasonable is recognizing that "dissent is often a source of insight."[29]

Trickster Politics

In light of Native American critiques of Euro-American colonialism, another type of narrative and rhetorical practice is essential: the explicit recognition of errors, atrocities, and betrayals. We need our own trickster stories, ones that recount actual acts of folly and greed and can remind us of the ways our cleverness can blind us, and our self-interest trap us. Native traditions have much to teach us about the content of such narrative (unfettered accounts of folly and abuse of power), as well as the enlivening and freeing effect of a nondualistic rhetoric of accountability, irony, and humor.

Many incidents in American history reflect the nondualistic interaction of good and evil, vitality and excess reflected in Native trickster stories. Ronald Takaki's account of the work of John Collier is illustrative. In 1934 John Collier, commissioner of Indian affairs in the Roosevelt administration, implemented the Indian Reorganization Act. Unlike many Euro-Americans, Collier saw in the Pueblo and Navajo peoples of New Mexico a type of social order that he thought was superior to the individualism of much of American society, a culture that should be seen as what he called "a gift for us all." Collier valued the deep sense of community expressed in communal landholding and in the Indian view of reciprocity between individuals and their society. He thought, "Only the Indians . . . were still the possessors and users of the fundamental secret of human life—the secret of building great personality through the instrumentality of social institutions."[30] Collier argued that this way of life should be preserved and could exist alongside the structures of modern life. He put in place, therefore, policies to protect Native self-government and Native communal land ownership.

Despite Collier's significant recognition of the importance of returning control of tribal affairs to the tribes themselves, he was still limited by colonial assumptions of superior knowledge. In 1933 he concluded, over the objections of the Navajo, that existing sheep herds should be dramatically reduced by half a million to prevent overgrazing, the severe erosion of Navajo lands, and eventual famine. He was also concerned that erosion caused by overgrazing threatened Boulder Dam and the water needed to support economic development in Arizona and southern California. Referring to the Navajo as "crying children," Collier cast himself and the government as parents attempting to "find the cause of the tears": "The youngster will not always understand a dose of castor oil may sometimes be more efficacious than a stick of candy."[31]

Navajos resolutely challenged Collier's plan. They told him that erosion was caused by periodic droughts and no such destruction was necessary: "We know something about that by nature because we were born here and raised here and we knew about the processes of nature on our range." Unwilling or unable to recognize the communal knowledge of the Navajo, Collier insisted on implementing his policy and ordered the destruction of over 400,000 sheep and goats. Takaki writes that the results were devastating. With their source of livelihood destroyed, many became dependent on government programs for survival. Furthermore, by 1950 scientists recognized that the Navajo were right: the primary cause of erosion was not overgrazing. The destruction of the herds had been unnecessary.[32]

Other trickster stories take place closer to our time. At the height of its growth, Enron was touted as the company of the future—a brilliant example of corporate innovation and risk taking. In the *New York Times*, David Barboza describes the way in which such daring led to dangerous missteps. He cites the words of a former executive at Enron: "Enron's appetite for risk was huge . . . We could set some limits, but we couldn't stop the train."[33] Kurt Eichenwald, writing for the same newspaper, describes the context for the scandalous charges of corporate malfeasance against major companies (Enron, Arthur Andersen, WorldCom, Qwest Communications, Tyco) in 2002: "Most everyone knows of the business cycle of boom and bust, but what is less well known is capitalism's cycle of scandal." Eichenwald cites Stephen L. Meagher, professor at Stanford University: "Fraud scandals follow bumps in the market as night follows day . . . Once there are pressures put on profits, the obvious incentive for management to maintain their lifestyle or their stock prices is to fiddle with the books."[34] Charles Kindleberger recounts the similarity of these current instances of illegal trading with a pattern of swindling dating back to at least 1600, when corrupt practices in Asia enriched the British East India Company and the Dutch East India Company.[35]

In the past, such scandals have sparked outrage and reform. Kindleberger and Eichenwald expect the same to happen now, but Eichenwald draws a further lesson from the history of business corruption: "The lesson of all this, experts said, is that investors should never grow so comfortable as to believe that the financial markets have been cleansed of potential scandal. Another will come along, on another day in another industry. The only question is when."[36]

These stories of corruption and excess need to be told and remembered fully as part of who we are. Narratives of vision, greed, and excess are all necessary as we shape and regulate our economic and social life. We need one another to check these tendencies in ourselves. Our reason can become rationalization, our will and energy self-deluding, without the checks provided by others who know these stories and remember them for us, just as we remember them for others.

Limitations of the Social Contract

There is another trickster story yet to be told: the ways in which the social contract itself—so deeply influential in the foundation of the American republic—can be manipulated, becoming an instrument of self-aggrandizement rather than social responsibility.

Dennis McPherson and Vine Deloria offer a thought-provoking critique of social contract theory. McPherson focuses on the centrality of property rights in classical social contract theory and on Locke's claim that property rights stem from the right of humans to "improve upon the state of nature, through their labor."[37] McPherson argues that this assumption reflects a dangerously fragmented view of the relationships of human beings to land: "To an aboriginal person, the natural world as it exists in the state of nature does not need improvement; man [*sic*] is . . . meant to . . . live in harmony with it. Therefore, Aboriginal people do not see themselves as entities separate from the state of nature."[38]

Deloria offers a second critique of the centrality of property rights: that this focus led to a fundamental distortion of the social contract. Rather than working on limits within a finite base, European settlers evaded their social problems by moving away from them and seizing new lands from other peoples. Deloria argues that a viable social contract requires a willingness to accept boundaries and "create a sense of nationality among diverse peoples." Furthermore, a just social contract includes close attention to what we can learn from the specific land base that is our home: "Certainly many Americans chafe at the idea that only Indians should be called 'Native Americans,' and they argue, quite properly, that anyone born in the United States is a native American. But their allegiance is to democracy, a powerful idea, but it has no relationship to the earth upon which we walk and the plants and animals that give us sustenance."[39]

Feminist critics, including Susan Okin, have pointed to other limitations in classical social contract theory. Okin argues that political theorists describe the social contract in ways that exacerbate masculine delusion and self-aggrandizement. If, for example, the focus is on the individual and his perception of his needs and responsibilities, there is no acknowledgment of the social and natural matrix from which we emerge and to which we belong, and the ways in which male autonomy is, and has been, sustained by female subordination.[40] The atomized, isolated, autonomous individual of Rousseau is a fiction, albeit one with dangerous "effects of truth." Rousseau writes, "I owe nothing to those whom I have promised nothing . . . Civil association is the most voluntary act in the world; since every individual is born free and his own master, no one is able, on any pretext whatsoever, to subject him without his consent."[41]

Feminist theory, along with the collectivist anthropology and epistemology articulated by Weaver, Deloria, and Sanchez, helps us untangle some contradictions in Rousseau's social contract theory. According to political philosopher Patrick Riley, Rousseau was as critical of the extreme individualism of his age and a polity based on "petty self-interest" as he was of authoritarian societies based on "paternal authority, the right of the strongest, and obligation derived from slavery."[42] Rousseau sought a form of social interdependence that did not sacrifice freedom, and he resolutely upheld the benefits of social cooperation: "Although in civil society man loses some of the advantages that belong to the state of nature, he gains far greater ones; his faculties exercised and developed, his mind enlarged, his sentiments ennobled, and his whole spirit elevated."[43] Rousseau wanted both "perfect independence" and a unified state sustained by the willing consent of the governed.[44]

Contrast Rousseau's perfectly independent individual with Grace Jantzen's articulation of a philosophy of natality, an epistemology and ethic predicated on our embeddedness in networks of care. Without years of sustained nurture, we would die as infants and as children, and even our achievements as adults reflect the gifts of those who have gone before and who accompany us along the way—welcoming our existence and providing education, care, and support. The understanding of religion developed by Jantzen is also helpful here. Jantzen suggests that it is fruitful to understand religion as a symbolic of desire, and not merely or primarily as a logic of belief and unbelief. She extols a feminist understanding of religion and spirituality in shaping our desire for human flourishing in a vibrant, fragile, resilient, interconnected world. She highlights our dependence on other people and on the natural world, stating the obvious but oft-ignored fact that we are all natals, born of woman, alive only because of networks of human care and an abundant ecosphere.[45]

Native American and feminist philosophers also lead us to a compelling critique of another core aspect of social contract theory, "the original position," John Rawls's criterion for making rational and ethical judgments about social policies. Rawls argues that we can make just decisions about the structure of society if we do so imagining that we do not know in advance what our position in society will be. Will we be male or female, factory worker or factory owner, able-bodied or disabled? According to Rawls:

> Just principles for the "basic structure" of society are the principles that free and rational persons concerned to further their own interests would accept in an initial position of equality as defining the fundamental terms of their association . . . This way of regarding the principles of justice I shall call justice as fairness.
>
> No society can, of course, be a scheme of cooperation which men enter voluntarily in a literal sense . . . yet a society satisfying the principles of justice as fairness comes as close as a

society can to being a voluntary scheme, for it meets the principles which free and equal persons would assent to under circumstances that are fair. In this sense its members are autonomous and the obligations they recognize self-imposed.[46]

Although the goal of Rawls's method is to redress social injustice, it is unlikely that his method can allow us to do so as thoroughly as he would desire. Rawls's solution—that we order society as though we could be born into any of the conditions that now exist—misses the fact that what we want and see as socially valuable for ourselves and for others is already shaped by where we are now.

In orchestrating the allotment of Indian communal lands and forcing Native children to attend boarding schools, many government officials were acting out of the best of motives. They genuinely thought Western education and individual landowning were best for everyone and most conducive to social order and social justice. They could not imagine a radically different conception of education, of the collective and individual good, so they rejected Native land claims as primitive and untenable, and they dismissed Native resistance to Western education as pagan and superstitious.

Another constitutive limitation in many versions of social contract theory is a focus on consent and obligation shaped by reason and not by desire. Patrick Riley examines the negative relationship between will and desire, and the difficulty of distinguishing between them. How do we distinguish between what we desire and what, for rational and moral reasons, we may legitimately will?[47]

Native American and feminist philosophers argue that the opposition between desire and reason is a false one. Our desire for connection, for collective flourishing, and to honor and celebrate the rich matrix of life leads us to face and see our errors, atrocities, and betrayals. This desire leads us to use the best of our reason, collectively and for generations, to imagine and implement just ways of living in concert.

Young's interpretation of inclusive democracy helps us avoid imposing, albeit unwittingly, our views on others. We are motivated to such inclusion as we are aware of the many ways in which, in the name of our highest ideals, we have severely damaged the integrity of other cultures. Our goal is a form of justice in which we evaluate critically the interests of all groups, ours included. As Young so clearly states, no standpoint is privileged, and no particular view can claim superiority.[48] Rather, we struggle together, using the best of our insight and judgment to see the strengths, as well as the weaknesses, of every perspective.

Power and Desire

Responding to the critiques and insights of Sanchez, Young, Weaver, and Deloria, I propose a version of the social contract that is closely aligned with the critical work of the French philosopher Michel Foucault. Following Nietzsche, Foucault reminds us of the absurdity, irony, and "lowly beginnings" of our noble institutions. With Foucault we find a way of seeing the importance of inclusive democracy that highlights Young's insights. Not only can studying different perspectives be the best way to expose misunderstandings, but the encounter with difference is the most fruitful way of recognizing the limits of our own concepts of truth, justice, and the good.

We learn two lessons from contemporary Native American activists, historians, and scholars. The first is the history of our "nobly" justified genocide. The second lesson is alternative ways of shaping the will and of shaping desire that can provide an ongoing check to justifying brutality in the name of our highest ideals. As we follow these lessons, I think it helpful to realize that we do so more in the spirit of Foucault than Habermas, and more in the spirit of what Foucault finds of value in Nietzsche (an unabashed and relentless questioning of our pretensions) than in the Nietzschean will to power. Schooled in our history of conquest and domination, schooled by ceremonies of attention and respect, the social contract can be expressed as a system of shaping and directing our desire for power, not denying it.[49]

We note now another dimension to our social contract: ironic rather than exalted, as well as historical and collective rather than counterfactual and individualistic.

Rejecting Torture

What difference does this make? Let me give a concrete example that reflects the significance of this way of thinking: William Schulz's refutation of Alan Dershowitz's argument for torture warrants. Both Dershowitz and Schulz argue within the frame of social contract theory, but with a significant difference. Dershowitz's arguments are counterfactual, and Schulz's grounded in history. Dershowitz bases his argument for torture warrants on a counterfactual example: the legitimacy of torturing a suspect to find the location of a ticking bomb before innocent people are killed. Schulz delineates the fallacies of this counterfactual example:

> For what the ticking bomb case asks us to believe is that the authorities know that a bomb has been planted somewhere; know it is about to go off; know that the suspect in their custody has the information they need to stop it; know that the suspect will yield that information accurately in matter of minutes if subjected to torture; and know that there is no other way to obtain it. The scenario asks us to believe, in

other words, that the authorities have all the information that authorities dealing with a crisis never have.[50]

Schulz bases his argument against torture in any circumstances on the information that we *do* have: the act of torture violates the Constitution of the United States and the Convention against Torture, ratified by the United States in 1994. Furthermore, these laws are based on a careful process of deliberation, one grounded in our collective history. Schulz reminds us of the historical reasons for the rejection of torture: we know its actual impact on those who are tortured, and we know the actual reasons that it is practiced by governments throughout the world: "Almost three-fourths of the world's countries practice [torture]. But not to find ticking bombs. To punish political opponents. To intimidate their allies. To cow a citizenry." [51]

A social contract based on history, on the "collective wisdom of humankind," leads us to recognize the temptations of tyranny, to resolutely support the laws and institutions that hold us (as well as others) accountable for the ramifications of our actions, and to a resolute defense of human rights.[52]

A Collective, Historical Social Contract

There are four elements of a collective, historically aware social contract:

1. The purpose for engaging in social cooperation is ethical and spiritual: acknowledging the sacred gift of life and the joy of living in harmony and Beauty.
2. The primary task is one of close attention, noticing the world around us, our effects on that world, and what that world has to show us of patterns of reciprocity and vitality.

3. We experience our human rights and our individual responsibilities and opportunities as embedded in a collective social and natural matrix—part of nature and within history. In this collective matrix we find creativity, equally expressed in autonomy and responsibility.
4. There are ceremonies of attention and gratitude that can enable us to reach the heights of creativity demonstrated in the "great Law" of the Iroquois.

We can see our struggles—first to establish a bill of rights and a governmental system of checks and balances, and then to maintain those rights and that separation in the face of pressures to disregard them—as part of a similar process. In his book *In Our Own Best Interest*, William Schulz acknowledges both the critical importance of human rights and the paucity of support for those rights within the United States. He reminds us that most Americans put national self-interest before human rights and see the violation of human rights in Burma, China, and Chiapas as having little connection with our concerns in the United States. In response, Schulz proposes a "new realism," gives pragmatic reasons why those violations matter, and describes how they affect our collective security:

[A new realism] would view human rights as more than the release of prisoners of conscience or an end to torture but as a comprehensive effort to shape democratic communities of rights that will be peaceful neighbors, fair trading partners, and collaborators in the effort to preserve a green planet . . .

If a country employs child soldiers or persecutes gay, lesbian, bisexual, and transgendered people or intimidates religious minorities or tolerates acid burnings of women, for example, it is a good bet that that country will be guilty of other abuses—that it may tolerate environmental toxins, fail to regulate cyberfraud, or ignore treaty commitments at will.

A new realism will understand human rights violations in a holistic fashion.[53]

Schulz recounts the dismay that often greets his line of reasoning from those who claim that human rights are an end in themselves, valuable whether or not they are in our own interests.[54] The logic of his argument, however, accrues with the moral wisdom of Sanchez, Weaver, and Deloria. In a world of close observation of natural and social interactions, it makes sense that we value human rights because we see the individual and collective impact of the violation of those rights. This is not an ethics of altruistic self-sacrifice or of charity for the less fortunate. This is a system of reciprocity, of grateful and critical acknowledgment of the threads of connection that sustain us. It makes sense for the Hotinonshonni, then, to create the Great Law and it makes sense for us to outlaw torture. Just as the Hotinonshonni saw the dire effects of unrestrained warfare, we see the horrific costs of torture as a means of social control. We check not just the excesses and evil actions of others, but of ourselves—for we, too, can become torturers; we, too, can justify the violation of human rights in the name of national security.

Rather than our system of values and our governmental policies being grounded in Manifest Destiny, in absolute truths born with self-righteous certainty, they are the hard-won insights of generations, the fruit of collective wisdom, attuned as much to our folly and excess as to our wisdom and responsibility. Schulz writes, "Human rights represent the boundaries of the acceptable, the limits beyond which an international consensus agrees that we may not go, regardless of the proclivities of a culture or tradition . . . The human rights advocate believes not necessarily that values are absolute but that we have in hand a global vision of 'best practices' with which to order our common life together."[55]

As we fully embrace this collective task, the lessons are hard, but the resources are vast. We can also learn from ethical and spiritual traditions that systematically develop resilience in the face of suffering, and insight and compassion in the face of social injustice. We now turn to other voices, also critical of the overweening power of the United States yet also evocative of other forms of individual and national identity and power.

chapter 6

audacity

The ennobling truths are not just challenges to act with wisdom and compassion but challenges to act with creativity and aesthetic awareness . . . The human world is like a vast musical instrument on which we simultaneously play our part while listening to the compositions of others. The creation of ourself in the image of awakening is not a subjective but an intersubjective process. We cannot choose whether to engage with the world, only how to.

—Stephen Batchelor[1]

Among the hundreds of demonstrators angrily shouting, fiercely denouncing the design of first-strike nuclear weapons at Draper Labs in Cambridge, Massachusetts, was a small group of robed Buddhist monks, smiling, chanting, beating their drums in the graceful, calming cadences of the human heart. As I participated in demonstrations in Boston and New England in the mid-1980s, I was captivated by the energy of the monks. Their very presence was a gift of healing and beauty, a sharp contrast to the voices of rage and despair. Many of my students and colleagues were equally moved, and we tried to be present in demonstrations in ways that denounced what we saw as military and economic aggression and simultaneously expressed beauty, joy, wonder, and peace. We were rarely successful.

Only now, twenty years after the demonstrations in Boston and Cambridge, do I realize that the Buddhist monks were as much an evocative, albeit nonjudgmental, "protest" against us as they were a protest of the making of nuclear weapons and the support of military action throughout the world. The presence of those gracious, calm, joyful monks was as much a challenge and gift to us angry peace demonstrators as they were to those who created and supported the creation of nuclear weapons. It is surprising that it has taken me so long to recognize this challenge and this gift. The power of righteous indignation is a remarkable thing.

Engaged Buddhism

As I studied the writing of Thich Nhat Hanh and Masao Abe, I learned what was behind the healing, open presence of the Buddhist monks in our loud, fierce demonstrations. Born in 1926, Thich Nhat Hanh is known throughout the world for his teaching and his activism. As a young man, he participated in the movement of Buddhist renewal in Vietnam and was a leader of Buddhist efforts to stop the war in Vietnam. He founded the School of Youth for Social Services, a form of what he called "engaged Buddhism." The purpose of the school was to involve students in working with villagers to redress the devastation of the war by repairing buildings, conducting schools, and providing basic health care. After he traveled to the United States in 1966 to talk about the cost of the war to all parties, the Vietnamese and Americans, he was not allowed to return to Vietnam. Since that time, he has been in exile in France. He has established the Order of Interbeing in the West, which includes monastic houses in France, Vermont, and California.[2]

I have been profoundly challenged by Thich Nhat Hanh's critique of the peace movement in the United States:

> In the peace movement there is a lot of anger, frustration, and misunderstanding. The peace movement can write very good protest letters, but they are not yet able to write a love letter . . . The way you speak, the kind of understanding, the kind of language you use should not turn people off. The President is a person like any of us.[3]

Masao Abe is the leading philosophical exponent of Zen Buddhism to the West since the death of D. T. Suzuki. He belongs to the Kyoto School and has written many insightful analyses of Western philosophy and the theology and ethics of Western Christianity.[4] Masao Abe offers the following critique of peace movements, human rights movements, and social reform movements in the West: "Even if those who participate in such movements are full of much good will and possess a strong sense of justice, if they lack an awakening to the original nature of self and others, their actions are without real power, or worse, they create more confusion."[5]

Within the tradition of engaged Buddhism, as articulated by Thich Nhat Hanh, Masao Abe, and others, there is a way of acting that is in itself a form of "being peace," a type of political engagement that is grounded in a profound experience of the "wondrous fullness" of life. In explaining this experience, Thich Nhat Hanh draws on the words of the Zen master Lin Chi, "The real miracle is to walk on earth."[6] How is this miraculous? Thich Nhat Hanh writes, "Every day we are engaged in a miracle which we don't even recognize: a blue sky, white clouds, green leaves, the black, curious eyes of a child—our own two eyes."[7]

What does it mean to fully walk on earth? In our open action and presence, we touch, even in the midst of oppression, pain, and suffering, the abundance and wonder of life.[8] The focus of engaged Buddhism is not a set of beliefs about life, self, society, and justice, but a nondualistic way of experiencing suffering and joy, self and others, friends and "enemies," good and evil. Buddhism, or dharma practice, is a set of actions that create or evoke "contentment with joy, and equanimity in the face of suffering."[9] These nondualistic ways of experiencing good and evil, self and others, provide a distinct way of holding hope, suffering, anger, and fear, and a distinct way of imagining and engaging in creative political action.[10]

Examples of Engaged Buddhism

While Thich Nhat Hanh was the first to use the phrase *engaged Buddhism*, other examples of work for social transformation based on Buddhist practices can be seen throughout the world. One example is the movement in 1956–1966 among the Untouchables of India. This movement, led by Dr. B. R. Ambedkar, was part of a struggle of millions of people against the caste system. In Sri Lanka, the Sarvodaya Shramadana movement worked to end rural poverty. Throughout Asia, there are movements for the rights of lay women and nuns. In Japan we find the work of Soka Gakkai and other Nichiren-inspired movements. The peace work of Aung San Suu Kyi, the Nobel Peace laureate of Myanmar, is exemplary, as is the work of Sulak Sivaraksa of Thailand challenging sexism, economic exploitation, and militarization.[11] These forms of social action come from many different streams of Buddhism—Theravada Buddhism as practiced in the Sarvodaya Shramadana movement and the work of Sulak Sivaraksa, the Zen Buddhism of Thich Nhat Hanh and Masao Abe, and the Tibetan Buddhism of the Dalai Lama. While rooted in varying interpretations of the teachings of the Buddha and in different cultures, these forms of dharma practice have a striking commonality. As the Dalai Lama states, "The existence of suffering in the world evokes in them a feeling of universal responsibility."[12]

According to Thich Nhat Hanh, "Meditation is not to get out of society, to escape from society, but to prepare for a re-entry into society."[13] Kenneth Kraft, professor of religious studies, claims that engaged Buddhism is both a clear development within the world of contemporary Buddhist traditions, and a way of practice that is in a period of experimentation and posing questions.[14] For example, what are the forms of social action that emerge from compassionate engagement with our pluralistic world and its multiple opportunities and challenges? If we remain open to the immense suffering caused by war, by poverty, by sexism and racism, and, if we remain equally open to the resources we have, the means of communication, of connection, our resources of economic and political power, how do we act with integrity and courage?

This is a challenging task, one best met by learning from other traditions while respecting and preserving the uniqueness of each. Not only are specific traditions, such as Western humanism and Buddhism, different from one another, but there are significant distinctions within ethical and religious traditions. Some Buddhists, for example, clearly differentiate engaged Buddhism from other forms of Buddhist practice, and others, like Stephen Batchelor, claim that the term is a misleading tautology, detaching action from other aspects of Buddhist practice. Batchelor describes insight and compassionate response as "two wings of a bird" and claims that "authentic Buddhist practice necessarily leads to . . . engagement with the world."[15]

Masao Abe, in contrast, distinguishes these newly emerging forms of social engagement from the practices of traditional

Buddhism. Abe finds that Buddhism's history, with only a few exceptions, evidences "an indifference to social evil." The focus in most of Buddhist history, even within the bodhisattva vow "to save all beings," has not been on society as a whole but on individuals. Christian liberation theology has persuaded Abe that the Buddhist focus on "interrelationality and compassion" may obscure inequality and injustice, creating a need for Buddhists to develop "a new notion of justice on the basis of wisdom and compassion."[16] Similarly, Christopher Queen, a scholar of Buddhist studies, calls engaged Buddhism "a 'new vehicle' . . . or a fourth *yana* in the evolution of the dharma," which emerges in the context of a "global conversation on human rights, distributive justice, and social progress."[17] Thich Nhat Hanh also considers the development of engaged Buddhism to be new, yet he grounds these developments in the history of Buddhism: "Buddhism is not one. The teaching of Buddhism is many. When Buddhism enters one country, that country always acquires a new form of Buddhism."[18] He sees it as appropriate, therefore, and to be expected, that the movement of Buddhism into the West will result in changes not only for the West but for Buddhism itself. The distinctive aspects of engaged Buddhism emerge, therefore, not merely from a Buddhist approach to social action but from a Western understanding of the interrelatedness of the individual and society, and Western commitments to freedom, human rights, and democracy.[19]

Practitioners of engaged Buddhism are involved in a vast array of social services: teaching meditation to prisoners, providing homes and food for refugees and for people who are homeless, and running small businesses that provide jobs in economically depressed urban centers. Engaged Buddhists are also involved in a wide array of activities for peace, including pilgrimages, public chanting, construction of peace pagodas, and meditation vigils at military and other government facilities. In addition, there is a growing network of educational institutions, from meditation and retreat centers to Buddhist colleges and universities.[20]

Within Buddhism, there is debate over what, if anything, is particularly Buddhist about the engaged Buddhists' work for economic and social justice. Darrel Wratten, a scholar of comparative religions, lays out four possible answers to this question. The first position is that none of these forms of activism are distinctively Buddhist; rather, they reflect a Protestant ethic of work and service. A second possibility is that the uniquely Buddhist nature of these actions is still nascent. For example, the small businesses that are run by Buddhists "may lead to new ways to actualize right livelihood." A third option is that these actions are already uniquely Buddhist. Because of the intrinsic link of inner and outer transformation, these forms of social engagement are substantially different from political and social activism based in other religious and ethical traditions. The fourth alternative—somewhat surprisingly, the one that is held most widely—is that it does not matter whether these actions are distinctively Buddhist or not.[21]

In considering the possible distinctiveness of Buddhist social engagement, it is important to hold in mind two distinctions. First, the visible form of an action (providing food and shelter for people who are homeless; providing hospice care to people with HIV/AIDS) may appear to be the same as that practiced by Christians, humanists, Jews, or Muslims, but the motivation for the action, and the attitude toward success and failure, may be radically different. Second, with regard to the different motivations and attitudes toward action found within Buddhism, it is important to remember that even the most renowned advocates of engaged Buddhism, Thich Nhat Hanh and Sulak Sivaraksa, are nondogmatic, holding the definitions of Buddhism lightly. Sivaraksa, for example, writes of small-*b* buddhism, cautioning against sectarianism.[22] In his analysis of engaged Buddhism, Kraft finds that many who participate in this movement are particularly willing to drop the religious affiliation if it "becomes a mark of attachment," distances them from others, or binds them to a constricting belief system. Furthermore, as Kraft points out, "the tradition's resources" are available to anyone; a person does not have to first take on the identity of a Buddhist.[23]

Compassion

If—as Masao Abe, Sulak Sivaraksa, and Thich Nhat Hanh say—they and other Buddhists have learned from a Western emphasis on human rights and social justice, we might next ask what engaged Buddhism brings to the West. Patricia Hunt-Perry and Lyn Fine describe the impact of Thich Nhat Hanh's form of engaged Buddhism on women who were peace activists before they became Buddhists. Now, in addition to opposing the policies and priorities of a militaristic society, they try to cultivate peace in themselves, as well as in society at large. They have not adopted different political goals, but the motivation for these same goals has changed. No longer motivated by anger and fear, Hunt-Perry and Fine find that the "cultivation of true love, compassion, and joy" can be a compelling impetus for social responsibility. They also find, through dharma practice, that fully experiencing the suffering and joy of oneself and others leads to a deep connection that overcomes the alienation that leads many political activists to see their political opponents as "enemies."[24]

Susan Moon finds a similar set of convictions in her conversations with four lifelong activists, Joanna Macy, Paula Green, Sala Steinback, and Melody Ermachild Chavis. Each of these women described the ways in which becoming Buddhist had changed her activism. All had come to the realization that "there's no enemy out there, no us and them." They had also found ways to work for justice without becoming attached to either immediate success or the assurance of inevitable progress. Paula Green, who has conducted nonviolence training in a refugee camp in Zaire, on the border of Rwanda, writes of having "no illusions about the pace of change, but planting seeds of peace for the future." These women also emphasized the importance of practices that help avoid burnout: equanimity through meditation, and the cultivation of kindness. Moon cites Joanna Macy, who describes social action as "the natural expression of being alive and awake." Macy told Moon, "We're all driven by ignorance, hatred, and greed. And we're all jewels in the net. Buddhism saves us not only from numbness, but also from cynicism."[25]

For many activists, dharma practice offers resources for long-lasting compassionate political engagement. In addition to examining how it is possible to overcome our attachment to results, our isolation, and our polarizing separation of allies and enemies, we will take up a further challenge. According to Cynthia Eller, many Buddhist activists are "politically disenfranchised" and doubt that the state is "an appropriate agent for the advancement of human welfare." It is not surprising, therefore, that most Buddhists choose to be involved in social service rather than political action—for example, nutrition programs, assistance to victims of natural disasters and nonviolence training—activities that take place on a small scale, mostly "outside the corridors of governmental power."[26] What would dharma practice mean for those of us who are not so politically disenfranchised and hold a fair measure of economic, political, cultural, and educational power? Kraft writes, in jest, of the need for a bodhisattva to be a politician or an economist.[27]

Kraft's jest is our task. There are efforts in the West to bring dharma practice to those who hold institutional power.

The Center for Contemplative Mind and Society leads meditation retreats for people in corporations, schools, and universities. Leonard Risken, an attorney and specialist in conflict resolution, has developed a program of mindfulness training for lawyers. In addition to reducing stress, Risken found that meditation enhances the practice of law. When attorneys are no longer locked into the habitual patterns of an adversarial mind-set, they are free to imagine appropriate responses to negotiations and court challenges. At times, advocacy and adversarial actions are appropriate to protect a clients' interest. But at other times, more conciliatory options may be more suitable. Meditative practices may well enhance our ability to imagine creative responses to complex problems.[28] Through dharma practice we can learn to become more resilient, more imaginative, and more honest in our use of power. For those of us who have social power, to merely "speak truth to power" is insufficient, if not disingenuous. We need to ask how we see and use the cultural, economic, and political power we have.

Dharma Practice and Social Action

Writing about the insights gained through the practice of Buddhism is a quixotic endeavor. Buddhism is not a philosophy, yet the mere descriptions of Buddhist perceptions of self and other, suffering and joy, good and evil, action and being, knowing and nonknowing appear to be concepts in a coherent philosophical and ethical system. Stephen Batchelor describes the problem well. By focusing on four noble truths, Batchelor states, "even sympathetic interpreters" miss "the crucial distinction that *each truth requires being acted upon in its own particular way (understanding* anguish, *letting go of* its origins, *realizing* its cessation, and *cultivating* the path)." The result of this misinterpretation is as profound as it is widespread: "Four ennobling truths to be acted upon are neatly turned into four propositions of fact to be believed."[29] Masao Abe concurs with this emphasis on practice, stating that it is misleading to see Zen as a philosophy. Although intellectual understanding certainly has a place in Zen, such understanding must be thoroughly grounded in practice.[30]

While daily practice is essential, the practitioners of engaged Buddhism are not dogmatic about the specific forms of practice. The teaching of Thich Nhat Hanh, for example, is notable for the prodigious array of activities he offers as ways of enhancing mindfulness: not merely attention to breathing, but mindful walking, driving, cleaning, even stopping to breathe before answering a ringing phone.[31] As Thich Nhat Hanh writes, "There are so many methods of stopping and seeing, and intelligent teachers will be able to invent ways to help you. In Buddhism it is said that there are 84,000 Dharma doors for you to enter reality."[32]

According to Thich Nhat Hanh, our ability to be aware can be cultivated as we pay close attention to even the seemingly mundane tasks of daily life.

> To my mind, the idea that doing dishes is unpleasant can occur only when you aren't doing them . . . I enjoy taking my time with each dish, being fully aware of the dish, the water, and each movement of my hands. I know that if I hurry . . . the time will be unpleasant and not worth living . . . If I am incapable of washing dishes joyfully, if I want to finish them quickly so I can go and have dessert, I will be equally incapable of enjoying my dessert. With my fork in my hand, I will be thinking about what to do next, and the texture and the flavor of the dessert, together with the pleasure of eating it, will be lost.
>
> Each thought, each action in the sunlight of awareness becomes sacred. In this light, no boundary exists between the

sacred and the profane. I must confess it takes me a bit
longer to do the dishes, but I live fully in every moment, and
I am happy.[33]

While meditation does take time and practice, Thich Nhat
Hanh claims that it can become an integral part of life, and not
a distraction or added burden to a life already filled with duties
and obligations. Acknowledging that "active, concerned people"
have much work to do, he advises, "Keep your attention focused
on the work, be alert and ready to handle ably and intelligently
any situation which may arise—this is mindfulness." He
explains that mindfulness is consistent with focusing fully on
one's work, with alertness, judgment, calm, and self-control.[34]

Mindfulness

The result of such meditative and ethical practice is intense
attention to life, a full engagement of mind, of senses, of heart
and imagination. As Batchelor states, "The stiller the mind, the
more palpable the dazzling torrent of life becomes."[35]

Dharma practice enhances the feelings of empathy that
lead us to recoil at the prospect of harming others. Dharma
practice leads us to respond to the suffering of another as if it
were our own, because, in a very real sense, it *is* our own.
Through dharma practice, our hearts are enlarged, and our
sense of the world is made more complex and more closely
intertwined. Through dharma practice, we see the illusory
nature of the boundaries that separate us and others. Linda
Holler analyzes this experience: "If tactile consciousness can
allow us to feel kinship with the myriad of things that create,
sustain, and nourish us, then that feeling of being comforted
may provide us with the moral strength to give that care back.
Morally, everything changes with the experience of emptiness

because one's incarnation as interbeing and impermanence creates a consciousness of gratitude and responsibility."[36]

In his attempt to mobilize people to support human rights throughout the world, William Schulz states that he is often asked, "But what does that suffering have to do with me?"[37] A Buddhist response to that question has three components: a shift in our perception of the suffering of others, a changed attitude toward those who do not empathize with that suffering, and a distinct attitude toward the one who is the perpetrator of suffering.

Schulz describes the gifts of "grace and kindness" that allows us to be moved by the suffering of others.[38] Meditation hones those gifts. The practice of meditation leads to a deep sense of interdependence with all people and all of nature, expanding the boundaries of our body and minds. Our knowledge of deep connection with those who suffer becomes as visceral as it is conceptual. Thich Nhat Hanh, for example, describes the complex awareness of both beauty and suffering that emerges through meditative practice:

> Meditation is to be aware of what is going on—in our bodies, on our feelings, in our minds, and in the world. Each day 40,000 children die of hunger. The superpowers now have more than 50,000 nuclear warheads, enough to destroy our planet many times. Yet the sunrise is beautiful, and the rose that bloomed this morning along the wall is a miracle. Life is both dreadful and wonderful. To practice meditation is to be in touch with both aspects.[39]

Empathy emerges from the cultivated awareness of interdependence. Thich Nhat Hanh calls his monastic order Tiep Hien, or the Order of Interbeing. The very name reflects the interdependence of all existence, a concept that he states is difficult to convey in English: "We have talked about the many in the one, and the one containing the many. In one sheet of paper, we see everything else, the cloud, the forest, the logger. I am, therefore you are. You are, therefore I am. That is the meaning of the word 'interbeing.'"[40]

As we meditate on the rich play of forces that makes up our life in the present, we realize that "our body is not limited to what lies inside the boundary of our skin."[41] We are dependent on the sun, the air, earth, and water, and we are equally dependent on other people. Not only do we depend on those who care for us when we are vulnerable infants and children, but our continued existence is possible only because of our physical links to light, food, water, and air. In mindful attention, we experience these physical connections. We also recall and embrace our physical and emotional connections with other people. The Buddhist scholar Anne Klein describes the interdependence of self and other people evoked in Tibetan traditions of meditation:

> In opening a meditation session, for example, one is often advised in Tibetan traditions to imagine oneself surrounded by male and female family members and friends. One might begin with one's mother and father on either side of oneself, and then visualize as well one's teacher and his or her teachers, each one taking the form of a Buddha whose body, composed entirely of light, vividly appears and then dissolves into oneself, thereby empowering one to accomplish the meditative task at hand. Thus, from the beginning, one practices as a self embodied and assisted by others. Buddhist traditions thus generally see no dichotomy between a sense of relatedness on the one hand and a sense of personal effectiveness on the other.[42]

What is the result of becoming aware, on a daily basis, of both our interdependence and our personal effectiveness?

Thich Nhat Hanh describes a profound healing of self and society that occurs as we touch the wonders that are around us, that constitute who we are in the core of our being. This healing has two components: equanimity in the face of danger and suffering, and a compassionate connection with other people. The "miracle of mindfulness" opens us to the depths of joy; the miracle of mindfulness enables us to embrace the truth of pain and suffering. Thich Nhat Hanh likens mindfulness to a mother calmly soothing a crying baby (a calm that those of us who are parents know is not always readily achieved!).[43]

Thich Nhat Hanh acknowledges that the world is dangerous, and that it is reasonable to be afraid and worried: "We don't know when the bombs will explode. We feel that we are on the edge of time. As individuals, we feel helpless, despairing. The situation is so dangerous, injustice is so widespread, the danger is so close." He claims, however, that full awareness of even the greatest danger can be met calmly and clearly. As an example, he describes the refugees who left Vietnam in small boats and the lifesaving importance of being able to remain calm even in the face of storms and rough seas. Just as the refugees in the boat had to "sit still and be able to smile," so our troubled world needs such people of calmness and peace.[44]

Skillful Means

There are two other dimensions to a Buddhist response to those who ask why they should care about the suffering of others. First, the question itself—what does the suffering of others have to do with me?—is not dismissed as a mark of moral or intellectual failing but is taken with utmost seriousness and answered with respect. Although Schulz is not a Buddhist, his response to those who challenge the relevance of human rights or ask if human rights should be abrogated to protect people from terrorist attacks is an example of the attitude that also emerges from dharma practice. Rather than denouncing or dismissing people for the questions they raise, he carefully responds to those questions, seeking ways to help people see the pragmatic reasons to support human rights, not only in times of peace but also in times of danger. A Buddhist would call this the exercise of "skillful means," taking seriously the concerns that people express and finding ways to bring them to wider and deeper connections with the suffering and joy of others.

As we learn to act out of wisdom and compassion, we try to find the skillful means of enabling ourselves and others to see the costs of injustice and the means of enabling ourselves and others to imagine ways of healing the damage caused by injustice. Kenneth Kraft writes of the long history of skillful means or "method as liberative art" within Buddhism.[45] Sulak Sivaraksa also describes the intricate connection among compassion, wisdom, and the development of skillful means of social engagement and institutional transformation: "To oppose those who kill and oppress, one must not only have a mind free of hostility, one must also be skilled in dealing with the complexities of the social system."[46]

Thich Nhat Hanh clearly describes a nuanced and creative way of responding to suffering. In his account of the practice of "Beginning Anew," he tells of his work with a Vietnam veteran who was so tormented by guilt over having killed Vietnamese children that he could not stand to be around children. Thich Nhat Hanh states, "Shame is not enough to change our heart," and offers a difficult, but transformative, practice: "You keep thinking about the five or six children that you killed in the past, but what about the children who are dying now? You still have your body, you still have your heart, you can do many things to help children who are dying in the present moment. Please give rise to your mind of love, and in the months and years that are left to you, do the work of helping children." The veteran was transformed by following this advice.[47] As this example shows, the practice of Beginning Anew and the focus on skillful means do not evoke shame or persuade people to accept an idea but rather evoke a deep-seated transformative insight, a fundamental alteration of heart, mind, and will.

Beyond Us vs. Them

Dharma practice takes us in a spiral movement that reframes ethical action. It changes how we see the suffering of others; it changes how we address those who do not see the depth of suffering or feel the urgency to redress suffering; and it changes how we see the perpetrators of suffering. Patricia Hunt-Perry and Lyn Fine discovered that some political activists who became Buddhists no longer saw opponents as the enemy to be silenced or defeated. However, the commitment to prevent others from doing violence and harm remains as strong as the commitment to avoid doing harm oneself. Thich Nhat Hanh describes the startling gift of compassion even for those who cause suffering for others.[48] We do not condone or ignore the harm that we and others may do, but our basis for trying to prevent the damage done by others, and by ourselves, now emerges from compassion, not from a desire to punish or blame. Of the person who harms us, Thich Nhat Hanh says, "He may think that his suffering will be lessened if he can cause us to suffer. Once we are in touch with his suffering, our enmity and bitterness towards him will vanish, and we will long for him to suffer less. The spring water of the compassionate mind begins to flow, and we ourselves are the first to be cleansed by it."[49]

Compassion for the suffering of one's enemies does not mean complacency in the face of evil and injustice. On the contrary, Thich Nhat Hanh calls understanding and compassion "very powerful sources of energy" that enhance our ability to

stop violence and injustice. He cites the example of the powerful work of Mahatma Gandhi. Like Gandhi, Thich Nhat Hanh
claims that it is possible to stand against violence and injustice
without hating those who are the bearers of violence and injustice: "Our enemy is not the other person. Our enemy is the violence, ignorance, and injustice in us and in the other person.
When we are armed with compassion and understanding, we
fight not against other people, but against the tendency to
invade, to dominate, and to exploit."[50]

The fruit of compassion is wisdom: seeking the most efficacious means of stopping injustice and violence, rather than trying to defeat or destroy those who are violent. We bring the
same persistent, nonviolent care to the suffering of others as
we do to the pain we ourselves endure.[51]

In engaged Buddhism we find the coherence of a particular
set of practices that evokes a healing shift in the perception
and experience of self and others, of pain and joy, of responsibility and possibilities for creative political and ethical action.

Fruits of Dharma Practice

As Abe so pointedly warns, such disciplined practice may lead
to quietism. As he and other practitioners of engaged
Buddhism also acknowledge, dharma practice may instead provide a solid foundation for ethical action. Ethical action or compassion and wisdom do not spring primarily from the will or
the intellect but from a changed perception of self and others.
This fundamental change in experience leads to a different
direction for the will and another task for the intellect—that of
seeking skillful means of responding to injustice, and of evok-
ing empathy and compassion in others.

What happens as we cultivate mindfulness in our daily
lives? For some, the effects are sudden and dramatic; for others,

there is a gradual unfolding of a different way of seeing the world, a different way of experiencing our belonging to the world. I, for one, am a very slow learner. It was only after over twenty years of sporadic meditation and ten years of sustained daily practice of concentration and mindfulness meditation that my sense of self and others was transformed. On a clear spring day, enjoying the warmth of the sun and the fresh green of the budding tees and slim shoots of growing flowers, I realized as I walked across campus that I could no longer think in terms of us against them. No longer the outsider calling others to change, I felt that I was in a very real sense my "enemy." Even someone like Jesse Helms, whose policies I abhorred, felt like part of me. We belong to the same world, and the success of his appeals to bigotry and fear cannot be separated from my fail-ures and the failures of other liberals and progressives to reach fearful people with compassion, vitality, humor, and insight. To denounce him seemed as odd as to denounce my foot when it cramps. Suddenly, a different perception of work for social jus-tice also emerged, grounded in the extent to which I am in and with the world, so much so that the use of *I* seems odd, unable to indicate accurately the nexus of awareness that is the human experience of being in, being constituted by a cherished, yet dangerous, world of forces, opportunities, beauty, and pain.

Dharma practice dissolves the division of "us and them" yet enables the creative exploration of skillful means of helping people see the horror of injustice and find resources to bring about healing and balance. Dharma practice also changes the way we experience the force of ethical standards of compassion, justice, and responsibility. Just as the four ennobling truths are injunctions to act and not propositions to be believed, the four-teen precepts, the ethical commitments of Thich Nhat Hanh's monastic order, are not injunctions to be obeyed but commit-ments that emerge from a deepening awareness of the rich interconnectedness of life. In 1996, each of the fourteen precepts that are followed by members of the Order of Interbeing were reworded to avoid misleading connotations of submission and obedience. According to Thich Nhat Hanh, the imperative form of the precepts "conveyed obedience to external authority, a dynamic of rules and of shame if the rules were broken." The precepts were inadequate in another way—failing to fully express not only individual concerns and responsibilities, but social concerns and opportunities.[52] Consider the significance of the change in the ninth precept. Originally it said, "Do not say untruthful things for the sake of personal advantage or to impress people." In its new form, it becomes a statement of awareness and social and individual commitment:

> Aware that words can create suffering or happiness, we are committed to learning to speak truthfully and constructively, using only words that inspire hope and confidence. We are determined not to say untruthful things for the sake of personal interest or to impress people, nor to utter words that might cause division or hatred. We will not spread news that we do not know to be certain nor criticize or condemn things of which we are not sure. We will do our best to speak out about situations of injustice, even when doing so may threaten our safety.[53]

As currently revised, the fourteen precepts followed by laity, monks, and nuns who belong to the order founded by Thich Nhat Hanh, the Order of Interbeing, express a nondogmatic ethic of awareness and compassion.

Some of the fruits of dharma practice are fairly easy to grasp: dissolution of the rigid boundaries between our bodies and the natural world, between ourselves and all others, including our so-called enemies. The implications for social action also are fairly straightforward: the renunciation of violence and the practice of compassion. There is, however, another form of dissolution that is harder for many of us who are trained in Western ethical and religious traditions to grasp, yet it is an insight that carries immense ethical and political significance. Masao Abe poses the issue starkly: "Should we not honestly recognize that being and non-being, life and death, good and evil have equal powers and roles in human existence?"[54]

Abe states that as we become deeply aware of the extent of human suffering, and as we are honest about the difficulties of our own struggle to live with compassion and integrity, we realize, "[The] priority of good over evil is an ethical imperative but not an actual human situation. In human beings good and evil have equal power. I cannot say that my good is stronger than my evil although I should try to overcome my evil by my good . . . It is not that I *have* a dilemma between good and evil, but that I *am* that dilemma."[55]

A Buddhist Ethos of Social Engagement

This realization of the equal power of good and evil, even within ourselves, does not diminish the ethical imperative of choosing good over evil but recasts it. Given this connection of good and evil, the goal of action is not defeating evil but learning how to act in light of the power and connection of both good and evil. The easy divide between those of us who are righteous and those others who are malevolent and corrupt is dissolved. Thich Nhat Hanh writes that the negative dynamics of society we so often rightly denounce are also within us.[56] To see good and evil in their interdependence lessens an unwarranted pride in our righteousness and makes it impossible to honestly indulge in polarizing denunciations of the evil of others. According to Thich Nhat Hanh, this experience also leads us to see the ways in which moral evil is not so far from natural evil.

Impatience and anger directed at a person who hurts us are, in this view, as unreasonable as those feelings directed at an earthquake or a flood: "We have to see hardships brought about by others as a sort of natural disaster. These people make our lives difficult because they are ignorant, prisoners of their desires or their hatreds. If we speak angrily to them, and treat them as our enemy, then we are just doing what they are doing, and we are no different from them."[57]

Experiencing ourselves as the dilemma of good and evil, forthrightly seeing the power of each in our individual and social worlds, short-circuits the comfort of any sense of self-righteousness and moral superiority. Not only are we intertwined with the evil in the world, but our virtuous separation from evil may itself become a vice. Batchelor claims that moral dangers accompany even the seemingly benign practice of compassion: "fantasies of moral superiority" and an inflated sense of our own purity and wisdom. He explains, "Exaggerated rejection of self-centredness can detach us from the sanity of ironic self-regard. Once inflation has taken hold—particularly when endorsed by supporters and admirers—it becomes notoriously difficult to see through it." As a corrective to these dangers, Batchelor advocates remembering that even a compassionate heart "still feels anger, greed, jealousy, and other such emotions. But it accepts them for what they are with equanimity, and cultivates the strength of mind to let them arise and pass without identifying with or acting upon them."[58]

Masao Abe claims that Buddhist and Western traditions have much to learn from each other. Like Sulak Sivaraksa, Abe sees the dangers of quietism and withdrawal within Buddhism and recognizes the merit of a focus on social justice and institutional change. While taking from Christian liberation theology and Western Enlightenment ethical traditions a concern with political structures, Abe and Sivaraksa claim that motivations for and the means of social engagement, as based in dharma practice, help avert some of the dangerous messianic and isolating tendencies within Western ethical and religious traditions. According to Abe, although the Western concentration on justice and love may compel us to work for social reform, it may as easily keep us from seeing the "original nature of self and others," seeing fundamental differences between peoples where there are actually deep similarities and connections. He warns us of the dangers of reifying the division "between the just and the unjust, the righteous and the unrighteous," and names the dynamics we see so often in Western history: the pursuit of justice, grounded in absolute truth, leads to "punishment, conflict, revenge, and even war."[59]

Abe's critique recognizes flaws in both Buddhist and Christian ethics: "Buddhism tends to put priority on enlightenment over practice and thereby threatens to become quietism. Conversely, Christianity tends to put priority on action over prayer and threatens to become a crusade."[60]

An ethos of political engagement based on wisdom, compassion, and thus the cultivation of skillful means of social transformation is somewhat different from the type of activism known to many of us in the West who are veterans of various movements for social change. The whole enterprise of social engagement is radically reconfigured, however, with the addition of a third element of Buddhist practice. Rather than an ethical system in which social action is grounded in justice, love, and truth, let us imagine an ethos in which social action is grounded in wisdom, compassion, and nonknowing.

The focus on skillful means by the practitioners of engaged Buddhism may sound as though reformers know what is best for society and are finding the "liberative arts" to bring others to our insights. This misses, however, what is most challenging about engaged Buddhism: the freedom and honesty of a genuine acceptance of the limits of our knowledge, and of the unsettling and refreshing possibility of the new. Thich Nhat

Hanh states that the avoidance of dogmatism, expressed in the first of the fourteen mindfulness trainings, is "the roar of lion. Its spirit is characteristic of Buddhism."[61] The avoidance of dogmatism is central to the first three mindfulness trainings:

> *Aware of the suffering created by fanaticism and intolerance,* we are determined not to be idolatrous about or bound to any doctrine, theory or ideology, even Buddhist ones . . . *Aware of the suffering created by attachment to views and wrong perceptions,* we are determined to avoid being narrow-minded and bound to present views . . . We are aware that the knowledge we presently possess is not changeless, absolute truth . . . *Aware of the suffering brought about when we impose our views on others,* we are committed not to force others, even our children, by any means whatsoever—such as authority, threat, money, propaganda, or indoctrination—to adopt our views.[62]

The basic reason that Buddhists avoid dogmatism, even about the teachings of the Buddha, is that understanding is important only as it functions as an opening and not as an end. Thich Nhat Hanh describes the apparent paradox: "Understanding means to throw away your knowledge. You have to be able to transcend your knowledge the way people climb a ladder . . . The Buddhist way of understanding is always letting go of our views and knowledge in order to transcend."[63]

After an intense workshop with fellow activists—trying to find ways of holding together our deepest convictions about the imperative of justice and the horror of suffering along with our recognition that we could not honestly assert that the good we so valued would inevitably triumph over the evils we abhorred—I finally understood more fully the concept of not-knowing. It requires simultaneously knowing, bringing with deep conviction all that you have learned and experienced, and at the same time, being ready in any interchange for a startling shift in perception, a new way of framing the world, of seeing depths and insights that you could not grasp before. This stance of nonknowing is far from tentative. To do it, one has to genuinely put one's knowledge to the test, to bring that knowledge to one's interactions with others with conviction, clarity, and power (for example, knowledge that genocide, war, and torture are wrong, and not an inevitable part of human experience). At the same time, one has to hold these truths lightly, offering them, the best of who we are and what we know, in genuine interaction with the best of what others are and know. Our nonknowing is only as open and profound as our knowing is well grounded and clear.

To offer all that we are and know and simultaneously to be mindful of what we cannot see and could not imagine—this is not relativism; this is audacity.

Audacity is not a word that often comes to mind to characterize the fruits of Buddhist meditation. More often, practitioners and scholars extol the relaxation, tranquility, and clarity that result from insight and concentration meditation. There is, however, far more to mindfulness than serenity.

Our audacity may serve us well as we act ethically and politically. The ambiguity of existence invites creativity and courage. Ambiguity is not an excuse for indecision or indifference but leads to an ethic of risk. Batchelor describes this challenge well: "If our actions in the world are to stem from an encounter with what is central in life, they must be unclouded by either dogma or prevarication."[64]

What is entailed in an ethic of empathy and risk? We may act as nonattached catalysts, offering the best of our knowledge and insight as ingredients in a process we can neither control nor predict.[65] Our goal, then, is no longer leading others to accept the rightness of our insights and solutions to social injustice but is, rather, open-minded participation together in "intelligent political action."[66] As we bring all of who we are and all of what we know into our political work, we may find our work enlivened by an ability to see our own foibles and failures without shame and paralyzing self-blame. Instead, we can willingly acknowledge our errors and injustice and try to rectify the damage that we do to others and to ourselves.

Batchelor writes of an additional fruit of mindfulness: given the inevitability of risk and uncertainty, we may learn to recognize the difference between moral certainty and ethical integrity. The former is a chimera; the latter can be a tangible, readily attainable adventure. Batchelor claims that we can learn to seek not the right thing to do, but the compassionate thing to do.[67] We can also seek the daringly beautiful course of action, the form of engagement that boldly acknowledges the multiple possibilities of what sociologist Jonathan Rieder calls our "vibrantly imperfect culture."[68]

As we are grounded in compassion, wisdom, and nonknowing, as we seek ethical integrity but not moral certainty, our model for political action is neither the ringing judgment of the prophet nor the confident witness of the martyr. Our model is, rather, the ironic vitality of the trickster, the audacity and connection of the artist, and the virtuosity of the jazz musician, playing with skill and verve the rhythms and risks of life.

In this work, we are enjoined to remain mindful of the particular constellation of actions in the past and the problems and opportunities in the present. Thich Nhat Hanh poses an embedded alternative to utopian idealism as a basis for social action. He writes that *hope itself can become an obstacle*, and he urges us to embrace the fullness of the present, rather than utopian dreams of perfection. He acknowledges the challenges of remaining in an unjust social order yet sees this immersion in the present as the most fruitful basis for social action.[69]

As we work for peace, firmly rooted in society rather than in utopian dreams of perfect peace and justice, we have important tasks. Sivaraksa and Thich Nhat Hanh both claim that it is not enough to protest the outbreak of war. They repeatedly emphasize the greater importance of persistent and creative attention to the roots of war, and a steady focus on preventing war and enhancing nonviolent means of conflict resolution.[70] It is not enough to decry the costs of violence. Sivaraksa encourages us to develop further the "art of transforming conflict" and claims that far more can be done through institutions such as the United Nations to prevent war.[71]

Given how our adversarial culture is enthralled with dreams of conquest and military glory, given the military and terrorist threats to peace, stability, and justice, given how much of our economy is tied to the production and development of weapons, and given that our political vocabulary defines power in terms of military prowess, the goal of preventing war may well seem less audacious than quixotic and foolhardy.

If we are, however, fully rooted in the present, we are able to see the multiple possibilities for preventing war. In the final chapter, we return to the challenge of imperial power and the vision of enduring peace. There is an ethos of peace, available to us and practiced by people throughout the world, that can serve us well as we strive as individuals, and as a nation, to creatively embrace the responsibilities of global citizenship and the mandate of social justice.

chapter 7

risk

We loved the risk. We loved getting lost. We loved having to make something happen out of thin air.
> —Herbie Hancock, on playing with Miles Davis, Wayne Shorter, Ron Carter, and Tony Williams[1]

If we in the peace movement embraced the present and its challenges with the insight and compassion of engaged Buddhism and with a full awareness of the atrocities and suffering caused by our conquest of Native American nations, how would we read the opportunities we have for abolishing or lessening the risk of war? The challenges are obvious: the spiral of violence in the Middle East, the threat of terrorism throughout the world, the tensions between the United States and North Korea, the tensions between India and Pakistan. These threats to peace are real, have deadly consequences, and require immediate response. At the same time, there are numerous opportunities for peace and nonviolent conflict resolution, and manifold opportunities to institutionalize alternatives to war.

We need to remain fully aware of both the reality of violence and the opportunities for peace. Bob Herbert, editorial writer for the *New York Times*, poses the challenge succinctly: "The terrorists will not achieve their ends by blowing up innocents. And we will not be able to bomb the terrorists into submission . . . It is time for all of us to begin searching for alternatives . . . We need to overcome our feelings of helplessness, and channel our rage and our anguish toward constructive ends."[2]

Following the guidance of engaged Buddhism and remaining within the Beauty Way, we can respond to the widespread support for military force by many people in the United States not by merely denouncing these responses, but by understanding them more deeply. The reasons for resorting to military force are simple, and not merely thoughtless arrogance and deeply ingrained bellicosity. People are responding to danger with the tools they have. While we may be able to imagine alternative responses—the use of international mediators, an international court, and so forth—these responses lack the known status and evident power of military forces. The International Criminal Court, a plausible venue for prosecuting terrorists, has only recently been ratified and does not have a solid history or acceptance. It was, in fact, soundly resisted by the Bush administration. By turning to the use of the military, people in the United States are responding to threats to national and international security with the institutions and the means that they have, know, and trust.

What is most needed now is not a mere denunciation of militarism. We can do far more. We can strengthen other institutional forms of response to terrorism and violence and make them more useful and usable. We can also be deeply grateful that these other forms of response do not need to be invented. Our task is to nurture the seeds of what is already in place.

Responses to the Threat of War

In our current situation, many people are acting out of two well-known and long-established Western responses to the brutality of war: the just-war tradition and a pacifist critique of war. Those, like Jean Bethke Elshtain, who advocated the use of military force in response to the terrorist attacks of 9/11 did so in the language of the just-war tradition, claiming that its essential conditions were met: the use of force was a response to the provocation and attacks of others, and the cause for which one fought was itself legitimate and warranted. Elshtain and many political and military leaders also argued that the means used were proportionate to the threat, and that all feasible means were taken to safeguard civilian populations: the targets were military installations and personnel, not civilian populations, and any civilian casualties were tragic errors, to be avoided if all possible.[3]

There are also people who continue the Western and Gandhian traditions of ethical and religious pacifism, refusing to be drawn into pragmatic rationales for the destruction of human life and the ecological devastation of war. They powerfully decry what is lost in human lives, political rights, economic and ecological resources, and the brutalization of heart necessary to kill other human beings.

We desperately need such protests and such clear denunciations of the folly and horror of war. We need the courage of those who refuse to serve in unjust situations. We need the presence of the Israelis and Palestinians who demonstrate for peace, declaring, "We are not each other's enemy." We need the people in the United States who stand at post offices and crowded streets in solidarity with those who suffer and in silent witness to the horror of war. Without such principled objections to war, without such resolute commitment to peace, I would question our humanity. Without other actions, however—without sustained, concerted attempts to institutionalize means of preventing war—I question our creativity and wisdom.

The Art of Peacemaking

We need not invent other institutional responses to the threat of war. We can, rather, build on the work of those who have seen the horror of war and have imagined concrete alternatives. In sixteenth-century Europe, Desiderius Erasmus, Europe's most renowned intellectual, passionately advocated "the art of peacemaking," an art he saw as more noble, and far more difficult, than that of waging war.[4]

Erasmus was critical of the way just-war theory was applied in his time: used by Christian princes to justify both their wars against one another and their wars against the Turks. His refutation of the critical leverage of the just-war theory was succinct and simple; in his *Adages* in 1517, he challenged those who claimed, "It is a sin to fight in a spirit of vengeance, but not if it is for love of justice," with a pointed rejoinder: "Who does not think his own cause just?" As Erasmus wrote, "The greatest evils have always found their way into the life of men under the semblance of good." Like Erasmus almost five hundred years ago, many people now are critical of the just-war tradition and decry the enormous suffering caused by war. *Dulce bellum inexpertis*—war is sweet to those who have not experienced it.[5]

Erasmus did not deny the reality and possible utility of conflict. Conflict does not always escalate to the point that René Girard refers to as "double bind" and "mimetic doubles"— the point where the parties become mirrors of the other, each seeing the annihilation of the other as the condition of their survival, each justifying their violence against the other as righteous violence.[6]

Despite their resolute advocacy of enduring peace and the arts of peacemaking, Erasmus and Kant did not think that humans can learn to live without serious conflict, between and within states. Sissela Bok, professor of philosophy, writes that

Erasmus and Kant "had no illusions that peace was somehow natural to the human species." Nor did they share the faith of some utopians "in some convulsive political or religious transformation that would bring permanent harmony—the more so as they had seen at close hand the corrupting and brutalizing effects of unrestrained violence both on perpetrators and on victims, no matter how humane the original motives."[7] Their core assumption about human nature is just the opposite: without regularized institutions to resolve conflict between nations and peoples, we will turn to violence and war.

Modern Peacemakers

There are constructive alternatives to war, fitting vehicles for our rage, anguish, passion, and creativity. One such project is Global Action to Prevent War, an international coalition-building effort to prevent war, terrorism, and genocide. The goals of the Global Action project are comprehensive and wide ranging: "Now instead of working for peace in fragments, it is time to bring together these diverse approaches—conventional force reductions, limits on arms production and trade, cuts in military spending, measures to stop proliferation and build confidence, training for peaceful conflict resolution, and means for conflict resolution, peace building, and peacekeeping—in a unified program to prevent war."[8]

The Global Action program is a coalition of international peace groups and nongovernmental organizations, working on a forty- to fifty-year project to institutionalize alternatives to war. It was developed in 1998 by Randall Forsberg, founder and director of the Cambridge-based Institute for Defense and Disarmament Studies; retired ambassador Jonathan Dean, adviser on international security issues for the Union of Concerned Scientists; and Saul Mendlovitz, Dag

Hammarskjöld Professor of International Law, Peace and World Order Studies at Rutgers University Law School, and founder and codirector of the World Order Models Project in New York City.

Global Action has three major components: (1) prevention of war, genocide, and terrorism by institutionalizing alternative means of dispute resolution and supporting the international rule of law; (2) limitation of national military forces to defense and the development of international peacekeeping forces, under the control of the United Nations; and (3) promotion of a culture of peace.[9] While the goals of Global Action are dramatic and far-reaching, the basis of those goals is concrete, immediate, and tangible. Global Action works with organizations and resources that are already in place. It is an effort to bring together initiatives, to coordinate long-term and short-term efforts, in a comprehensive program to abolish war.

The broad goals of Global Action can be met by working within and strengthening existing institutions. For example, the coalition has identified four ways that the United Nations could strengthen its peacekeeping and war prevention capacities. The first would be to establish "a corps of 50 professional mediators at the disposal of the Secretary General and the Security Council." Another would be to set up a committee of the UN General Assembly charged with conflict prevention; this committee could dispatch teams to possible conflict sites and invite witnesses to the UN in New York. The third measure would be to create a 4,000- to 6,000-member "standing volunteer police force" at the UN. Finally, member states could promote the "effective implementation of the International Criminal Court."[10]

Our understanding of the art and science of conflict mediation has expanded dramatically within the last twenty years. In nearly every school system within the United States, from elementary through high school, peer mediation programs are in place to train young people to resolve conflicts without violence.

Many law schools have conflict mediation programs, providing training in alternative means of dispute resolution.[11] This expertise can be fostered, and these people who are already trained in nonviolent means of conflict resolution can be brought together under a number of different auspices, beginning with a permanent center for conflict mediation within the United Nations.

The second component of Global Action—the limitation of national military forces to defense and the development of international peacekeeping forces—will take longer and is more far-reaching. When people are threatened, they do not have to invent strategies for the use of military force, nor do they have to create ad hoc military alliances; those organizations are already in place in regional security organizations. Peacekeeping resources should be equally available. Global Action addresses this imbalance with its goal to "strengthen the mediation and peacekeeping capabilities of existing universal-membership regional security organizations." These organizations include the Organization for Security and Cooperation in Europe (OSCE), the Organization of American States (OAS), the African Union (formerly the Organization of African Unity), and the Association of Southeast Asian Nations (ASEAN). Other regions, notably the Middle East, South Asia, and the East Asia–Pacific region, could benefit from the creation of similar organizations.[12]

Another important component of providing alternatives to war is now in place. The International Criminal Court has been ratified by over ninety countries, including Canada, all European Union countries, twenty-four countries in Africa, and eleven Asian countries. The purpose of the court is to "prosecute individuals for genocide, crimes against humanity, and other war crimes."[13] Defense secretary Donald H. Rumsfeld rejected the court as a threat to U.S. sovereignty and warned of dire consequences (which, to many of us, hardly seem undesirable): "By putting U.S. men and women in uniform at risk of politicized prosecutions," Rumsfeld said, the court "could well create a powerful disincentive for U.S. military engagement in the world."[14] Others, such as Senator Russ Feingold, saw more promise in cooperation with the court and pointed to the dangers of forgoing this opportunity for international justice: "Beyond the extremely problematic matter of casting doubt on the U.S. commitment to international justice and accountability" such resistance casts doubts about "our country's credibility in all multilateral endeavors."[15]

The 2003 revision of the Global Action program also addresses alternative means of responding to the 2001 terrorist attacks on the United States. The program, developed by members of the Task Force on Peace and Security of the United Nations Association, National Capital Area, and described recently by Jonathan Dean, has two components, one immediate, the other preventive and long term. An immediate proposal is that UN member nations conduct international tribunals to publicly try al-Qaeda leaders for crimes against humanity. Dean argues that the value of such a tribunal could be as vast as that of the Nuremberg trials. Those public trials of Nazi war criminals served a dual purpose, bringing the people responsible for genocide to justice and, of equal significance, exposing those crimes to public view and thereby delegitimizing Nazi ideology among former supporters of fascism within Germany and throughout the world.[16]

Another immediate need is for the United States to work with the European Union and Muslim states to prepare a joint proposal for the settlement of the Israeli-Palestinian conflict. As many analysts of terrorism have pointed out, a sense of profound humiliation and frustration at the inability to resolve this conflict is a key component of this current wave of terrorism. Other efforts are more long term—support for economic development, health care, education, and improved governance in Middle Eastern societies.[17]

The Risks of International Cooperation

Four major criticisms have been raised against the Global Action project: (1) it requires the United States to give up its sovereignty; (2) it could be misused by U.S. or multilateral forces; (3) it does not eradicate the root causes of war; and (4) it is the expression of a deluded, if not dangerous, utopianism.

Sovereignty at Stake

Many people will be threatened by the loss of U.S. sovereignty if we support the International Criminal Court and subject ourselves to its laws. Many will resist our reliance on multilateral efforts when we now have the military power to act alone.[18] William Schulz addresses these concerns and offers a pragmatic rationale for cooperating in the institutionalization of the rule of law, shaping that law, and willingly subjecting ourselves to it: "The United States is a mighty power, but it is not omnipotent. If history is any guide, it will not remain even a mighty power forever. Wouldn't it be wiser, then, while we have the power, to enter wholeheartedly into the creation of international norms, be they legal or behavioral, that best reflect our values and then respect those norms and their attendant procedures even when we may be found in violation?"[19]

Checks on the Peacekeepers

Other critics might well claim that it is dangerous to work within existing institutions because of their complicity in the past with oppressive actions, even torture. Furthermore, a turn to peacekeeping in the future may become a justification for perpetual war. This danger is very real. At times, conflict prevention and mediation will fail. Not all disputes in the private sphere can be resolved without litigation, nor can all public and international disputes be resolved without force. An international criminal court is necessary, as is a multilateral force to stop genocide. Such force is less likely, however, to serve as a mask for empire building if it is a multinational force, under the global checks and balances of multinational control. When military force is required to stop genocide or to restore order, a culture of vigilance and institutionalized checks to the use of force by peacekeepers is as necessary as are checks on the power of police forces within nation-states. We need to be continually aware of how we could turn the mechanisms of international law to the interests of domination and exploitation.

Causes of War

There are many who will resist the Global Action project—some because it is too far-reaching, others because it is not far-reaching enough. The third major criticism of Global Action highlights its limitations. Even if all of its proposals were implemented, the root causes of war would remain: imperial aggression, racism, and poverty. Even if war were abolished, other fundamental forms of injustice would also remain: racism, sexism, environmental degradation, homophobia, poverty, and child abuse. My response to these criticisms is both simple and complex. The simple answer is that the critics are right. Global Action does not remove the root causes of war, nor does it address a whole set of equally urgent social issues. In her dialogue with Elise Boulding and other peace scholars, Randall Forsberg clearly articulates the nonutopian vision of Global Action as a part of our collective work for justice, rather than all that must be done to create a just world. Forsberg says,

"The idea that we can create a genuinely egalitarian participatory society that meets human needs is a concept that goes far beyond the absence of war."[20] As a component of work for justice, Global Action complements other initiatives; it does not replace them.

At the same time, my response is far more complex. Steeped in the tradition of biblical prophecy and American utopianism, I and many others of my generation have seen our work as revolutionary activists to be that of establishing justice on earth now, in our generation, and for all future generations. Half measures and incremental changes were anathema. We did not want reform, we wanted revolution: a world in which all peoples live equitably, in harmony with one another and with all of nature. The watchword for this type of activism was simple: "No one is free until everyone is free."

In the life and writings of Carol Lee Sanchez and the writings of other members of the Pueblo Nation, we see a different way of establishing justice. Within the Pueblo Nation, living wisely and seeing life as sacred is all-encompassing *and* differentiated. No one knows all the requisite ceremonies and stories. No one is responsible for all tasks. Rather, everyone has a particular role and an invaluable part in the mosaic of collective life. No one, however, is responsible for definitively establishing or maintaining justice in his or her lifetime, much less for all time.

What sheer arrogance and folly to think otherwise! Why did we think that our perspective on injustice was the sole fulcrum to move the massive burden of oppression? How sane, how freeing, to realize we only see a fragment of what it takes to live well! We are called to a particular task, and we are not alone. Others are as compelled to establish a sound, just economic order as we are compelled to establish nonviolent alternatives to war. We need one another's efforts. We respond to the task of living in Beauty and live out the gift of wisdom and compassion in innumerable ways: some work in shelters for battered women; others work on providing equitable and affordable health care; others seek environmentally sound agricultural practices. Does another slogan come to mind—"Let a hundred flowers bloom"? The campaign and its subsequent reality, the suppression of dissent and diversity by many Chinese communists, demonstrates how difficult it is to truly welcome the countless paths to peace and to justice, the countless ways of living with wisdom and compassion.[21]

Dangerous Delusion or Creative Challenge?

We have a vision: a world in which conflicts are settled largely through peaceful means and in which war is as rare as it is abhorrent. This is a goal shared by some and derided by many. The strongest critique of such a vision of international order based on global citizenship and global responsibility is that it is dangerously deluded utopian fantasy.[22]

Jean Bethke Elshtain reminds us that international institutions have often failed to prevent violence and doubts that "endangered people around the globe" will be able to turn to such institutions for protection, and for justice. She indicts the failure of the United Nations peacekeeping forces, "handcuffed by the rules of disengagement in Bosnia, watch[ing] as people were being shot to pieces before their very eyes." Elshtain doubts that adequate reform of such institutions is possible and claims that "liberal and neoliberal internationalist entities have great difficulty reckoning with the determined and the ruthless."[23]

While she questions the efficacy of liberal internationalism in restraining violence and punishing those who violate human rights and international law, Elshtain is equally wary of the power of such international institutions to override the legitimate interests of particular nations and peoples: "We must not lose sight of our national interest in favor of a utopian vision of a world in which states are diminished and international institutions work their will to the exclusion of the self-interests of particular polities."[24]

Given the risks of international cooperation, given the past failures of multilateral peacekeeping forces, is it possible that international institutions can be made more effective in preventing war and protecting human rights?

I do not know. I do know that we have managed to contain some of our proclivities for violence—moving from anarchic vigilantism to the rule of law within nations. We do have a democratic government with a system of checks and balances, albeit one that is often poorly understood and frequently undermined by citizens and politicians seeking short-term political gains or security at the expense of freedom.[25]

We know why we contain to some degree governmental coercion, monarchical despotism, and vigilantism. We contain these because we have a social contract based on the recognition that monarchs, governments, and military and police forces have the capacity to abuse power. What could lead us even further in this direction, to significant limitations on our proclivity to wage war?

Quite likely, the proposal for an international rule of law was utopian when Kant and Erasmus first raised it as a possibility for European nations. When Kant called for the rule of law as the foundation of an enduring peace, when Erasmus asked for international councils to arbitrate the conflicts between Christian princes, the rule of law was barely established within nations, much less between nations.[26] Now, however, the rule of law is taken for granted as the foundation of civil order within nations, and there are movements by other countries to establish the rule of law between nations through the ratification of the International Criminal Court. Furthermore, the field of conflict mediation has been developed greatly in the West, and we can amplify and learn from Buddhist and other traditions of conflict mediation. We also know and see the costs and folly of war. We know that a Pax Americana established and maintained by military force will be accompanied by the death, coercion, and humiliation of millions of people. Let us pose the question differently. Instead of asking, "Are we so naive as to think a Pax Humana, an international rule of law, is realistic?" let us ask, "Are we daring enough and creative enough to find the political, cultural, and ethical resources to make it real?"

The Folly of Empire

Our reading of U.S. history leads us to challenge two assumptions held by advocates of the legitimacy of Empire.

1. Such power can be used to benefit humanity as a whole, and it is more likely that imperial power can be so well used by the United States than by other nations.
2. Other forms of action and international cooperation are the fruit of weakness, not strength. The only real power is military or economic coercion.

Our common history teaches us the folly of the first assumption; specific aesthetic, ethical, and political practices may enable us to see the limits of the second.

Although he claims that the United States could become a beneficent wielder of imperial power, Robert Kagan acknowledges that "the young United States wielded power against weaker peoples on the North American continent."[27] He does not explore, however, the details of that use of power. To do so would bring him to see the ways in which imperial power destroys both the victims of imperial power and the people that wield it. Recall the indictment of the Narragansett after the British massacre of the Pequot people; recall the slaughter of the Yana, Yuki, Pomo, and hundreds of other Native peoples in California.[28] The atrocities of Empire are many, the costs borne for generations.

There are many critiques of imperial power, two widely known and one equally compelling but less often articulated. I will begin with the first two: first, Empire is destructive of the humanity of the colonized, and second, Empire also destroys the humanity of the colonizer.

Effects on the Colonized

In contemplating the possibilities and perils, the responsibilities and rewards of imperial power, the course of our reflection and the conclusions we draw are inexorably shaped by our conversation partners. Whose experiences of Empire do we ponder? Niall Ferguson and Robert Kagan, for example, acknowledge the costs, risks, and limitations of imperial power, but they are the beneficiaries as well as the champions of Empire. Ferguson admits that there were costs to the spread of the British Empire: the degradation and deaths of the slave trade, the deaths of those who resisted imperial rule, and the humiliation of forced labor. He argues, however, that the worst violations of human dignity were mitigated by the criticism they met from within Britain itself, most notably in the eventually successful campaign to abolish slavery. He also argues that, in the long run, the gains of British imperial rule far outweigh the losses in human dignity and life. He cites such gains as "the free movement of goods, capital and labour" and the imposition of "Western norms of law."[29]

This calculus of benefits and costs involves two fundamental dangers. The first is the problem of denying or evading the immensity of loss. The second danger is that, when acknowledging damage to the humanity of others, we choose to value our own humanity more. With violence to others comes a cost to us: we become brutal in the doing and callous in the disregard. To emphasize as a fair calculus their death and humiliation for our gain reflects a tragic lack of empathy and imagination. The most telling critique of Ferguson's defense of the overall benefits of the British Empire is in the frontispiece of the book itself: a well-dressed white man, calmly smoking a pipe, surrounded by scenes of the most horrifying racial and sexual violence: a black woman, stripped and hung by her wrists from a barren tree; a black man, also stripped, being whipped by two other black men; three bare-breasted black women, two calmly observing the scene of horror and the other pouring a drink for a white man, who has his back turned to the violence and degradation around him.

Any defense of colonialism and Empire must be weighed against the ongoing indictment of imperial power by those who know its costs. From Frantz Fanon through Gayatri Spivak and to the contemporary fiction of Sherman Alexie, we find voices of protest and outrage being raised throughout the world, powerfully denouncing the soul-rending costs of imperial domination.[30]

Let us enter this same calculus of gain and loss, guided, however, by an awareness that comes from either being the dominated oneself or having had empathy instilled through the stories of those who have borne those costs and known torture, rape, death, domination, and humiliation. Let us also enter this same calculus with two classic Western ethical principles, one developed by Immanuel Kant, the other by John Rawls. Rawls proposes a simple yet potentially revolutionary moral criterion, the principle of justice as fairness. If we were to choose the structure of our society "behind a veil of ignorance," unaware of our status in society, we would choose a system in which all are treated fairly, in which all have basic human rights and equality of opportunity.[31]

Rawls's principle of justice is eminently logical but easily and persistently avoided. Ferguson describes the benefits his family received from Empire, calling the years they lived in Kenya a "magical time" of comfort and security: "We had our bungalow, our maid, our smattering of Swahili—and our sense of unshakeable security."[32] Would he have experienced the same security if his mother had been the maid, if his father and grandfather had been killed in resistance to British rule, if his daughters and sons had been humiliated and confined in mind- and body-destroying menial jobs or, in an earlier time, sold into slavery? The critique of Peter Berger in *Pyramids of Sacrifice* is still pertinent. We do well to be suspicious of any intellectuals or political leaders, whether from the right or the left, who sacrifice other people and other people's children for the greater good but do not suffer or die themselves.[33] At stake in these arguments is a clear moral imperative: the inauthenticity of claiming the necessity, for the greater good, of a sacrifice that you and your family do not make.

We might wish to modify Kant's categorical imperative. Rather than requiring ourselves to will as ethical only that which we would will as universal law,[34] we can say, "Accept as tolerable only a set of consequences that you would willingly bear and see borne by your children and grandchildren."

In our analysis of imperial power in the present, these principles apply: do we focus primarily on our experiences as the beneficiaries of Empire, or do we acknowledge as well the lives lost in conquest, lives marred by the limitations and humiliations of occupation and domination? To stop the undeniable cruelty of one despotic leader and prevent possible harm to ourselves and other nations, by late June 2004, 847 American soldiers had been killed, and more than 10,000 Iraqi soldiers and civilians had been killed, wounded, or displaced from their homes.[35]

While the U.S. military and the U.S. media regularly reported, as they should, the numbers of U.S. and allied soldiers wounded and killed, they were not so forthcoming about the numbers of Iraqi casualties. An independent investigation by the Associated Press found that at least 3,240 civilians had been killed by June 11, 2003, only three months after the war had begun. Patrick Tyler, reporting for the *New York Times*, cited a much larger figure from a British-American research group: 5,534 to 7,207 civilian deaths. The investigators for the Associated Press also found that the U.S. and British governments did not count, and did not *intend* to count, civilian casualties. The report cites Lt. Col. Jim Cassella, a spokesman for the Pentagon, who said, "Our efforts focus on destroying the enemy's capabilities, so we never target civilians and have no reason to try to count such unintended deaths." Patrick Tyler also found that the U.S. military was similarly reluctant to count even Iraqi soldiers killed in battle, citing the difficulty of separating civilian and military deaths and claiming that such an accounting was "just not significant information."[36] There is something chilling about the logic that upholds, as well we should, the numbers of American lives lost yet refuses to even try to account for the numbers of Iraqi people killed.

How do we face the horror that people may well have been killed and maimed in vain? We are just beginning to discover ways of breaking the poisonous cycle of bitterness and rage, learning to honoring lives lost in war and terrorism, mourning and protesting their deaths without vengeance and retaliation.[37] We are just beginning to find other means of bringing tyrants to justice and other means of safeguarding security and dignity. We must decisively turn to another path—remembering these deaths, and honoring their lives by doing all that we can to prevent such horrors from happening again.

Niall Ferguson could be right: it could make a difference that the United States is the current imperial power. It could even make an immense difference, but not for the reasons he imagines—that we can wield imperial power with beneficence and justice. Rather, recognizing the impossibility of that goal, we might honor and acknowledge the costs and horrors of our imperial past and then use our power cooperatively with others, putting in place international structures that can check imperial ambitions and excesses, ours included.

Costs of Coercion

We can thereby creatively challenge the second assumption at the core of the defense of imperial power: power equals control, so power requires coercion. There are three fundamental reasons to question the assumption that order and security require coercive power, one pragmatic, the other two ethical and aesthetic. Despite his advocacy of the beneficence of liberal imperial power, Niall Ferguson also points to the pragmatic limits of unilateral, coercive economic or military power. He criticizes Robert Kagan on this point and delineates the necessity of multilateral institutions and multilateral cooperation to meet transnational challenges: "Yet today's transnational threats such as terrorism, nuclear proliferation and organized crime—to say nothing of disease pandemics, climate change and water shortages—put a premium on cooperation, not competition, between states. The attractions of unilateralism are undeniable, since demanding allies can be more irksome than invisible foes, but a solo strategy offers little prospect of victory against any of these challenges: the successful prosecution of the 'wars' against all of them depends as much on multilateral institutions as does the continuation of free trade."[38]

Hannah Arendt, in her analysis of totalitarianism, gives an ethical critique of coercion: "Power and violence are opposites; where the one rules absolutely, the other is absent."[39] Behind this seemingly counterintuitive statement is Arendt's definition of genuine power as not merely the ability "to act but to act in concert." Jonathan Schell concurs. Violence may create temporary cooperation and temporary submission; it cannot create sustained relationships of willing "action in common." Arendt argues that the terror of totalitarian rule destroys the support any government needs to survive, thus destroying the ruler's genuine power. Schell affirms Arendt's critique of totalitarianism and applies it to the choices and challenges now faced by the United States: "Do American leaders imagine that the people of the world, having overthrown the territorial empires of the nineteenth and twentieth centuries, are ready to bend the knee to an American overlord in the twenty-first? Do they imagine that allies are willing to become subordinates? Have they forgotten that people hate to be dominated?"[40]

The Tedium of Domination

A third critique of Empire is that imperial power is not only corrosive and destructive, but also profoundly unimaginative. Ferguson laments that citizens of the United States may lack the staying power necessary to not only establish but to maintain an Empire. He fears that we lack the requisite commitment and dedication to spend generations developing the linguistic and managerial skills required to govern colonies far from our native home.[41] I am focusing, however, on a different type of boredom, an aesthetic reason to turn from imperial power, a twist to Arendt's insight into the banality of evil. Imperial power is as tedious as it is deadly. The saga of a supposedly superior civilizing power bolding controlling "lesser" peoples and nations, then falling to its own excesses, is as devoid of aesthetic novelty and interest as it is rife with horrific violence and loss. Have we not seen this movie far too many times?

Cooperative Power

Can there be other forms of world order? I do not know, but these are the reasons to try; these are the ingredients of a different ceremony of audacity, power, responsibility, and compassion. We know, from our own history, the workings of Empire. Empire is the creation, the fruit, of Truth, Goodness, and Power. The conviction of the right to rule, the presumed knowledge of what is required for order and peace, from the splendor of Pax Romana to the "civilizing" rule of the British Empire and the prosperity, security, and democracy promised by American internationalism—in all, domination is masked as benevolent leadership in the inevitable exercise of power to those wielding power. But it is not, of course, so masked to its victims. They see its other face—that of arrogance, of self-righteousness, even the face of those who take pleasure in dominating others and inflicting pain. Lest we too hastily repeat another self-deluding and polarizing divide, let us remember that we who distrust imperial power often do so because we know, in our own hearts and minds, its appeal. We know the pleasure that can accompany domination and victory over others, and the checks we seek are checks to our own self-righteous hubris, our own excesses in the pursuit of our visions of justice and truth.

It would be a mistake, however, to fail to recognize the risk of choosing other ways of using power. We may fail; we may find innumerable ways to abuse even forms of cooperative, nonviolent power. Here we can apply the logic of Schulz's critique of simple declarations that terrorism is evil. Just as it is not enough to name evil as evil, it is not enough to name good as good. Such righteous certainty may lead to an illusion of inevitability that prevents us from doing the hard work required to implement and sustain institutional structures of cooperation and balance.[42]

Jonathan Schell gives us direction for that work, along with a clear definition of cooperative power: "Power is cooperative when it springs from action in concert of people who willingly agree with one another."[43] The political philosopher Iris Marion Young gives a lucid description of democratic international order based on such cooperative power: "We should envision global democracy as the interaction of self-determining peoples and locales on terms of equality in which they understand obligations to listen to outsiders who claim to be affected by their decisions or actions and to resolve conflicts with them through settled procedures in a global framework of regulatory principles democratically decided on together by all the self-determining entities."[44]

Schell and Young also acknowledge the risks of such forms of international order and the limits of cooperative power. Young warns that "global interdependence" may lead to "cultural homogenization."[45] Schell reminds us of the unfamiliarity of this form of power. Although he charts the history of cooperative power, or nonviolent action, he is disturbed by the fact that not only is the history relatively unknown, but there is no good term in the English language for nonviolent action. As Schell so rightly points out, it's like calling action "noninaction." Like Schell, I prefer the power of a positive term, rather than the negative connotations of *nonviolence*—a term that connotes passivity and holds violence as the norm. Gandhi's term *satyagraha* is deeply meaningful within Indian culture; it has a rich array of connotations—holding to truth, soul force, truth force—that are, however, impossible to translate into English.[46]

For the time being, *cooperative power* may be the best term, especially if it can be enlivened by other connotations: an aesthetic appreciation of jazz performance, the splendor and audacity that emerges from working with resources, limits, insights, and mistakes; a resolute yet ironic memory of our ability to let our good intentions keep us from seeing the damaging effects of our actions; a determined realization that our strategies for acting cooperatively or justly may not work for all situations or for all peoples. As Schell so clearly states, the forms of cooperative or nonviolent action are vast:

> At the street level, this would mean choosing satyagraha over violent insurrection—the sit-down or general strike or "social work" over the suicide bombing or attack on the local broadcasting station. At the level of the state it would mean choosing democracy over authoritarianism or totalitarianism . . . At the level of international affairs, it would mean choosing negotiation, treaties, and other agreements and institutions over war and, in general, choosing a cooperative, multilateral international system over an imperial one; at the level of biological survival, it would mean choosing nuclear disarmament over the balance of nuclear terror and proliferation.[47]

In each of these examples, Schell points out, there is more than a choice to accept or reject violence; there is also selection of a cooperative alternative to violence.

What leads us to choose the risk of cooperative forms of power over the seeming certainties of coercive power? While we can do so for moral or religious reasons, claiming, as did Gandhi and King, obedience to the will of God, Schell rightly recalls Arendt's compelling warnings of the dangers of "Robespierre's terror of virtue."[48] When ethical and spiritual insights are predicated not on our virtue but on the inextricable skeins of virtue and vice, our ethical and spiritual practices may not be the source of unconditional moral truths but, rather, the means of helping us see our constitutive failings, greed, and imbalances.

Trickster stories keep us honest, just as compassion leads us to want to work with, rather than against, other peoples.

Schell argues for a cooperative international order based on love and freedom. Such order is more likely to be sustained, rather than the product of individual whim or inclination, as we learn from traditions that systematically nurture the capacity for and direction of respect and compassion. Buddhist and Native traditions contain complex practices that evoke and shape love, that evoke respect for others and an awareness of and freedom in the face of our own flaws—the "triple fires" of greed, hatred, and delusion, which are central to us and not just our enemies.

Nations can enter into a social contract and ground the willingness to do so not in what Schell calls "Hobbesean or Lockean fear." Rather, their willingness can arise from ceremonies of awakening and gratitude.[49] Here Buddhist and Native American philosophers have much to offer. They write of communities and practices that evoke and shape awareness, respect, gratitude, and compassion for others. A freedom shaped by respect and awareness of limits is more than individual inclination. It can be the fruit of social, collective stories and ceremonies of attention and memory. The foundation of this ethic is not spirit or religion per se, but particular communities and their shaping of the power of spirit, of deep connections to other peoples and to nature, for moral, self-critical ends.

As we develop cooperative forms of power, Erasmus's advice to the Christian princes of Europe applies also to us: "Think not only of what you wish to gain, but of what you lose to gain it."[50] In this journey there will be loss. Just as many children, young people, and adults were killed and beaten in non-violent struggles led by Gandhi and in the civil rights movement in the United States, so others may die and suffer in this struggle. The difference, though, in this calculus of risk and gain is that Gandhi, as well as King and other leaders of the Civil Rights Movement, were willing to bear the costs themselves, willing, as Gandhi said so often, to die but not to kill. I do not know yet the full costs of this wager, but I do know that, as we see them, we cannot deny them nor simply pass them on to be borne by others.

There is a final challenge to the choice of cooperative rather than imperial power, one only seemingly trivial. It is the challenge to make the rhetoric of cooperative power, democracy, freedom, human rights, international order, and the rule of law as energizing as the rhetoric of Empire. We must consider whether it is possible to develop persuasive political rhetoric without polarizing dualisms and ringing certainties.

This alternative rhetoric will be powerful to the degree that it corresponds to the aesthetic power of jazz, a form of beauty and vitality predicated on open confrontation with failure, differences, limits, multiple options, and risk. Lest we think it impossible to honor and respond to suffering and, at the same time, relish the joys and challenges of life, let us allow our hearts to be lifted and our imaginations enlivened by the audacity, bravado, suffering, and beauty that is found in the best jazz performances—what Ann Douglas called "an impossible mix of intellect and rapture."[51] Let us take up the challenge so clearly posed by William Schulz: "What is of supreme importance is that I live my life in a posture of gratitude—that I recognize my existence and, indeed, Being itself, as an unaccountable blessing . . . What is always helpful and absolutely necessary is to look kindly on the world, to be bold in pursuit of its repair, and to be comfortable in the embrace of its splendor."[52]

Power can be wielded with a different logic and ethic. Rather than coercion, we may create a dazzling play of difference that highlights with crystalline clarity the particular strengths of others and ourselves. Rather than an American internationalism, we have in place the ingredients of a jazz internationalism. On October 21, 2001, Danilo Perez, an internationally renowned jazz pianist named as cultural ambassador by his native Panama, performed in Columbia, Missouri, with artists from Brazin, Nigeria, and the United States. Perez told the audience that he and the members of the quintet felt blessed to have the opportunity to demonstrate a form of internationalism other than that seen on September 11 of that year: a vision of beauty and vitality that emerges from the creative interaction of people from different cultures, with varied gifts and insights.[53]

The internationalism envisioned and embodied by Perez emerges from an improvisational ethic, an ethos expressed both in the artistry of performance and of living. These are the ingredients of this improvisational ethic:

Beauty: a deep, nuanced appreciation of the world around us, its foibles and limitations as much as its graceful splendor.

Irony: continuously remembering that our best efforts may produce the worst and our worst serve as the catalyst for the best; acknowledging that what we do not know is always far greater than what we do perceive and comprehend.

Suffering: being present to agony and pain, even when we cannot understand or grasp its genesis and scope; refusing to evade, dismiss, or deny the depth and cost of tragedy and loss.

And finally, **joy in the continued challenges of life:** the satisfaction of belonging to generations who care deeply about suffering and yet relish the wonders of friendship, connection, and beauty; the freedom of an open heart and a lively imagination; the sustenance of knowing that, whether we win or lose, we have seen and cherished the wondrous gift of life.

In framing a new international order, we build on the work of others, sustaining habits of heart and will that lead to creativity and self-critique. In so doing, we create the matrix of possibility for other peoples to live in balance, with justice, knowing that their way will be as much of a challenge for them as ours is for us. For every age is the pivotal age, every age is the fulcrum; the time is now, for *us*, if not for all time.

acknowledgments

I would like to thank the Office of Minority Affairs and Faculty Development at the University of Missouri–Columbia for funding the development leave that allowed time for research and reflection. I also thank my colleagues in the Department of Religious Studies for their consistent support and inspiration.

I am grateful to Jonathan Dean for his helpful criticisms of chapter seven. I am also appreciative of the critical insights and suggestions made by Carol Lee Sanchez, Elaine Lawless, Saul Mendlovitz, and Anna Peterson, who read the entire manuscript with care and rigor. Michael West and Karen Schenkenfelder provided the kind of superb copy-editing that authors dream of receiving! This work is clearer because of them. The faults that remain, of course, are all mine.

In writing this book I have been challenged and sustained by many sources—my parents and their continued impact on their families and community since their deaths in 1997, friends near (Karen Touzeau, Carol Lee Sanchez, and Elaine Lawless) and far (Amy Shapiro, Karen Baker-Fletcher, Garth Kasimu Baker-Fletcher, Mary McClintock Fulkerson, and

Betty Deberg), and my ebullient, creative family, Jon, Zoë, and Hannah. My understanding of jazz, ethics, and democracy has been transformed by the musicians with whom I have led workshops, Bobby Watson, Ray Drummond, and James Williams. James Williams passed away July 20, 2004, and we honor his legacy of celebrating the generations of jazz musicians and the artistry they have inspired and sustained. I am grateful to Bobby, Ray, and James for their generosity and insight, and appreciative of the work of my husband, Jon Poses, who has made all of this happen. I am also grateful to Jon for the love, support, and entertainment that continuously enriches my life and work.

notes

preface: pax americana, pax humana

1. Many people are critical of the use of the term *America* to refer to the United States. The term is, of course, incorrect, taking as it does the name of an entire continent for the name of one nation within that continent. In *Terrible Honesty*, Ann Douglas writes of the period in the 1920s when the term was widely adopted by people in the United States: "The nation was usually referred to not as the 'United States,' but as 'America' ... Americans in the 1920s liked the term ... precisely for its imperial suggestions of an intoxicating and irresistible identity windswept into coherence by the momentum of destiny." Douglass, *Terrible Honesty: Mongrel Manhattan in the 1920s* (New York: Farrar, Straus, and Giroux, 1995), 3. Given that such an imperial identity is now the subject of debate, it seems fitting to continue using the term.

2. Robert Kagan, *Of Paradise and Power: America and Europe in the New World Order* (New York: Knopf, 2003); Jean Bethke Elshtain, *Just War against Terror: The Burden of American Power in a Violent World* (New York: Basic Books, 2003), 6–7, 169–70; Niall Ferguson, *Empire: The Rise and Demise of the British World Order and the Lessons for Global Power* (New York: Basic Books, 2003), 367–70; Jonathan Schell, *The*

Unconquerable World: Power, Nonviolence and the Will of the People (New York: Henry Holt, 2003), 265; Zbigniew Brzezinski, *The Choice: Global Domination or Global Leadership* (New York: Basic Books, 2004), vii, 4, 18, 135–38, 217–18; William F. Schulz, *Tainted Legacy: 9/11 and the Ruin of Human Rights* (New York: Nation Books, 2003), 211, 152.

3.President of the United States of America, *The National Security Strategy of the United States of America* (September 2002); Joseph Nye Jr., "U.S. Power and Strategy after Iraq," *Foreign Affairs* 82:4 (2003): 65–69.

4. Schulz, *Tainted Legacy*, 61; Ferguson, *Empire*, xii, 367–70.

5. *The National Security Strategy of the United States of America* reflects these goals. In its preface, President Bush states, "The United States enjoys a position of unparalleled military strength and great economic and political influence." The document defends "a distinctly American internationalism" in which the United States will retain military supremacy and will use its influence to spread "freedom, democracy and free enterprise" (preamble, letter by President Bush, and 30).

6. Kagan, *Of Paradise and Power*, 13, 28–29, 37, 55–57, 73–74, 86–87.

7. *National Security Strategy*, 11, 14.

8. Schulz, *Tainted Legacy*, 60–64, 212.

9. Noam Chomsky, *Hegemony or Survival: America's Quest for Global Dominance* (New York: Henry Holt, 2003).

10. Kagan, *Of Paradise and Power*, 95, 88.

11. Tyler, "New Overseer Arrives in Baghdad in Sudden Revision of Top Positions by Washington," *New York Times*, May 13, 2003.

12. Michel Foucault, "Michel Foucault and Zen: A Stay in a Zen Temple," in *Religion and Culture*, ed. Jeremy R. Carrette (New York: Routledge, 1999).

13. See David Chidester, *Savage Systems: Colonialism and Comparative Religion in Southern Africa* (Charlottesville: University Press of Virginia, 1996); and Charles H. Long, *Significations: Signs, Symbols and Images in the Interpretation of Religion* (Philadelphia: Fortress Press, 1986).

14. In addition to the work of Long and Chidester, see Thomas Dean, ed., *Religious Pluralism and Truth: Essays on Cross-Cultural Philosophy of Religion* (Albany: State University of New York Press, 1995).

15. Karen McCarthy Brown, *Mama Lola: A Vodou Priestess in Brooklyn* (Berkeley: University of California Press, 1991).

16. Ania Loomba provides a thorough discussion of the complexities of postcolonial studies, analyzing the difficulties with the term *postcolonial* itself. Not only may it imply that domination has ceased, but we run the danger of missing the different forms of colonialism and of resistance to colonialism; we also run the danger of missing the different ways aspects of "precolonial" culture continued to exist even during colonization. She argues, however, that "the word 'postcolonial' is useful in indicating a general process with some shared features across the globe. But if it is uprooted from specific locations, 'postcoloniality' cannot be meaningfully investigated, and instead, the term begins to obscure the very relations of domination that it seeks to uncover." Loomba agrees with Jorge de Alva, who defines postcolonialism "not just as coming literally after colonialism and signifying its demise, but more flexibly as the contestation of colonial domination and the legacies of colonialism. Such a position would allow us to include people geographically displaced by colonialism such as African-Americans or people of Asian or Caribbean origin in Britain as 'postcolonial subjects' although they live within metropolitan cultures. It also allows us to incorporate the history of anti-colonial resistance with contemporary resistances to imperialism and to dominant Western culture." Loomba, *Colonialism/Postcolonialism* (London: Routledge, 1998), 12, 19.

See also the works of Frantz Fanon, *Black Skin, White Masks*, reissue ed. (New York: Grove, 1991), and *The Wretched of the Earth* (New York: Grove, 1963); Chinua Achebe, "An Image of Africa: Racism in Conrad's *Heart of Darkness*," amended version of the second Chancellor's Lecture at the University of Massachusetts, Amherst, February 1975, in *The Norton Anthology of Theory and Criticism*, ed. Vincent B. Leitch, 1783–94 (New York: Norton, 2001); Homi K. Bhabha, *The Location of Culture* (London: Routledge, 1994); Edward W. Said, *Orientalism* (New York: Pantheon, 1978); Gayatri Chakravorty Spivak, *A Critique of Postcolonial Reason: Toward a History of the Vanishing Present* (Cambridge, MA: Harvard University Press, 1999).

17. See Long, *Significations*; Brown, *Mama Lola*; Chidester, *Savage Systems*; Vine Deloria Jr., *Spirit and Reason: The Vine Deloria, Jr. Reader* (Golden, CO: Fulcrum, 1999); and Vine Deloria Jr., *God Is Red: A Native View of Religion* (Golden, CO: Fulcrum, 1992).

18. James Wilson, *The Earth Shall Weep: A History of Native America* (New York: Grove, 1998).

19. Ferguson, *Empire*, 358–70.

20. Paul Tillich, *Systematic Theology, Three Volumes in One*, vol. 3, *Life and the Spirit: History and the Kingdom of God* (Chicago: University of Chicago Press, 1967), 339–42.

chapter 1: memory

1. Karen Baker-Fletcher and Garth Kasimu Baker-Fletcher add the category "generations" to core concepts of constructive theological and ethical reflection in their systematic theology. See Baker-Fletcher and Baker-Fletcher, *My Sister/My Brother: Womanist and Xodus God-Talk* (Maryknoll, NY: Orbis, 1997).

2. Carol Lee Sanchez, "Animal, Vegetable, Mineral: The Sacred Connection," in *Ecofeminism and the Sacred*, ed. Carol J. Adams (New York: Continuum, 1993).

3. I am no longer a Christian, but a religious humanist. This particular form of humanism, while critical of much within the Jewish and Christian traditions, cannot be understood apart from those same traditions: it emerges from the Jewish and Christian traditions of commitment to justice and the worth of every human being. For a further discussion of the development of religious humanism, see William F. Schulz, *Making the Manifesto: The Birth of Religious Humanism* (Boston: Skinner House, 2002); and Anthony Pinn, *By These Hands: A Documentary History of African American Humanism* (New York: New York University Press, 2001).

4. Mark S. Heim, *Salvations: Truth and Difference in Religion* (Maryknoll, NY: Orbis, 1995), 175.

5. Jim Harrison, *The Road Home* (New York: Washington Square Press, 1998), 383.

6. Katie Cannon, *Black Womanist Ethics* (Atlanta: Scholars Press,

1988), and *Katie's Canon: Womanism and the Soul of the Black Community* (New York: Continuum, 1995). I respond to Cannon's work and analyze the ethical resources in selected novels by African American women in *A Feminist Ethic of Risk* (Minneapolis: Fortress Press, 1990; rev. ed., 2000).

7. Ralph Ellison, cited in Gerald Early, *Tuxedo Junction: Essays on American Culture* (New York: Echo, 1992), 289. I address these concerns in more detail in *Feminist Ethic of Risk* and in *Sweet Dreams in America: Making Ethics and Spirituality Work* (New York: Routledge, 1999).

8. I saw in them joy, resilience, and belonging to and honoring this wonderful gift of life. As I attempt to understand and express this legacy of joyous service, I find deep resonance with the moral wisdom of working in spite of deep obstacles, as this wisdom is found in the writings of African American women, eloquently described by Katie Cannon; and of African American peoples as described by Emilie Townes and Karen and Garth Kasimu Baker-Fletcher and in the novels of Patrick Chamoiseau, Toni Cade Bambara, Toni Morrison, and Mildred Taylor. See Patrick Chamoiseau, *Texaco* (New York: Pantheon, 1997); Emilie M. Townes, *Breaking the Fine Rain of Death: African American Health Issues and a Womanist Ethic of Care* (New York: Continuum, 1998); Emilie M. Townes, *In a Blaze of Glory: Womanist Spirituality as Social Witness* (Nashville, TN: Abingdon, 1995); Karen Baker-Fletcher and Garth Kasimu Baker-Fletcher, *My Sister, My Brother*; Karen Baker-Fletcher, *Sisters of Dust, Sisters of Spirit: Womanist Wordings on God and Creation* (Minneapolis: Fortress Press, 1998); Toni Cade Bambara, *The Salt-Eaters* (New York: Vintage, 1981); Toni Morrison, *Paradise* (New York: Knopf, 1998); Mildred Taylor, *Roll of Thunder, Hear My Cry* (New York: Bantam, 1984); Theophus Smith, *Conjuring Culture: Biblical Formations of Black America* (New York: Oxford University Press, 1994); Patricia Hill Collins, *Fighting Words: Black Women and the Search for Justice* (Minneapolis: University of Minnesota Press, 1998); Anthony B. Pinn, *Varieties of African American Religious Experience* (Minneapolis: Fortress Press, 1998); Anthony B. Pinn, *Terror and Triumph: The Nature of Black Religion* (Minneapolis: Fortress Press, 2003); and Patricia Williams, *The Alchemy of Race and*

Rights: Diary of a Law Professor (Cambridge, MA: Harvard University Press, 1991).

9. There was substantial opposition from scientists and military leaders to the decision to use atomic weapons against Japan. In the *Franck Report* (June 11, 1945) a panel of seven scientists from the University of Chicago, including Leo Szilard, argued against the use of the weapons in war and argued for a test demonstration "before the eyes of representatives of all United Nations, on the desert or a barren island." *The Franck Report,* June 11, 1945, U.S. National Archives, Washington, D.C., Record Group 77, Manhattan Engineer District Records, Harrison-Bundy File, folder #76. Available as e-text, copyright 1995–98 by Gene Dannen: http://www.dannen.com/decision/franck.html. These recommendation were rejected by a scientific panel including J. R. Oppenheimer, E. Fermi, A. H. Compton, and E. O. Lawrence, who claimed that there was "no acceptable alternative to direct military use."

Recommendations on the Immediate Use of Nuclear Weapons, by the Scientific Panel of the Interim Committee on Nuclear Power, June 16, 1945, U.S. National Archives, Record Group 77, Records of the Office of the Chief of Engineers, Manhattan Engineer District, Harrison-Bundy File, folder #76. Available as e-text, copyright 1995–98 by Gene Dannen: http://www.dannen.com/decision/. The Manhattan Committee, under the leadership of Secretary of War Henry Stimson, recommended on June 1 that "we could not give the Japanese any warning, that we could not concentrate on a civilian area; but that we should seek to make a profound psychological impression on as many of the inhabitants as possible. At the suggestion of Dr. Conant the Secretary agreed that the most desirable target would be a vital war plant employing a large number of workers and closely surrounded by workers houses." Notes of the Interim Committee Meeting, May 31, 1945, available at http://www.nuclearfiles.org. Also available in Martin J. Sherwin, *A World Destroyed* (New York: Vintage, 1977), app. L, 302. In a 1960 article in *U.S. News and World Report,* Leo Szilard recounts the fear that led Stimson to choose to bomb people rather than an unoccupied site: "I certainly have to take exception to the article Stimson wrote after Hiroshima in Harper's Magazine. He wrote that a 'demonstration' of the A-bomb was impossible because we had only two bombs. Had we staged a 'demonstration' both bombs might have been duds and then we would have lost face." *U.S. News and World Report*, August 15, 1960, online at http://www.dannen.com/decision/.

10. David Gushee, *Righteous Gentiles of the Holocaust: A Christian Interpretation* (Minneapolis: Fortress Press, 1994).

11. The terms *American Indian* and *Native American* are problematic and contested. Jace Weaver argues that they reflect the denials and erasures of American history, denying the diversity and complexity of the nations that existed for tens of thousands of years before the European invasion, and denying the ongoing struggles to maintain national identity and integrity. The term *Native American*, used primarily by well-meaning whites, is quite likely only a temporary solution. Most native peoples prefer referring to a particular nation, and in much of Canada, the preferred terminology is *First Nations*. When a collective term is required, many scholars use the terms *American Indian, Indian*, and *Native American* interchangeably. Weaver, *Other Words: American Indian Literature, Law, and Culture* (Norman: University of Oklahoma Press, 2001), xii; and Weaver, ed., *Native American Religious Identity: Unforgotten Gods* (Maryknoll, NY: Orbis, 1998), xiii.

Gerald Vizenor describes the inaccuracy of *Indian* ("Manifestly, the *indian* is an occidental misnomer, an overseas enactment that has no referent to real native cultures of communities") and coins another term, *postindian*, to refer to contemporary Native peoples, the "new storiers of convergence and survivance." Vizenor, *Manifest Manners: Narratives on Postindian Survivance* (Lincoln: University of Nebraska Press, 1999), vii–viii.

The solution proposed by Lee Francis is one I find compelling but did not follow because it would be confusing in this discussion of the interaction of different cultures and nations. Francis writes, "The word *People* is used whenever I refer to the people of the sovereign nations, tribes, bands, villages, pueblos, rancherias, and communities. *People* with a capital *P* is how we refer to ourselves in our respective languages. For example, in my Keresan language, we call ourselves *Hano* which, loosely translated, means 'the People.'" Francis, *Native Time: A Historical Time Line of Native America* (New York: St. Martin's, 1996), 330.

12. Castro County Historical Commission, *Castro County 1891–1981* (Dallas: Taylor Publication, 1981), 11.

13. Carol Lee Sanchez, personal conversation, March 2002. See also James Wilson, *The Earth Shall Weep: A History of Native America* (New York: Grove, 1998), chap. 9.

14. Philip Arnold, "Black Elk and Book Culture," *Journal of the American Academy of Religion* 67:1 (March 1999).

15. Michel Foucault, *Power / Knowledge: Selected Interviews and Other Writings, 1972–1977* (New York: Pantheon, 1980), 135–37.

16. For a discussion of the divisions within feminism, see Angela Y. Davis, *Women, Race and Class* (New York: Vintage, 1983); Gloria Anzaldua, ed., *Making Face / Making Soul* (San Francisco: Spinsters Press, 1990); Jane Flax, "The End of Innocence," in *Feminists Theorize the Political*, ed. Judith Butler and Joan W. Scott (New York: Routledge, 1992); Janet Jakobsen, *Working Alliances and the Politics of Difference: Diversity in Feminist Ethics* (Bloomington: Indiana University Press, 1999); and bell hooks, *Feminist Theory: From Margin to Center* (Boston: South End, 1984).

chapter 2: laughter

1. Elenore Smith Bowen, *Return to Laughter: An Anthropological Novel* (New York: Anchor Books, 1964).

2. For a comprehensive collection of the writings of people who have lived lives of faith-based activism for social justice, see Roger Gottlieb, ed., *Liberating Faith: Religious Voices for Justice, Peace and Ecological Wisdom* (New York: Rowman and Littlefield, 2003).

3. For a thorough analysis of the relationship between religion and violence, see Marc Gopin, *Between Eden and Armageddon: The Future of World Religions, Violence, and Peacemaking* (Oxford: Oxford University Press, 2000); Oliver McTernan, *Violence in God's Name: Religion in an Age of Conflict* (Maryknoll, NY: Orbis, 2003); John L. Esposito, *Unholy War: Terror in the Name of Islam* (Oxford: Oxford University Press, 2002); Mark Wallace and Theophus H. Smith, eds., *Curing Violence* (Sonoma, Calif.:

Polebridge, 1994); Cheryl A. Kirk-Duggan, *Refiner's Fire: A Religious Engagement with Violence* (Minneapolis: Fortress Press, 2000).

4. Brian Victoria, *Zen at War* (New York: Weatherhill, 1997), 87.

5. Ibid.

6. Ibid., 27.

7. For an analysis of the process of "moral disengagement" that justifies violence in the name of a greater good, see the work of Alfred L. McAlister, "Moral Disengagement: Measurement and Modification," *Journal of Peace Research* 38:1 (2001): 87–89; and Anthony Bandura, "Mechanisms of Moral Disengagement," in W. Reich, ed., *Origins of Terrorism: Psychologies, Ideologies, Theologies, States of Mind* (Cambridge: Cambridge University Press, 1990), 161–91. Oliver McTernan also provides a sobering account of the use of religion to justify violence, and gives contemporary examples from Judaism, Catholicism, Buddhism, Protestantism, Islam, and Hinduism. McTernan, *Violence in God's Name*, 28–36.

8. Jonathan Schell, *The Unconquerable World: Power, Nonviolence and the Will of the People* (New York: Henry Holt, 2003), 224.

9. Jean-Luc Marion, *God without Being* (Chicago: Univ. of Chicago Press, 1991).

10. Grace Jantzen, *Becoming Divine: Towards a Feminist Philosophy of Religion* (Bloomington: Indiana University Press, 1999), 86.

11. Thee Smith, "W/Riting Black Theology," *Forum* 5:4 (December 1980): 50–51.

12. For a representative critique of the claims of metaphysical theology and the methods of ontotheology, see Jantzen, *Becoming Divine*; Philippa Berry and Andrew Wernick, *Shadow of Spirit: Postmodernism and Religion* (New York: Routledge, 1992); and Paul Lakeland, *Postmodernity: Christian Identity in a Fragmented Age* (Minneapolis: Fortress Press, 1997).

13. Jantzen, *Becoming Divine*, 97.

14. Luce Irigaray writes:

Religion marks the place of the absolute *for us*, its path, the hope of its fulfillment. All too often that fulfillment has been postponed or

> transferred to some transcendental time and place. It has not been interpreted as the infinite that resides within us and among us, the god in us, the Other for us, becoming with and in us . . . This God, are we capable of imagining it as a woman? Can we dimly see it as the perfection of our subjectivity?

Irigaray, *Sexes and Genealogies*, trans. Gillian C. Gill (New York: Columbia University Press, 1993), 63.

15. Sharon D. Welch, *A Feminist Ethic of Risk* (Minneapolis: Fortress Press, 1990).

16. Karl Barth, "The Question of Natural Theology," in *Church Dogmatics: A Selection*, selected by Helmut Gollwitzer, trans. and ed. G. W. Bromiley, 49–86 (New York: Harper, 1962). See also Jacques Derrida's contrast between legitimate and illegitimate forms of messianic expectation:

> Now, if there is a spirit of Marxism which I will never be ready to renounce, it is not only the critical idea or the questioning stance (a consistent deconstruction must insist on them even as it also learns that this is not the last or first word). It is even more a certain emancipatory and *messianic* affirmation, a certain experience of the promise that one can try to liberate from any dogmatics and even from any metaphysico-religious determination, from any *messianism*. And a promise must promise to be kept, that is, not to remain "spiritual" or "abstract," but to produce events, new effective forms of action, practice, organization, and so forth.

Derrida, *Specters of Marx: The State of the Debt, the Work of Mourning, and the New International,* trans. Peggy Kamuf (New York: Routledge, 1994), 89. See also John D. Caputo's thorough discussion of the critique of concrete messianism, religious violence, and coercion in *The Prayers and Tears of Jacques Derrida: Religion without Religion* (Bloomington: Indiana Univ. Press, 1997), introduction, chap. 3, and conclusion.

17. Jacques Derrida, *The Gift of Death*, trans. David Willis (Chicago: Univ. of Chicago Press, 1996); Emmanuel Lévinas, *Basic Philosophical*

Writings, ed. Adriaan T. Peperzak, Simon Critchley, and Robert Bernasconi (Bloomington: Indiana Univ. Press, 1996), 29. See also Caputo's exploration of the theological and philosophical significance of Derrida's thought, *The Prayers and Tears of Jacques Derrida*.

18. Richard Rorty, *Consequences of Pragmatism (Essays: 1972–1980)* (Minneapolis: Univ. of Minnesota Press, 1982), 208. See also Friedrich Nietzsche, *Twilight of the Idols: Or How One Philosophizes with a Hammer,* trans. Richard Polt (Indianapolis: Hackett, 1997), and his "revaluation of all values" and critique of "the four great errors": confusing cause and effect, false causality, imaginary causes, and free will.

19. Toni Morrison, *Paradise* (New York: Knopf, 1998), 306.

20. Karen Baker-Fletcher and Garth Kasimu Baker-Fletcher, *My Sister, My Brother: Womanist and Xodus God-Talk* (Maryknoll, NY: Orbis, 1997), 180; see also Birch and Cobb's discussion of trusting "life as the creative good" in Charles Birch and John B. Cobb Jr., *The Liberation of Life: From the Cell to the Community* (Cambridge: Cambridge University Press, 1981), 180.

21. Rosabeth Moss Kanter extols the creativity of global capitalism and argues that it is fed by the skills and worldviews of "cosmopolitans":

> Cosmopolitans are rich in three intangible assets . . . that translate into preeminence and power in a global economy: concepts—the best and latest knowledge and ideas; competence—the ability to operate at the highest standards of any place anywhere; and connections— the best relationships, which provide access to the resources of other people and organizations around the world.

Kanter, *World Class: Thriving Locally in the Global Economy* (New York: Simon and Schuster, 1995), 23.

22. Approximately 146 scientists from the Chicago Metallurgical Laboratory, the Manhattan Project at Oak Ridge,Tennessee, and from the Manhattan Project at Los Alamos, New Mexico, did recognize the danger posed by atomic weapons. These scientists had worked to develop atomic weapons in response to the threat that Germany was developing such

weapons. After the defeat of Germany, they argued that production should cease, and that the weapons should not be used against Japan. In the first petition, circulated by Leo Szilard in July 1945, Szilard argued that atomic weapons were "ruthless weapons for the annihilation of cities." Drawing analogies to the moral choices faced by Nazi scientists, he urged other scientists to join him in condemning the use of such weapons. His work inspired other similar petitions at Oak Ridge. Sixty-seven scientists signed the Oak Ridge petition and asked that President Truman conduct a test demonstration of the weapons before an international audience but that he not use them against Japan:

> The last few years show a marked tendency toward increasing ruthlessness. At present our Air Forces, striking at the Japanese cities, are using the same methods of warfare which were condemned by American public opinion only a few years ago when applied by the Germans to the cities of England. Our use of atomic bombs in this war would carry the world a long way further on this path of ruthlessness. Atomic power will provide the nations with new means of destruction. The atomic bombs at our disposal represent only the first step in this direction and there is almost no limit to the destructive power which will become available in the course of this development. Thus a nation which sets the precedent of using these newly liberated forces of nature for purposes of destruction may have to bear the responsibility of opening the door to an era of devastation on an unimaginable scale.In view of the foregoing, we, the undersigned, respectfully petition that you exercise your power as Commander-in-Chief to rule that the United States shall not, in the present phase of the war, resort to the use of atomic bombs.

Oak Ridge petition, mid-July 1945, U.S. National Archives, Record Group 77, Records of the Chief of Engineers, Manhattan Engineer District, Harrison-Bundy File, folder #76. See also the Szilard Petition, First Version, July 3, 1945Source: U.S. National Archives, Record Group 77, Records of the Chief of Engineers, Manhattan Engineer District,

Harrison-Bundy File, folder #76; and the Oak Ridge petition, July 13, 1945, U.S. National Archives, Record Group 77, Records of the Chief of Engineers, Manhattan Engineer District, Harrison-Bundy File, folder #76. Available as e-text, copyright 1995–98 by Gene Dannen: http://www.dannen.com/decision/franck.html.

23. Theophus Smith, *Conjuring Culture: Biblical Formations of Black America* (Oxford: Oxford University Press, 1994), 3–12, 18. Smith's understanding of "conjure" is different in emphasis from that of Derrida in *Specters of Marx*. Derrida also refers to "conjuration" as "the appeal that causes to come forth . . . what *is not there* at the present moment of the appeal." Yet his focus is on conjure as exorcism, the "destruction" and "disavowal" of a "malignant, demonized, diabolized force." Smith's "conjure" is performative and creative: the evocation of freedom, of particular forms of life, and not primarily "certifying death." Derrida, *Specters of Marx*, 41, 48.

24. Smith, *Conjuring Culture*, 31, 43; Jacques Derrida, "Plato's Pharmacy," in *Dissemination*, trans. Barbara Johnson (Chicago: University of Chicago Press, 1981).

25. Anthony B. Pinn, *Varieties of African American Religious Experience* (Minneapolis: Fortress Press, 1998), 101–2.

26. Ibid., 72. For a thorough exploration of the moral sense of Haitian Vodou, see also Karen McCarthy Brown, "Alourdes: A Case Study of Moral Leadership in Haitian Vodou," in *Saints and Virtues*, ed. John Hawley (Berkeley: University of California Press, 1987); and Karen McCarthy Brown, *Mama Lola: A Vodou Priestess in Brooklyn* (Berkeley: University of California Press, 1991).

27. Pinn, *Varieties of African American Religious Experience*, 102. See also Charles H. Long's discussion of the role of interpretive communities in *Significations: Signs, Symbols, and Images in the Interpretation of Religion* (Philadelphia: Fortress Press, 1986).

28. Toni Morrison, *Sula* (New York: Bantam, 1973), 90.

29. Patrick Chamoiseau, *Texaco*, trans. Rose-Myriam Rejouis and Val Vinokurov (New York: Pantheon, 1997), 119, 263–64.

30. Ibid., 341.

31. Ibid., 310.

32. Jantzen argues that "it would be more accurate to see atheism/theism not as itself the relevantly significant binary, but as one *pole* of a binary, the repressed other being everything else which is unacknowledged in the centrality of this pair." Jantzen claims that "the repressed other" is the "opening of desire that interrupts this emphasis on belief." Following Irigaray, she looks for a "new morning of the world," "developing a feminist philosophy of religion whose founding gesture is not the justification of beliefs which separates the 'true' from the 'false', but rather an imaginative longing for the divine in a reduplication of desire not content with the old gods but seeking the horizon and the foundation needed to progress between past and future" (Irigaray). Jantzen, *Becoming Divine*, 65, 99.

33. This is an atheistic version of the theistic symbolic of "spirit and dust" developed by Karen Baker-Fletcher in *Sisters of Dust, Sisters of Spirit: Womanist Wordings on God and Creation* (Minneapolis: Fortress Press, 1998). The "atheism" highlights our acceptance of finitude and imperfection. I agree with Jantzen's symbolic of natality, but think the force of our full affirmation of finitude is clearer if we relinquish Irigaray's symbolic of perfection and Jantzen's symbolic of becoming divine. It is important to note however that, for Jantzen, "becoming divine" does not mean that finitude is devalued: "A symbolic of natality is not in any sense a denial of death or a pretense that death does not matter." "The acceptance of life is an acceptance of limits, which, after all, enable as much as they constrain: the boundless is beyond capacity. The obligation to become divine is not an obligation to become limitless; the quest for infinity would be a renunciation, not a fulfillment, of our gendered, embodied selves." "Rather than squander our energy in a futile struggle against finitude, we can rejoice in the (limited) life we have as natals and act for love of the world." Jantzen, *Becoming Divine*, 152, 154, 155.

34. In our affirmation of the present and the everyday, we address the critique voiced by Jonathan Rieder: "For some time now, the cultural left has been going around in a funk, deconstructing everything in sight, wavering between scolding a culture that seems hostile to liberation and conducting a promiscuous search for signs of resistance to that culture's dominating symbols. But in all this rage for representation, the left has often committed soul murder too, projecting disappointment onto the

objects of its gaze, representing itself rather than the complex reality of a vibrantly imperfect culture." Rieder, *New York Times Book Review,* December 26, 1998, 15.

35. Cynthia Willett, for example, contrasts a patriarchal (and elitist) symbolic of self and desire with resources for self, community, freedom, and desire seen in African American experience and in the mother-child interaction. She describes the sensually mediated logic of intersubjectivity found in the writing of Frederick Douglass, who evoked the power of the touch of his mother and grandmother to create a self correlated with community and openness. She also turns to Daniel Stern and the analysis of the activity of the infant in relationship to the mother to show the limits of views that see this experience as inchoate and passive, as either one-sided or amorphous and prior to meaning, meaning occurring only through the phallic intervention of language. Willett, *Maternal Ethics and Other Slave Moralities* (New York: Routledge, 1995), 8, 170, 24, 43, 47.

36. Irigaray claims that "the (male) ideal other has been imposed upon women by men. Man is supposedly woman's more perfect other, her model, her essence. The most human and the most divine goal woman can conceive is to become *man.* If she is to become woman, if she is to accomplish her female subjectivity, woman needs a god who is a figure for the perfection of *her* subjectivity. Irigary, *Sexes and Genealogies,* 64. In sharp contrast to Irigaray, Mary McClintock Fulkerson uses poststructuralist tools to describe the unconventionally transformative modes of women's subjectivity, agency, and use of language in three particular groups of women (Pentacostal women, Presbyterian lay women, feminist theologians). Fulkerson, *Changing the Subject :Women's Discourses and Feminist Theology* (Minneapolis: Fortress Press, 1994).

Iris Marion Young describes five faces of oppression and their constraints on agency and subjectivity in *Justice and the Politics of Difference* (Princeton: Princeton University Press, 1990).

37. Central to the work of womanist theologians and ethicists is the recognition that these limits have not completely shaped the agency and subjectivity of people of color. D. Soyini Madison, for example, begins her collection of writings by women of color by explaining the significance of

this saying: "I remember my mother standing, in 'colored woman' style, her arms akimbo and her head tilted to the side, speaking quietly but forcefully in a tone that could scare a bull. She would willfully declare: 'Being the woman that I am I will make a way out of no way.' These were *mother's* words, but they are also the words and the will of *all* women of color who assert who they are, who create sound out of silence, and who build worlds out of remnants. . . . *The Woman That I Am* is a proclamation of the 'I' in each individual woman's identity, but it is also a testament to the collective power of women of color." Madison, *The Woman That I Am: The Literature and Culture of Contemporary Women of Color* (New York: St. Martin's, 1994), 1.

As an example of womanist theology and ethics, see also the works of Karen Baker-Fletcher; Emilie M. Townes, *In A Blaze of Glory: Womanist Spirituality As Social Witness* (Nashville: Abingdon, 1995); Emilie M. Townes, ed., *Embracing the Spirit: Womanist Perspectives on Hope, Salvation and Transformation* (Maryknoll, N.Y.: Orbis, 1997); Katie G. Cannon, *Black Womanist Ethics* (Atlanta: Scholars, 1988); Delores Williams, *Sisters in the Wilderness: The Challenge of Womanist God-Talk* (Maryknoll, N.Y.: Orbis, 1993).

38. Patricia J. Williams, *The Alchemy of Race and Rights: Diary of a Law Professor* (Cambridge, MA: Harvard Univ. Press, 1991), 163.

39. For an alternative examination of the significance of the diversity of religious experience, see Laurel C. Schneider, *Re-imaging the Divine: Confronting the Backlash against Feminist Theology* (Cleveland, Ohio: Pilgrim, 1998). Schneider argues for a monistic polytheism that "lends authority and legitimacy to revelatory religious experience in all of its diversity" (p. 175). Where I differ, fundamentally, from Schneider's thought-provoking proposal is her use of metaphors of divine certainty, finality, power, and goodness.

40. Chamoiseau, *Texaco*, 33.

41. Eric Lott uses this metaphor to describe the artistic power of the jazz musician Charlie Parker: "Jazz was a struggle which pitted mind against the perversity of circumstance, and . . . in this struggle blinding virtuosity was the best weapon." Lott, "Double V, Double-Time: Bebop's

Politics of Style," in *Jazz among the Discourses*, ed. Krin Gabbard (Durham, NC: Duke Univ. Press, 1995), 243.

42. William James, *The Varieties of Religious Experience* (Cambridge, MA: Harvard University Press, 1985). James's critique of "healthy-mindedness" is found in lectures 4 and 5. These lectures were delivered as the Gifford Lectures on Natural Religion at Edinburgh University in 1901 and 1902.

43. Chamoiseau, *Texaco*, 34.

44. Rita Nakashima Brock and Susan Brooks Thistlethwaite, *Casting Stones: Prostitution and Liberation in Asia and the United States* (Minneapolis: Fortress Press, 1996), 279.

45. Chamoiseau, *Texaco*, 34.

46. Leslie Marmon Silko, "Landscape, History and the Pueblo Imagination," in Madison, *The Woman That I Am*, 499, 502.

47. Morrison, *Paradise*, 318.

48. Chamoiseau, *Texaco*, 294.

49. Ibid., 340.

50. Brock and Thistlethwaite, *Casting Stones*, 279.

51. Baker-Fletcher and Baker-Fletcher, *My Sister, My Brother*, 203–4.

52. Ibid., 178, 184.

53. Silko, "Landscape, History and the Pueblo Imagination," 506.

54. Pinn, *Varieties of African American Religious Experience*, 99–103.

55. Williams, *The Alchemy of Race and Rights*, 165.

56. Sanchez states, "The most fundamental meaning of the word *Sacred* for Native Americans is 'entitled to reverence and respect' . . . American Indians believe the universe and everything in it is 'entitled to reverence and respect.'" Carol Lee Sanchez, "Animal, Vegetable, and Mineral," in *Ecofeminism and the Sacred*, ed. Carol J. Adams, 207–28 (New York: Continuum, 1994), 224.

57. Martin Buber, *I and Thou* (New York: Charles Scribner's Sons, 1970).

58. See Jantzen's thorough critique of Lévinas's reification of the "vulnerable" face:

What sort of symbolic does it bespeak and reinforce if the most insistent thing that comes to mind in being face to face with the Other is the desire to kill? Even granting that this is what Lévinas sees as the violent logic of western ontology, in which mastery is the founding gesture and killing is its logical conclusion, to speak of this in terms of individual desire and temptation is shocking . . . Why the impulse to kill? Why not, say, an impulse to smile, or feed, or kiss, or converse? Why the assumed hostility, what Lévinas later writes of as "the face of the neighbor in its persecuting hatred"? . . . . Could he say what he does if the face which confronts him is the face of an infant? a mother? one natal greeting another?

Jantzen, *Becoming Divine*, 239; see also 237–53.

59. For feminist and womanist explorations of mutuality and reciprocity, see, for example, Rosemary Radford Ruether, *Women and Redemption: A Theological History* (Minneapolis, Fortress Press, 1998); Rosemary Radford Ruether, *Gaia and God: An Ecofeminist Theology of Earth Healing* (San Francisco: Harper San Francisco, 1992); Carter Heyward, *Touching Our Strength: The Erotic as Power and the Love of God* (San Francisco: Harper and Row, 1989); Catherine Keller, *From a Broken Web: Separation, Sexism and Self* (Boston: Beacon, 1986); Chung Hyun Kyung, *Struggle to Be the Sun Again: Introducing Asian Women's Theology* (Maryknoll, N.Y.: Orbis, 1990); Ada Maria Isasi-Diaz, *Mujerista Theology* (Maryknoll, N.Y.: Orbis, 1997); Rebecca Chopp, *The Power to Speak: Feminism, Language, God* (New York: Crossroad, 1989); Mary Daly, *Gyn / Ecology: The Metaethics of Radical Feminism* (Boston: Beacon, 1985); Paula Cooey, *Religious Imagination and the Body: A Feminist Analysis* (New York: Oxford Univ. Press, 1994); Rita Nakashima Brock, *Journeys by Heart: A Christology of Erotic Power* (New York: Crossroad, 1991); and Sallie McFague, *The Body of God: An Ecological Theology* (Minneapolis: Fortress Press, 1993).

60. Chamoiseau, *Texaco*, 300.

61. I have been an activist in left and feminist politics all of my adult life. This is not the attitude that fueled our protests, our demands

for social justice, and our denunciations of oppressive institutions and individuals.

62. I have followed here the example set by Roger S. Gottlieb in "The Transcendence of Justice and the Justice of Transcendence: Mysticism, Deep Ecology and Political Life," *Journal of the American Academy of Religion* 67:1 (March 1999): 149–66. Gottlieb disavows any metaphysical grounding for his vision of mysticism, describes the mysticism of "deep ecology" clearly, and yet describes what he sees as four intrinsic dangers of this form of mysticism.

63. Pinn, *Varieties of African American Religious Experience*, 184.

64. Gottlieb writes:

> The vision of mysticism offered here will not satisfy everyone. It is a particularly non-metaphysical view in which ultimate reality is pretty much exhausted by "ordinary" reality. Of course, when illuminated by the sparks of mystical experience, "ordinary" reality can shine quite brightly—as in the old Zen story that identifies true enlightenment with simply seeing "a mountain as a mountain and a river as a river."

Gottlieb, "The Transcendence of Justice," 164.

65. Morrison, *Paradise*, 306. For another discussion of the importance of generational connections with a recognition of the oppressive potential and actuality of those connections, see Isasi-Diaz, *Mujerista Theology*, 137–44.

66. *Return to Laughter* is an anthropological novel written by Laura Bohannen under the pseudonym of Elenore Smith Bowen and first published in 1954. Bohannen, an American anthropologist, describes her attempts to "objectively" study tribal peoples in Nigeria. Bohannen tells of the breakdown of her conviction of cultural superiority, from her initial arrogant impatience with education into the names of different plants to her discovery of a communal social logic of rage, laughter, forgiveness, and intensity that proved more resilient in the face of social crisis than her own dualistic moral vocabulary of good and evil, friend and foe:

They knew how to live at close quarters with tragedy, how to live with their own failure and yet laugh. They knew the terror of a broken society, where brother's hand is raised against brother in hate and fear; they knew how to come back, brother to brother, and create life anew . . . These people . . . who all know they may themselves be faithless and crippled, and who all know that they build on shifting sand, have yet the courage to build what they know will fall . . . It is the laughter of people who value love and friendship and plenty, who have lived with terror and death and hate.

Elenore Smith Bowen, *Return to Laughter: An Anthropological Novel* (New York: Anchor, 1964), 297.

chapter 3: virtuosity

1. Carol Lee Sanchez, *Excerpts from a Mountain Climber's Notebook: Selected Poems 1971–1984* (San Francisco: Taurean Horn Press, 1985), 18. Used by permission.

2. Vine Deloria Jr., *Spirit and Reason: The Vine Deloria, Jr. Reader* (Golden, CO: Fulcrum, 1999), 204–5.

3. David L. Moore, "Return of the Buffalo: Cultural Representation as Cultural Property," in *Native American Representation: First Encounters, Distorted Images, and Literary Appropriations*, ed. Gretchen M. Bataille (Lincoln: University of Nebraska Press, 2001), 53.

4. James Wilson, *The Earth Shall Weep: A History of Native America* (New York: Grove, 1998), 121.

5. Carol Lee Sanchez, "Animal, Vegetable, Mineral: The Sacred Connection," in *Ecofeminism and the Sacred*, ed. Carol J. Adams (New York: Continuum, 1993), 209.

6. Wilson, *The Earth Shall Weep*, 105.

7. Ibid., 106

8. Ibid., 115–16.

9. Ibid., 121.

10. Ibid.

11. Ibid., 129.

12. Regis Pecos, foreword to Joe S. Sando, *Pueblo Nations: Eight Centuries of Pueblo Indian History* (Santa Fe, N.Mex.: Clear Light, 1992, 1998), xii, xiv.

13. Kathryn Shanley, "The Indians America Loves to Love and Read: American Indian Identity and Cultural Appropriation," in *Native American Representation: First Encounters, Distorted Images, and Literary Appropriations*, ed. Gretchen M. Bataille (Lincoln: University of Nebraska Press, 2001), 26–27.

14. Patrick Riley, *Will and Political Legitimacy: A Critical Exposition of Social Contract Theory in Hobbes, Locke, Rousseau, Kant, and Hegel* (Cambridge, MA: Harvard University Press, 1982), 1.

15. See William Schulz's discussion of political consensus as a basis for human rights, *Tainted Legacy: 9/11 and the Ruin of Human Rights* (New York: Nation Books, 2003), chap. 5.

16. Hobbes, *Leviathan*, chap. 13.

17. Martin Jay, "Lafayette's Children: The American Reception of French Liberalism" *SubStance* 31:1 (2002): 9–26, 3.

18. Ibid., 4–7.

19. Ibid., 8.

20. Patricia J. Williams, *The Alchemy of Race and Rights: The Diary of a Law Professor* (Cambridge, MA: Harvard University Press, 1991), 163.

21. An initial piece of such work is the groundbreaking writing of Ronald Takaki. In *A Different Mirror: A History of Multicultural America*, Takaki brings us the complex history of America seen through the narratives of Native Americans, African Americans, Mexicans, and Asian, Irish, and Jewish immigrants. Ronald Takaki, *A Different Mirror: A History of Multicultural America* (Boston: Little, Brown, 1993).

22. Jace Weaver, preface to *Native American Religions: Unforgotten Gods* (Maryknoll, N.Y.: Orbis, 1998), ix.

23. June M. Collins, "Kinship, Social Class, and Religion of Northwest Peoples," in *North American Indian Anthropology: Essays on Society and Culture*, ed., Raymond J. Demallie and Alfonso Ortiz (Norman: University of Oklahoma Press, 1994), 82–105.

24. Sattler describes the marked difference in gender roles found in the

early eighteenth and nineteenth centuries among the Muskogee (Creek) of Georgia, Alabama, and northern Florida and the Cherokee of western North and South Carolina, eastern Tennessee, and northeastern Georgia, and the differences that persisted among Oklahoma Cherokee during the 1970s and Seminole and Creek traditionalists in the 1980s. Among the Muskogee, female sexuality was tightly controlled and women "lacked direct, formal access to power." Among the Cherokee, women not only had greater sexual freedom before and after marriage but had official authority through the position of "Beloved Woman or War Woman." Richard A. Sattler, "Women's Status among the Muskogee and Cherokee," in *Women and Power in Native North America,* edited by Laura F. Klein and Lillian A. Ackerman, 214–30 (Norman: Oklahoma Univ. Press, 1995), 218, 222.

25. Archie Fire Lame Deer and Richard Erdoes, *Gift of Power: The Life and Teachings of a Lakota Medicine Man* (Santa Fe, N.Mex.: Bear Company, 1992), 226–27, 238.

26. Alfonzo Ortiz, "The Dynamics of Pueblo Survival," in *North American Indian Anthropology: Essays on Society and Culture,* ed. Raymond J. Demallie and Alfonso Ortiz (Norman: Univ. of Oklahoma Press, 1994), 299, 304.

27. Gerald Vizenor, *Manifest Manners: Narratives on Postindian Survivance* (Lincoln: Univ. of Nebraska Press, 1999), vii–viii.

28. Ibid., x.

29. Jace Weaver, *Other Words: American Indian Literature, Law, and Culture* (Norman: University of Oklahoma Press, 2001), 134.

30. In this work I primarily depend on the synthesis of diverse Native views found in the work of three Native American philosophers and activists: Jace Weaver, trained in law and religious studies; Vine Deloria Jr., philosopher and cultural critic; and Carol Lee Sanchez, poet, artist, and philosopher. I have also learned from the eloquent writing of poets and novelists Joy Harjo (Cree), Leslie Marmon Silko (Laguna Pueblo), James Welch (Blackfoot/Gros Ventre), Gerald Vizenor, Paula Gunn Allen (Laguna Pueblo), Luci Tapahonso (Navajo), and N. Scott Momaday (Kiowa). All of these contemporary authors offer find a richly intricate depiction of contemporary Native ethics, community, and epistemology, as

well as an incisive and compelling critique of Euro-American constructions of and domination of the "Native American Other."

31. Sherman Alexie, *Ten Little Indians: Stories* (New York: Grove,
2003), 11.

32. Weaver, *Other Words*, 321.

33. Moore, "Return of the Buffalo," 66.

34. Vine Deloria Jr. and Clifford Lytle, *The Nations Within: The Past
and Future of American Indian Sovereignty* (New York: Pantheon Books,
1984).

35. U.S. 2000 Census, U.S. Census Bureau, http://www.census.gov.

36. Leslie Marmon Silko, *Almanac of the Dead* (New York: Penguin,
1991), 712.

37. Moore, "Return of the Buffalo," 66–67.

38. Weaver, *Other Words*, 183–86, 219–26.

39. Christopher Columbus, *The Journal of Christopher Columbus*,
trans. Cecil Jane, revised and annotated by L.A. Vigneras with an appen-
dix by R. A. Skelton (London: Hakluyt Society, 1960), 24, 28.

40. V. Deloria, *Spirit and Reason*, 372.

41. Weaver, *Other Words*, 179.

42. Joe S. Sando, *Pueblo Nations: Eight Centuries of Pueblo Indian
History* (Santa Fe, NM: Clear Light, 1992), 2.

43. Weaver, *Other Words*, 185.

44. Ibid., 189.

45. President Ronald Reagan, cited by Wilson, *The Earth Shall Weep*,
419.

46. Wilson, *The Earth Shall Weep*, 46–49, 179–80, 253–60; Kendrick
Frazier, *People of Chaco: A Canyon and Its Culture* (New York: Norton,
1999), 218–19.

47. Weaver, *Other Words*, 42, 301.

48. Ibid., 42.

49. Ibid., 301.

50. Ibid., 302.

51. Ibid., 179–80.

52. V. Deloria, *Spirit and Reason*, 337.

53. Vine Deloria Jr., *God Is Red: A Native View of Religion* (Golden, CO: Fulcrum, 1992), 2. See also V. Deloria, *Spirit and Reason*, 337.

54. Weaver, *Other Words*, 303–4.

55. Carol Lee Sanchez, personal communication.

56. V. Deloria, *God Is Red*, 195–96.

57. Weaver, *Other Words*, 43.

58. Ibid., 54, 304.

59. Weaver, *Other Words*, 44 (citing Thomas King).

60. V. Deloria, *God Is Red*, 85, 88–89.

61. V. Deloria, *Spirit and Reason*, 50–52.

62. Sanchez, "Animal, Vegetable, Mineral," 217–18.

63. From *Sáanii Dahataal: The Women are Singing,* by Luci Tapahonso. ©1993 Luci Tapahonso. Reprinted by permission of the University of Arizona Press.

64. Weaver, *Other Words,* 77.

65. Linda Hogan, selection from "Department of the Interior," in *Wise Women*, ed. Susan Cahill (New York: Norton, 1996), 276.

66. Ibid., 279.

67. Ibid.

68. Weaver, *Other Words*, 38.

69. V. Deloria, *God Is Red*, 68.

70. Anne Makepeace, "American Masters: Edward Curtis," http://www.thirteen.org/americanmasters/curtis/ (discussion of Curtis's work).

71. Christopher Cardozo, *Native Nations: First Americans as Seen by Edward Curtis* (Boston: Little, Brown, 1993), 19.

72. Ibid.

73. V. Deloria, *God Is Red*, 43.

74. Weaver, *Other Words*, 36.

75. McPherson and Rabb, cited in ibid.

76. Charles Eastman, cited in V. Deloria, *God Is Red*, 86.

77. Christopher Ronwanien:te Jocks, cited in Weaver, *Other Words*, 45.

78. Frazier, *People of Chaco*, 174–80, 218, 221, 231; Neil Salisbury, "The Indians' Old World: Native Americans and the Coming of Europeans," in *American Encounters: Natives and Newcomers from*

European Contact to Indian Removal, 1500–1850, ed. Peter C. Mancall and James H. Merrell (New York: Routledge, 2000), 10.

79. V. Deloria, *God Is Red*, 195.

80. Leslie Marmon Silko, *Storyteller* (New York: Arcade, 1981), 227.

81. Weaver, *Other Words*, 47.

82. V. Deloria, *God Is Red*, 195.

83. Ibid., 66–68.

84. Paula Gunn Allen, "Return of the Buffalo," described in Moore, 59.

85. Sanchez, "Animal, Vegetable, Mineral," 225.

86. Weaver, *Other Words*, 56.

87. Ibid., 249.

88. Lewis Hyde, cited in ibid., 252.

89. Ibid., 250–51.

90. Vizenor, *Manifest Manners*, ix, 76, 83.

91. Ibid., 14–15.

92. Weaver, *Other Words*, 254.

93. Hyde, cited in ibid, 253.

94. Weaver, *Other Words*, 253.

95. Philip Deloria, *Playing Indian* (New Haven, Conn.: Yale Univ. Press, 1998), 4.

96. Ibid., 191.

97. Ibid., 5.

98. Sanchez, "Animal, Vegetable, Mineral," 215–16.

99. Ibid., 218.

100. Ibid., 214, 223.

101. Ibid., 226.

102. Ibid.

chapter 4: respect

1. Carol Lee Sanchez, *From Spirit to Matter: New and Selected Poems 1969–1996* (San Francisco: Taurean Horn Press, 1996), 144–45. Used by Permission.

2. Wilson, *The Earth Shall Weep: A History of Native America* (New York: Grove, 1998), 20, 41.

3. Ibid., 49, 79.

4. Jace Weaver, *Other Words: American Indian Literature, Law, and Culture* (Norman: Univ. of Oklahoma Press, 2001), 93.

5. Philip Deloria, *Playing Indian* (New Haven, Conn.: Yale Univ. Press, 1998), 64.

6. Ibid.

7. Ibid., 63–64.

8. Ibid., 138.

9. Vine Deloria Jr., *Spirit and Reason: The Vine Deloria, Jr. Reader* (Golden, Colo.: Fulcrum, 1999), 137–43.

10. William Schulz, *In Our Own Best Interest: How Defending Human Rights Benefits Us All* (Boston: Beacon, 2001), 197.

11. Ibid., 179.

12. Cornelius J. Jaenen, "Amerindian Views of French Culture in the Seventeenth Century," in *American Encounters: Natives and Newcomers from European Contact to Indian Removal 1500–1850*, ed. Peter C. Mancall and James H. Merrell (New York: Routledge, 2000), 84.

13. Ibid., 70.

14. Ibid., 85.

15. Ibid., 88–90.

16. V. Deloria, *Spirit and Reason*, 160.

17. James Axtell, "The White Indians of Colonial America," in *American Encounters: Natives and Newcomers from European Contact to Indian Removal 1500–1850*, ed. Peter C. Mancall and James H. Merrell (New York: Routledge, 2000), 325.

18. Ibid., 325–26.

19. Benjamin Franklin, cited in ibid., 326.

20. Ibid., 327.

21. Rebecca Kugel, "Of Missionaries and Their Cattle: Ojibwa Perceptions of a Missionary as Evil Shaman," in *American Encounters: Natives and Newcomers from European Contact to Indian Removal 1500–1850*, ed. Peter C. Mancall and James H. Merrell (New York: Routledge, 2000), 163–64.

22. Ibid., 164, 168.

23. Cited in Jaenen, "Amerindian Views," 85.

24. LaVonne Brown Ruoff, "Reversing the Gaze: Early Native American Images of Europeans and Euro-Americans," in *Native American Representation: First Encounters, Distorted Images, and Literary Appropriations*, ed. Gretchen M. Bataille (Lincoln: University of Nebraska Press, 2001), 207.

25. Ibid.

26. Cited in Jaenen, "Amerindian Views," 85.

27. Wilson, *The Earth Shall Weep*, 42.

28. Virginia Irving Armstrong, ed., *I Have Spoken: American History through the Voices of the Indians* (New York: Pocket Books, 1972), 43.

29. Wilson, *The Earth Shall Weep*, 279; Charles Eastman, cited in Ruoff, "Reversing the Gaze," 206.

30. Wilson, *The Earth Shall Weep*, 264, 270.

31. *The Journal of Columbus*, trans. Cecil Jane (London: Hakluyt Society, 1960), 28.

32. Lee Francis, *Native Time: A Historical Time Line of Native America* (New York: St. Martin's, 1996), 30.

33. Cited in Gerald Vizenor, *Manifest Manners: Narratives on Postindian Survivance* (Lincoln: Univ. of Nebraska Press, 1999), 110–11.

34. Wilson, *The Earth Shall Weep*, 196.

35. Ibid., 196–98.

36. Ibid., 212–13.

37. Cited in Ruoff, "Reversing the Gaze," 213–14.

38. Wilson, *The Earth Shall Weep*, 64–69.

39. Ibid., 70–71.

40. Ibid., 88.

41. Ibid., 90–91.

42. Ibid., 96, 127.

43. Ibid., 75.

44. Ibid., 170.

45. Ibid., 14, 226.

46. Ibid., 228.

47. Ibid., 231.

48. Ibid., 232.

49. Ibid., 233.

50. Ibid., 237, 244–46.

51. Ibid., 253, 273.

52. Ibid., 273–74.

53. Ibid., 278.

54. Ibid., 275.

55. Ibid., 283, 295.

56. V. Deloria, *Spirit and Reason*, 162.

57. Wilson, *The Earth Shall Weep*, 311.

58. Ibid., 315.

59. Ruoff, "Reversing the Gaze," 218.

60. Weaver, *Other Words*, 15; and Wilson, *The Earth Shall Weep*, 318.

61. V. Deloria, *Spirit and Reason*, 309; and Wilson, *The Earth Shall Weep*, 407.

62. Wilson, *The Earth Shall Weep*, 407, 412, 415, 417.

63. Danny Hakim, "Off the Reservation, onto the Dealer's Lot," *New York Times*, May 14, 2002, C1–C2.

64. P. Deloria, *Playing Indian*, 7.

65. Vine Deloria Jr., *God Is Red: A Native View f Religion* (Golden, Colo.: Fulcrum, 1992), 76.

66. Ibid., 43; Weaver, *Other Words,* 137.

67. V. Deloria, *Spirit and Reason*, 189.

68. Dean Murphy, "U.S. Approves Power Plant in Area Indians Hold Sacred," *New York Times*, November 28, 2002, A32.

69. Weaver, *Other Words*, 19.

70. Ibid., 152.

71. V. Deloria, *God Is Red*, 263.

72. Ibid., 189–90.

73. Kathryn Shanley, "The Indians America Loves to Love and Read: American Indian Identity and Cultural Appropriation," in *Native American Representation: First Encounters, Distorted Images, and Literary Appropriations,* ed. Gretchen M. Bataille (Lincoln: Univ. of Nebraska Press, 2001), 26.

74. V. Deloria, *God Is Red,* 263, 265.

chapter 5: ceremony

1. Vine Deloria Jr., *Spirit and Reason: The Vine Deloria, Jr. Reader* (Golden, CO: Fulcrum, 1999), 256.

2. Ibid.

3. Jace Weaver, *Other Words: American Indian Literature, Law, and Culture* (Norman: University of Oklahoma Press, 2001), 303–4.

4. Iris Marion Young, *Inclusion and Democracy* (Oxford: Oxford University Press, 2000), 16.

5. Ibid., 16–17.

6. Ibid., 16.

7. Ibid., 17.

8. Michel Foucault, "Polemics, Politics, and Problematizations: An Interview with Michel Foucault," by Paul Rabinow, in *Michel Foucault, Ethics, Subjectivity and Truth, Essential Works of Foucault, 1954–1984*, vol. 1, ed. Paul Rabinow (New York: New Press, 1997), 111–13 (interview conducted in May 1984).

9. Michel Foucault, "The Masked Philosopher," interview by Christian Delacampagne, in *Michel Foucault, Ethics, Subjectivity and Truth, Essential Works of Foucault, 1954–1984*, vol. 1, ed. Paul Rabinow (New York: New Press, 1997), 327 (interview conducted on April 6–7, 1980).

10. Ronald V. Dellums and H. Lee Halterman, *Lying Down with the Lions: Public Life from the Streets of Oakland to the Halls of Power* (Boston: Beacon, 2000), 2–3.

11. Ibid., 17, 30, 76.

12. Ibid., 75–76.

13. Ibid., 49, 107.

14. Ibid., 144–45.

15. Ibid., 200–201.

16. Ibid., 201.

17. Foucault, "The Masked Philosopher," 326.

18. Carol Lee Sanchez, "Animal, Vegetable, Mineral: The Sacred Connection," in *Ecofeminism and the Sacred*, ed. Carol J. Adams (New York: Continuum, 1994), 227.

19. V. Deloria, *Spirit and Reason*, 141.

20. Ibid., 51, 134, 141.

21. William Jones, professor emeritus of Black Studies at the University of Florida, workshop on the "Grid of Oppression," University of Missouri–Columbia, October 1993.

22. Young, *Inclusion and Democracy*, 55.

23. Ibid., 3, 6.

24. Ibid., 7.

25. Ibid., 61.

26. Ibid., 29, 65.

27. Ibid., 7, 71–75.

28. Ibid., 76–77.

29. Ibid., 24.

30. Cited in Ronald Takaki, *A Different Mirror: A History of Multicultural America* (Boston: Little, Brown, 1993), 238.

31. Ibid., 239, 241.

32. Ibid., 244.

33. David Barboza, "Despite Denial, Enron Papers Show Big Profit on Price Bets," *New York Times*, December 12, 2002, C6.

34. Kurt Eichenwald, "After a Boom, There Will Be Scandal. Count on It," *New York Times*, December 16, 2002, C3.

35. Charles Kindleberger, "Corruption, Crime, Chicanery: Business through the Ages," *New York Times*, December 16, 2002, C3

36. Eichenwald, "After a Boom, There Will Be Scandal."

37. Dennis McPherson, in *Native American Religious Identity: Unforgotten Gods,* ed. Jace Weaver (Maryknoll, N.Y.: Orbis, 1998), 86.

38. Ibid.

39. V. Deloria, *Spirit and Reason*, 215, 218; and Vine Deloria Jr., *God Is Red: A Native View of Religion* (Golden, Colo.: Fulcrum, 1992), 61.

40. Susan Miller Okin, *Justice, Gender and the Family* (New York: Basic Books, 1989).

41. Patrick Riley, *Will and Political Legitimacy: A Critical Exposition of Social Contract Theory in Hobbes, Locke, Rousseau, Kant, and Hegel* (Cambridge, Mass.: Harvard Univ. Press, 1982), 9.

42. Patrick Riley, "A Possible Explanation of Rousseau's General Will," in *The Social Contract Theorists: Critical Essays on Hobbes, Locke, and*

Rousseau, ed. Christopher W. Morris, 167–78 (Lanham, Md.: Rowman and Littlefield, 1999), 170–71.

43. Jean Jacques Rousseau, *The Social Contract,* trans. Judith Masters (New York: St. Martin's , 1978), 56.

44. Riley, "A Possible Explanation of Rousseau's General Will," 170.

45. Grace Jantzen, *Becoming Divine: Towards a Feminist Philosophy of Religion* (Bloomington: Indiana Univ. Press, 1999) 99, 152–55.

46. John Rawls, *A Theory of Justice* (Cambridge, Mass.: Harvard Univ. Press, 1971), 11–13.

47. Riley, "A Possible Explanation of Rousseau's General Will," 209.

48. Young, *Inclusion and Democracy,* 30.

49. In an interview, "Revolutionary Action 'until Now,'" Foucault is critical of humanism and the type of freedom found in social contract theory:

By humanism I mean the totality of discourse through which Western man is told: "Even though you don't exercise power, you can still be a ruler. Better yet, the more you deny yourself the exercise of power, the more you submit to those in power, then the more this increases your sovereignty." Humanism invented a whole series of subjugated sovereignties: the soul (ruling the body, but subjected to God), consciousness (sovereign in a context of judgment, but subjected to the necessity of truth), the individual (a titular control of personal rights subjected to the laws of nature and society), basic freedom (sovereign within, but accepting the demands of an outside world and "aligned with destiny.") In short, humanism is everything in Western civilization that restricts the desire for power: it prohibits the desire for power and excludes the possibility of power being seized.

If our subjection is grounded in our own histories of domination and brutality, and confronting those tendencies in the present, subjection is not simply rejecting "the desire for power." It is more akin to what Foucault called becoming aware of the fascist within us all. Michel Foucault, "Revolutionary Action 'Until Now,'" in *Language, Countermemory, Practice:*

Selected Essays and Interviews by Michael Foucault, ed. Donald F. Bouchard (Ithaca, N.Y.: Cornell Univ. Press, 1977), 221–22.

50. William F. Schulz, "The Torturer's Apprentice," *The Nation*, May 13, 2002, 26.

51. Ibid.

52. Ibid., 27. As I write this book, while there have been reports from Amnesty International and the International Red Cross recounting torture and abuse, the full extent of the torture of prisoners in Iraq, Afghanistan, and Guantanamo Bay by United States personnel has not yet been uncovered. See for example the reports by James Risen and David Johnston, "Photos of Dead Show the Horrors of Abuse," *New York Times*, May 7, 2004, A11; and Don Van Natta Jr. "Interrogations Methods in Iraq Aren't All Found in Manual," *New York Times*, May 7, 2004, A11.

53. William F. Schulz, *In Our Own Best Interest: How Defending Human Rights Benefits Us All* (Boston: Beacon, 2001), 1, 193, 194.

54. Ibid., 196.

55. Ibid., 184.

chapter 6: audacity

1. Stephen Batchelor, *Buddhism without Beliefs: A Guide to Contemporary Awakening* (New York: Riverhead, 1997), 106.

2. Sister Annabel Laity, introd. to Thich Nhat Hanh, *Thich Nhat Hanh: Essential Writings*, ed. Robert Ellsberg (Maryknoll, N.Y.: Orbis, 2001).

3. Thich Nhat Hanh, *Being Peace* (Berkeley, CA: Parallax, 1987), 79–80.

4. William Lafleur, introd. to Masao Abe, *Zen and Western Thought*, ed. William R. LaFleur (Honolulu: Univ. of Hawaii Press, 1985).

5. Masao Abe, *Buddhism and Interfaith Dialogue*, ed. Steven Heine (Honolulu: University of Hawaii Press, 1995), 230.

6. Thich Nhat Hanh, *Essential Writings*, 23.

7. Thich Nhat Hanh, *The Miracle of Mindfulness: A Manual on Meditation* (Boston: Beacon, 1975), 17–18.

8. Thich Nhat Hanh, *Essential Writings*, 23.

9. Batchelor, *Buddhism without Beliefs*, 74, 89.

10. There is a significant debate about the Buddha nature. Is it cultivated or recognized through dharma practice? See ibid., 13; and Anne Carolyn Klein, *Meeting the Great Bliss Queen: Buddhists, Feminists, and the Art of the Self* (Boston: Beacon, 1995), 4.

11. Christopher Queen, "Introduction: The Shapes and Sources of Engaged Buddhism," in *Engaged Buddhism: Buddhist Liberation Movements in Asia*, ed. Christopher S. Queen and Sallie B. King (Albany: State University of New York Press, 1996), 2–5.

12. Cited in Queen, "Introduction: The Shapes and Sources," 5.

13. Thich Nhat Hanh, *Being Peace*, 45.

14. Kenneth Kraft, *The Wheel of Engaged Buddhism: A New Map of the Path* (New York: Weatherhill, 1999), 20.

15. Cited in Sandra Bell, "A Survey of Engaged Buddhism in Britain," in Queen, ed., *Engaged Buddhism in the West*, 413–14.

16. Abe, *Buddhism and Interfaith Dialogue,* 58–59. See also Masao Abe, *Zen and Comparative Studies*, ed. Steven Heine (Honolulu: Univ. of Hawaii Press, 1997), 186.

17. Christopher S. Queen, "Introduction: A New Buddhism," in Queen, ed., *Engaged Buddhism in the West*, 1–2, 18, 22.

18. Thich Nhat Hanh, *Being Peace*, 84.

19. Christopher Queen describes the interaction between Western ethical and religious values and Buddhist practices and perceptions:

While they [the concepts and practices of engaged Buddhism] are rooted in ancient conceptions of individual striving, such as discipline, virtue, and altruism: and in ideas of tribal identity, covenant community, and monastic order; they owe their distinctive character to notions of human rights, social justice, political activism, and due process that have evolved in the "Western" cultural tradition, with contributions from Judaism, Greek humanism, Christianity, Roman and Anglo-Saxon law, the scientific and social

Enlightenment of seventeenth and eighteenth century Europe, and the pragmatism and progressivism of nineteenth and twentieth century America.

Queen, "Introduction: A New Buddhism," 2–3.

20. Martin Bauman, "Work as Dharma Practice: Right Livelihood Cooperatives of the FWBO," in *Engaged Buddhism in the West*, ed. Christopher S. Queen (Boston: Wisdom Publications, 2000), 372; Kraft, *The Wheel of Engaged Buddhism*, 17; and Robert E. Goss, "Naropa Institute: The Engaged Academy," in Queen, ed., *Engaged Buddhism in the West*, 328–29.

21. Darrell Wratten, "Engaged Buddhism in South Africa," in Queen, ed., *Engaged Buddhism in the West*, 496–97.

22. Sulak Sivaraksa, *Seeds of Peace: A Buddhist Vision for Renewing Society*, edited by Tom Ginsburg (Berkeley, California: Parallax Press, 1992) 62–72.

23. Kenneth Kraft, "Prospects of a Socially Engaged Buddhism," *Inner Peace, World Peace: Essays on Buddhism and Nonviolence*, ed. Kenneth Kraft (Albany: SUNY Press, 1992), 14.

24. Patricia Hunt-Perry and Lyn Fine, "All Buddhism Is Engaged," in Queen, ed., *Engaged Buddhism in the West*, 60–61.

25. Susan Moon, "Activist Women in American Buddhism," in Queen, ed., *Engaged Buddhism in the West*, 247, 250, 256.

26. Cynthia Eller, "The Impact of Christianity on Buddhist Nonviolence in the West," in Kraft, ed., *Inner Peace, World Peace*, 100–101.

27. Kraft, *The Wheel of Engaged Buddhism*, 54.

28. Leonard L. Riskin, "The Contemplative Lawyer: On the Potential Benefits of Mindfulness Meditation to Students, Lawyers, and Their Clients," *Harvard Negotiation Law Review* 7 (Spring 2002): 1–66. See also the work of the Center for Contemplative Mind in Society: "The Center for Contemplative Mind in Society collaborates with individuals and organizations to assist in pioneering new approaches to learning, communication, decision making, leadership and social change. Our work is accomplished largely through teaching contemplative practices at retreats

and meetings in secular settings to help people change the way they relate to their world and move toward more compassionate action." See http://www.contemplativemind.org. The center works with people engaged in law, business, media, academics, philanthropy, youth leadership, and environmental activism.

29. Batchelor, *Buddhism without Beliefs*, 4–5.

30. Masao Abe, *Zen and Western Thought*, ed. William R. LaFleur (Honolulu: Univ. of Hawaii Press, 1985), 4–10.

31. Kraft, "Prospects of a Socially Engaged Buddhism," 20.

32. Thich Nhat Hanh, *Being Peace*, 110.

33. Thich Nhat Hanh, *Peace Is Every Step: The Path of Mindfulness in Everyday Life* (New York: Bantam, 1991), 27.

34. Thich Nhat Hanh, *The Miracle of Mindfulness*, 20–21.

35. Batchelor, *Buddhism without Beliefs*, 65.

36. Linda Holler, *Erotic Morality: The Role of Touch in Moral Agency* (New Brunswick, NJ: Rutgers University Press, 2002), 172 and chap. 5. See also Klein, *Meeting the Great Bliss Queen*, 190.

37. Schulz, *In Our Own Best Interest*, 1.

38. Ibid., 197.

39. Thich Nhat Hanh, *Being Peace*, 4.

40. Ibid., 47.

41. Thich Nhat Hanh, *Essential Writings*, 59, 65.

42. Klein, *Meeting the Great Bliss Queen*, 108.

43. Thich Nhat Hanh, *Essential Writings*, 23, 85.

44. Thich Nhat Hanh, *Being Peace*, 11–12.

45. Kenneth Kraft, "New Voices in Engaged Buddhist Studies," in Queen, ed., *Engaged Buddhism in the West*, 497.

46. Cited in Kraft, "Prospects of a Socially Engaged Buddhism," 137.

47. Thich Nhat Hanh, *Essential Writings*, 108.

48. Thich Nhat Hanh, *The Miracle of Mindfulness*, 89–90.

49. Thich Nhat Hanh, *Essential Writings*, 101.

50. Thich Nhat Hanh, *Anger: Wisdom for Cooling the Flames* (New York: Riverhead, 2001), 128–29.

51. Ibid., 70.

52. Hunt-Perry and Fine, "All Buddhism Is Engaged," 50–51.

53. Thich Nhat Hanh, *Interbeing: Fourteen Guidelines for Engaged Buddhism*, 3rd ed. (Berkeley, CA: Parallax, 1998), 17–18.

54. Abe, *Zen and Comparative Studies*, 37.

55. Abe, *Zen and Western Thought*, 191.

56. Thich Nhat Hanh, *Peace Is Every Step*, 112.

57. Thich Nhat Hanh, *Essential Writings*, 99.

58. Batchelor, *Buddhism without Beliefs*, 89–90.

59. Abe, *Zen and Comparative Studies*, 211–12.

60. Abe, *Buddhism and Interfaith Dialogue,* 242.

61. Thich Nhat Hanh, *Being Peace*, 89.

62. Thich Nhat Hanh, *Interbeing*, 17.

63. Thich Nhat Hanh, *Being Peace,* 43.

64. Batchelor, *Buddhism without Beliefs*, 38.

65. Klein, *Meeting the Great Bliss Queen*, 199–200.

66. Thich Nhat Hanh, *Anger*, 143.

67. Batchelor, *Buddhism without Beliefs*, 47.

68. Rieder, *New York Times Book Review*, December 26, 1998, 15.

69. Thich Nhat Hanh, *Being Peace*, 49–50.

70. Thich Nhat Hanh, *Anger*, 135.

71. Sulak Sivaraksa, *Seeds of Peace,* 115.

chapter 7: risk

1. "The Miles Davis Story," produced, directed, and narrated by Mike Dibbs, a Dibb Directions Production for Channel 4 Television Limited (UK), Sony Music Entertainment Inc. New York: Columbia Music Video, 2002.

2. Bob Herbert, "Betraying Humanity," *New York Times*, March 28, 2002.

3. Jean Bethke Elshtain, *Just War against Terror: The Burden of American Power in a Violent World* (New York: Basic Books, 2003), 18–25.

4. Sissela Bok describes four Western attitudes toward war: realist, just war, pacifist, and the arts of peacemaking, or "perpetual peace." The fourth pattern can be found in the works of Erasmus, William Penn, the

Abbé de Saint-Pierre, Immanuel Kant, and Jeremy Bentham, and as interpreters and critics, in the works of Leibniz, Rousseau, and Hegel:

> The plans that Erasmus, the Abbé de Saint-Pierre, Kant, and others offered for moving toward a universal and perpetual peace have long been dismissed as utopian or hypocritical, at times even suppressed as dangerously heretical. These thinkers challenged the common perception of war as an immutable aspect of the human condition and of lasting peace as possible, if at all, only in the hereafter . . . But two aspects of the best among their writings are as relevant today as in the past: first, their intrepid challenges to the common assumption that war will always be with us; and second, their suggestions for how to create a social climate conducive to the forging of a stable peace.

Bok, "Early Advocates of Lasting World Peace: Utopians or Realists?" in *Celebrating Peace*, ed. Leroy S. Rouner (Notre Dame, Ind.: Univ. of Notre Dame Press, 1990), 52–55.

5. Desiderius Erasmus, *The "Adages" of Erasmus: A Study with Translations*, ed. and trans. Margaret Mann Phillips (Cambridge: Cambridge University Press, 1964), 308, 317, 337.

6.René Girard, *Violence and the Sacred*, trans. Patrick Gregory (Baltimore, MD: Johns Hopkins University Press, 1977), 79. See also René Girard, *The Scapegoat*, trans. Yvonne Frecerro (Baltimore, MD: Johns Hopkins University Press, 1986); and René Girard with Jean-Michel Ourgoulian and Guy Lefort, *Things Hidden since the Foundation of the World* (Stanford, Calif.: Stanford Univ. Press, 1987).

Theophus Smith describes the phenomenon as follows: "Doubles are rivals whose mutual desire to displace the other renders them increasingly like one another as their conflict escalates. At the furthest extreme of mutually desired homicide the essential identity between antagonists is complete: each desires sole survival on the condition of the other's annihilation." Girard claims that the only way that societies have found to escape the double bind is through the displacement of violence onto a scapegoat:

former enemies join in vanquishing another enemy, one who is seen as a threat to the survival of both. However, Mark Wallace and Theophus Smith propose that disclosing the false projection of guilt on the scapegoat may stop the spiral of violence. Smith, *Conjuring Culture: Biblical Formations of Black America* (New York: Oxford University Press, 1994), 197–98; Mark Wallace and Theophus Smith, eds., *Curing Violence* (Sonoma, CA: Polebridge, 1994), 249.

7. Bok, "Early Advocates of Lasting World Peace," 55, 56, 60.

8. Global Action to Prevent War, *The Global Action Program*, rev. 10, April 1999, http://www.globalactionpw.org. I am a member of the Columbia chapter of Global Action to Prevent War and also serve on the U.S. steering committee. There are many other organizations doing closely related work, such as the Peaceful Prevention of Deadly Conflict project of the Friends Committee on National Legislation (FCNL) http://www.fcnl.org/; the European Center for Conflict Prevention, http://www.conflict-prevention .net/; Search for Common Ground, http://www.sfcg.org/; and the Carnegie Commission on the Prevention of Deadly Conflict, http://wwics.si.edu/sub-sites/ccpdc/index.htm. The Global Action program emerges from the attempts of scholars and activists to imagine and put in place constructive alternatives to existing policies and institutions. For an example of such an integrated analysis, see the following works: Saul Mendlovitz and R.B.J. Walker, eds., *Contending Sovereignties: Redefining Political Community* (Boulder, Colo.: L. Rienner, 1990); Saul Mendlovitz, ed., *On the Creation of Just World Order: Preferred Futures for the 1990s* (New York: Free Press, 1979); Saul Mendlovitz and Burns H. Weston, eds., *Preferred Futures for the United Nations* (Irvington-on-Hudson, N.Y.: Transnational Publishers, 1995).

9. Global Action to Prevent War, "A Coalition-Building Effort to Stop War, Genocide, and Internal Armed Conflict," Program Statement 2003, http://www.globalactionpw.org. The project is also open to revision and refinement through the input of more people and in response to new challenges—for instance, revision 18 includes specific recommendations on how to respond to the terrorist attacks on the United States (Global Action

to Prevent War, *The Global Action Program*, rev. 18, March 2002, http://www.globalactionpw.org).

10. Ibid.

11. See the work of the Alliance for International Conflict Prevention and Resolution, http://www.aicpr.org.

12. Global Action, *Global Action Program*, rev. 18.

13. Neil A. Lewis, "U.S. Is Set to Renounce Its Role in Pact for World Tribunal," *New York Times*, May 5, 2002; International Criminal Court (ICC), "States Parties," ICC Web site, http://www.icc-cpi.int/statesparties .html, May 3, 2004.

14. Lewis, "U.S. Is Set."

15. Neil A. Lewis, "U.S. Rejects All Support for New Court on Atrocities," *New York Times*, May 7, 2002, A9.

16. Jonathan Dean, "Are We Fighting the Right War against Terrorism?" public lecture, University of Missouri–Columbia, April 26, 2002.

17. Ibid.

18. Zbigniew Brzezinski writes of the danger of being shackled by recalcitrant allies: "An America that is scrupulously deferential to international rules, studiously avoids flexing its muscle in economic areas of special interest to major segments of its electorate, is obediently ready to limit its own sovereignty, and is prepared to place its military under international legal jurisdiction might not be the power of last resort needed to prevent global anarchy." Brzezinski, *The Choice: Global Domination or Global Leadership* (New York: Basic Books, 2004), 94. Like Brzezinski, Jean Bethke Elshtain warns that "liberal and neoliberal internationalist entites have great difficulty reckoning with the determined and the ruthless." Elshtain, *Just War against Terror*, 172.

19. William F. Schulz, *In Our Own Best Interest: How Defending Human Rights Benefits Us All* (Boston: Beacon, 2001), 190–91.

20. Elise Boulding and Randall Forsberg, *Abolishing War, Cultures and Institutions: Dialogue with Elise Boulding and Randall Forsberg* (Boston: Boston Research Center for the 21st Century, 1998), 46.

21. The daring photography of Li Zhensheng, taken surreptiously while officially documenting the Cultural Revolution, is one source that documents the terror and humiliation of this period of history. Li Zhensheng, *Red-Color News Soldier* (London: Phaidon, 2002), excerpt reprinted in Li Zhensheng, "Shooting Mao's Madness: Red-Color News Soldier," *Amnesty Now* (Winter 2003), 14–16.

22. Michiko Kakutani critizes Benjamin's Barbar's advocacy of a democratic and benevolent interdependece: "Mr. Barber's talk about 'preventive democracy' has a way of slip-sliding into half-baked utopian musings about 'global citizenship' and 'the newly empowered voice of global opinion.'" Kakutani, "The Trouble with Eagles and Owls," review of *Fear's Empire: War, Terrorism, and Democracy*, by Benjamin R. Barber, *New York Times*, September, 30, 2003.

23. Elshtain, *Just War against Terror,* 178, 172.

24. Ibid., 170, 178.

25. See William Schulz's critique of governmental policies since 9/11: William Schulz, *Tainted Legacy: 9/11 and the Ruin of Human Rights* (New York: Nation Books, 2003).

26. "The plans that Erasmus, the Abbé de Saint-Pierre, Kant, and others offered for moving toward a universal and perpetual peace have long been dismissed as utopian or hypocritical, at times even suppressed as dangerously heretical. These thinkers challenged the common perception of war as an immutable aspect of the human condition and of lasting peace as possible, if at all, only in the hereafter." Bok, "Early Advocates of Lasting World Peace," 52.

27. Robert Kagan, *Of Paradise and Power* (New York: Knopf, 2003), 9.

28. James Wilson, *The Earth Shall Weep: A History of Native America* (New York: Grove, 1998), 90, 226–40.

29. Niall Ferguson, *Empire: The Rise and Demise of the British World Order and the Lessons for Global Power* (New York: Basic, 2003), xxii–xxv.

30. See the work of Frantz Fanon, *Black Skin, White Masks,* reissued ed. (New York: Grove, 1991), and *The Wretched of the Earth* (New York: Grove, 1963); Gayatri Chakravorty Spivak, *A Critique of Postcolonial Reason: Toward a History of the Vanishing Present.* (Cambridge: Harvard

Univ. Press, 1999), and the novels and short stories of Sherman Alexie, including *The Toughest Indian in the World* (New York: Grove, 2000).

31. John Rawls, *A Theory of Justice* (Cambridge: Harvard Univ. Press, 1971).

32. Ferguson, *Empire,* xvii.

33. Peter Berger, *Pyramids of Sacrifice: Political Ethics and Social Change* (Garden City, N.Y.: Anchor, 1976).

34. "Act only according to that maxim by which you can at the same time will that it should become a universal law"; "Act as though the maxim of your action were by your will to become a universal law of nature." Immanuel Kant, *Groundwork of the Metaphysics of Morals*, ed. Mary Gregor (New York: Cambridge University Press, 1998), 422.

35. "Names of the Dead" report of the Department of Defense, printed in the *New York Times*, June 25, 2004; Amnesty International, "Iraq: One Year on the Human Rights Situation Remains Dire," March 18, 2004 (AI Index: MDE 14/006/2004).

36. Associated Press, "More than 3,240 Iraqi Civilians Killed During War," June 11, 2003; Patrick Tyler, "As U.S. Fans Out in Iraq, Violence and Death on Rise," *New York Times*, June 14, 2003.

37. See the thorough discussion of the nature of reconciliation and conflict resolution in Vern Neufeld Redekop, *From Violence to Blessing: How an Understanding of Deep-Rooted Conflict Can Open Paths to Reconciliation* (Ottawa, ON: Novalis, Saint Paul University, 2002).

38. Niall Ferguson, *Colossus: The Price of America's Empire* (New York: Penguin, 2004), 296–97.

39. Cited in Jonathan Schell, *The Unconquerable World: Power, Nonviolence, and the Will of the People* (New York: Henry Holt, 2003), 218.

40. Ibid., 221–22, 345.

41. Ferguson, *Empire,* chap. 4 and conclusion.

42. Schulz, *Tainted Legacy*, 19.

43. Schell, *The Unconquerable World,* 227.

44. Iris Marion Young, *Inclusion and Democracy* (Oxford: Oxford Univ. Press, 2000), 9.

45. Ibid.

46. Schell, *The Unconquerable World,* 350–51.

47. Ibid.

48. Ibid., 224.

49. Ibid., 265–66.

50. Erasmus, *The "Adages" of Erasmus.*

51. Ann Douglas, "Feel the City's Pulse? Be-bop, Man!" *New York Times,* August 28, 1998, B26.

52. William F. Schulz, *Making the Manifesto: The Birth of Religious Humanism* (Boston: Skinner House, 2002), xxiii.

53. Danilo Perez, performance at the Blue Note, Columbia, Missouri, October 21, 2001, sponsored by the We Always Swing Jazz Series.

index